Nutshell Series

of

WEST PUBLISHING COMPANY

P.O. Box 64526

St. Paul, Minnesota 55164-0526

Accounting—Law and, 1984, 377 pages, by E. McGruder Faris, Late Professor of Law, Stetson University.

Administrative Law and Process, 2nd Ed., 1981, 445 pages, by Ernest Gellhorn, Former Dean and Professor of Law, Case Western Reserve University and Barry B. Boyer, Professor of Law, SUNY, Buffalo.

Admiralty, 2nd Ed., 1988, about 362 pages, by Frank L. Maraist, Professor of Law, Louisiana State University.

Agency-Partnership, 1977, 364 pages, by Roscoe T. Steffen, Late Professor of Law, University of Chicago.

American Indian Law, 1981, 288 pages, by William C. Canby, Jr., Adjunct Professor of Law, Arizona State University.

Antitrust Law and Economics, 3rd Ed., 1986, 472 pages, by Ernest Gellhorn, Former Dean and Professor of Law, Case Western Reserve University.

Appellate Advocacy, 1984, 325 pages, by Alan D. Hornstein, Professor of Law, University of Maryland.

Art Law, 1984, 335 pages, by Leonard D. DuBoff, Professor of Law, Lewis and Clark College, Northwestern School of Law.

Banking and Financial Institutions, 1984, 409 pages, by William A. Lovett, Professor of Law, Tulane University.

Church-State Relations—Law of, 1981, 305 pages, by Leonard F. Manning, Late Professor of Law, Fordham University.

Civil Procedure, 2nd Ed., 1986, 306 pages, by Mary Kay Kane, Professor of Law, University of California, Hastings College of the Law.

Civil Rights, 1978, 279 pages, by Norman Vieira, Professor of Law, Southern Illinois University.

Commercial Paper, 3rd Ed., 1982, 404 pages, by Charles M. Weber, Professor of Business Law, University of Arizona and Richard E. Speidel, Professor of Law, Northwestern University.

Community Property, 2nd Ed., 1988, about 420 pages, by Robert L. Mennell, Former Professor of Law, Hamline University and Thomas M. Boykoff.

Comparative Legal Traditions, 1982, 402 pages, by Mary Ann Glendon, Professor of Law, Harvard University, Michael Wallace Gordon, Professor of Law, University of Florida and Christopher Osakwe, Professor of Law, Tulane University.

Conflicts, 1982, 470 pages, by David D. Siegel, Professor of Law, St. John's University.

Constitutional Analysis, 1979, 388 pages, by Jerre S. Williams, Professor of Law Emeritus, University of Texas.

Constitutional Federalism, 2nd Ed., 1987, 411 pages, by David E. Engdahl, Professor of Law, University of Puget Sound.

Constitutional Law, 1986, 389 pages, by Jerome A. Barron, Dean and Professor of Law, George Washington University and C. Thomas Dienes, Professor of Law, George Washington University.

Consumer Law, 2nd Ed., 1981, 418 pages, by David G. Epstein, Dean and Professor of Law, Emory University and Steve H. Nickles, Professor of Law, University of Minnesota.

Contract Remedies, 1981, 323 pages, by Jane M. Friedman, Professor of Law, Wayne State University.

Contracts, 2nd Ed., 1984, 425 pages, by Gordon D. Schaber, Dean and Professor of Law, McGeorge School of Law and Claude D. Rohwer, Professor of Law, McGeorge School of Law.

Corporations—Law of, 2nd Ed., 1987, 515 pages, by Robert W. Hamilton, Professor of Law, University of Texas.

Corrections and Prisoners' Rights—Law of, 2nd Ed., 1983, 386 pages, by Sheldon Krantz, Dean and Professor of Law, University of San Diego.

Criminal Law, 2nd Ed., 1987, 321 pages, by Arnold H. Loewy, Professor of Law, University of North Carolina.

Criminal Procedure—Constitutional Limitations, 4th Ed., 1988, about 461 pages, by Jerold H. Israel, Professor of Law, University of Michigan and Wayne R. LaFave, Professor of Law, University of Illinois.

Debtor-Creditor Law, 3rd Ed., 1986, 383 pages, by David G. Epstein, Dean and Professor of Law, Emory University.

Employment Discrimination—Federal Law of, 2nd Ed., 1981, 402 pages, by Mack A. Player, Professor of Law, University of Georgia.

Energy Law, 1981, 338 pages, by Joseph P. Tomain, Professor of Law, University of Cincinnatti.

Environmental Law, 1983, 343 pages by Roger W. Findley, Professor of Law, University of Illinois and Daniel A. Farber, Professor of Law, University of Minnesota.

Estate and Gift Taxation, Federal, 3rd Ed., 1983, 509 pages, by John K. McNulty, Professor of Law, University of California, Berkeley.

Estate Planning—Introduction to, 3rd Ed., 1983, 370 pages, by Robert J. Lynn, Professor of Law, Ohio State University.

Evidence, Federal Rules of, 2nd Ed., 1987, 473 pages, by Michael H. Graham, Professor of Law, University of Miami.

Evidence, State and Federal Rules, 2nd Ed., 1981, 514 pages, by Paul F. Rothstein, Professor of Law, Georgetown University.

Family Law, 2nd Ed., 1986, 444 pages, by Harry D. Krause, Professor of Law, University of Illinois.

Federal Jurisdiction, 2nd Ed., 1981, 258 pages, by David P. Currie, Professor of Law, University of Chicago.

Future Interests, 1981, 361 pages, by Lawrence W. Waggoner, Professor of Law, University of Michigan.

Government Contracts, 1979, 423 pages, by W. Noel Keyes, Professor of Law, Pepperdine University.

Historical Introduction to Anglo-American Law, 2nd Ed., 1973, 280 pages, by Frederick G. Kempin, Jr., Professor of Business Law, Wharton School of Finance and Commerce, University of Pennsylvania.

Immigration Law and Procedure, 1984, 345 pages, by David Weissbrodt, Professor of Law, University of Minnesota.

Injunctions, 1974, 264 pages, by John F. Dobbyn, Professor of Law, Villanova University.

Insurance Law, 1981, 281 pages, by John F. Dobbyn, Professor of Law, Villanova University.

Intellectual Property—Patents, Trademarks and Copyright, 1983, 428 pages, by Arthur R. Miller, Professor of Law, Harvard University, and Michael H. Davis, Professor of Law, Cleveland State University, Cleveland-Marshall College of Law.

International Business Transactions, 2nd Ed., 1984, 476 pages, by Donald T. Wilson, Late Professor of Law, Loyola University, Los Angeles.

International Law (Public), 1985, 262 pages, by Thomas Buergenthal, Professor of Law, Emory University and Harold G. Maier, Professor of Law, Vanderbilt University.

Introduction to the Study and Practice of Law, 1983, 418 pages, by Kenney F. Hegland, Professor of Law, University of Arizona.

Judicial Process, 1980, 292 pages, by William L. Reynolds, Professor of Law, University of Maryland.

Jurisdiction, 4th Ed., 1980, 232 pages, by Albert A. Ehrenzweig, Late Professor of Law, University of California, Berkeley, David W. Louisell, Late Professor of Law, University of California, Berkeley and Geoffrey C. Hazard, Jr., Professor of Law, Yale Law School.

Juvenile Courts, 3rd Ed., 1984, 291 pages, by Sanford J. Fox, Professor of Law, Boston College.

NUTSHELL SERIES

Labor Arbitration Law and Practice, 1979, 358 pages, by Dennis R. Nolan, Professor of Law, University of South Carolina.

Labor Law, 2nd Ed., 1986, 397 pages, by Douglas L. Leslie, Professor of Law, University of Virginia.

Land Use, 2nd Ed., 1985, 356 pages, by Robert R. Wright, Professor of Law, University of Arkansas, Little Rock and Susan Webber Wright, Professor of Law, University of Arkansas, Little Rock.

Landlord and Tenant Law, 2nd Ed., 1986, 311 pages, by David S. Hill, Professor of Law, University of Colorado.

Law Study and Law Examinations—Introduction to, 1971, 389 pages, by Stanley V. Kinyon, Late Professor of Law, University of Minnesota.

Legal Interviewing and Counseling, 2nd Ed., 1987, 487 pages, by Thomas L. Shaffer, Professor of Law, Washington and Lee University and James R. Elkins, Professor of Law, West Virginia University.

Legal Research, 4th Ed., 1985, 452 pages, by Morris L. Cohen, Professor of Law and Law Librarian, Yale University.

Legal Writing, 1982, 294 pages, by Lynn B. Squires and Marjorie Dick Rombauer, Professor of Law, University of Washington.

Legislative Law and Process, 2nd Ed., 1986, 346 pages, by Jack Davies, Professor of Law, William Mitchell College of Law.

Local Government Law, 2nd Ed., 1983, 404 pages, by David J. McCarthy, Jr., Professor of Law, Georgetown University.

Mass Communications Law, 3rd Ed., 1988, 538 pages, by Harvey L. Zuckman, Professor of Law, Catholic University, Martin J. Gaynes, Lecturer in Law, Temple University, T. Barton Carter, Professor of Public Communications, Boston University, and Juliet Lushbough Dee, Professor of Communications, University of Delaware.

Medical Malpractice—The Law of, 2nd Ed., 1986, 342 pages, by Joseph H. King, Professor of Law, University of Tennessee.

Military Law, 1980, 378 pages, by Charles A. Shanor, Professor of Law, Emory University and Timothy P. Terrell, Professor of Law, Emory University.

Oil and Gas Law, 1983, 443 pages, by John S. Lowe, Professor of Law, Southern Methodist University.

Personal Property, 1983, 322 pages, by Barlow Burke, Jr., Professor of Law, American University.

Post-Conviction Remedies, 1978, 360 pages, by Robert Popper, Dean and Professor of Law, University of Missouri, Kansas City.

Presidential Power, 1977, 328 pages, by Arthur Selwyn Miller, Professor of Law Emeritus, George Washington University.

Products Liability, 3rd Ed., 1988, about 350 pages, by Jerry J. Phillips, Professor of Law, University of Tennessee.

Professional Responsibility, 1980, 399 pages, by Robert H. Aronson, Professor of Law, University of Washington, and Donald T. Weckstein, Professor of Law, University of San Diego.

Real Estate Finance, 2nd Ed., 1985, 262 pages, by Jon W. Bruce, Professor of Law, Vanderbilt University.

Real Property, 2nd Ed., 1981, 448 pages, by Roger H. Bernhardt, Professor of Law, Golden Gate University.

Regulated Industries, 2nd Ed., 1987, 389 pages, by Ernest Gellhorn, Former Dean and Professor of Law, Case Western Reserve University, and Richard J. Pierce, Professor of Law, Southern Methodist University.

Remedies, 2nd Ed., 1985, 320 pages, by John F. O'Connell, Dean and Professor of Law, Southern California College of Law.

Res Judicata, 1976, 310 pages, by Robert C. Casad, Professor of Law, University of Kansas.

Sales, 2nd Ed., 1981, 370 pages, by John M. Stockton, Professor of Business Law, Wharton School of Finance and Commerce, University of Pennsylvania.

Schools, Students and Teachers—Law of, 1984, 409 pages, by Kern Alexander, President, Western Kentucky University and M. David Alexander, Professor, Virginia Tech University.

Sea—Law of, 1984, 264 pages, by Louis B. Sohn, Professor of Law, University of Georgia and Kristen Gustafson.

Secured Transactions, 2nd Ed., 1981, 391 pages, by Henry J. Bailey, Professor of Law Emeritus, Willamette University.

Securities Regulation, 3rd Ed., 1988, about 350 pages, by David L. Ratner, Dean and Professor of Law, University of San Francisco.

Sex Discrimination, 1982, 399 pages, by Claire Sherman Thomas, Lecturer, University of Washington, Women's Studies Department.

Taxation and Finance, State and Local, 1986, 309 pages, by M. David Gelfand, Professor of Law, Tulane University and Peter W. Salsich, Professor of Law, St. Louis University.

Taxation of Individuals, Federal Income, 3rd Ed., 1983, 487 pages, by John K. McNulty, Professor of Law, University of California, Berkeley.

Torts—Injuries to Persons and Property, 1977, 434 pages, by Edward J. Kionka, Professor of Law, Southern Illinois University.

Torts—Injuries to Family, Social and Trade Relations, 1979, 358 pages, by Wex S. Malone, Professor of Law Emeritus, Louisiana State University.

Trial Advocacy, 1979, 402 pages, by Paul B. Bergman, Adjunct Professor of Law, University of California, Los Angeles.

Trial and Practice Skills, 1978, 346 pages, by Kenney F. Hegland, Professor of Law, University of Arizona.

Trial, The First—Where Do I Sit? What Do I Say?, 1982, 396 pages, by Steven H. Goldberg, Professor of Law, University of Minnesota.

Unfair Trade Practices, 1982, 445 pages, by Charles R. McManis, Professor of Law, Washington University.

Uniform Commercial Code, 2nd Ed., 1984, 516 pages, by Bradford Stone, Professor of Law, Stetson University.

Uniform Probate Code, 2nd Ed., 1987, 454 pages, by Lawrence H. Averill, Jr., Dean and Professor of Law, University of Arkansas, Little Rock.

Water Law, 1984, 439 pages, by David H. Getches, Professor of Law, University of Colorado.

Welfare Law—Structure and Entitlement, 1979, 455 pages, by Arthur B. LaFrance, Professor of Law, Lewis and Clark College, Northwestern School of Law.

Wills and Trusts, 1979, 392 pages, by Robert L. Mennell, Former Professor of Law, Hamline University.

Workers' Compensation and Employee Protection Laws, 1984, 274 pages, by Jack B. Hood, Former Professor of Law, Cumberland School of Law, Samford University and Benjamin A. Hardy, Former Professor of Law, Cumberland School of Law, Samford University.

Hornbook Series

and

Basic Legal Texts

of

WEST PUBLISHING COMPANY

P.O. Box 64526

St. Paul, Minnesota 55164–0526

Admiralty and Maritime Law, Schoenbaum's Hornbook on, 1987, 692 pages, by Thomas J. Schoenbaum, Professor of Law, University of Georgia.

Agency and Partnership, Reuschlein & Gregory's Hornbook on the Law of, 1979 with 1981 Pocket Part, 625 pages, by Harold Gill Reuschlein, Professor of Law Emeritus, Villanova University and William A. Gregory, Professor of Law, Georgia State University.

Antitrust, Sullivan's Hornbook on the Law of, 1977, 886 pages, by Lawrence A. Sullivan, Professor of Law, University of California, Berkeley.

Civil Procedure, Friedenthal, Kane and Miller's Hornbook on, 1985, 876 pages, by Jack H. Friedental, Professor of Law, Stanford University, Mary Kay Kane, Professor of Law, University of California, Hastings College of the Law and Arthur R. Miller, Professor of Law, Harvard University.

Common Law Pleading, Koffler and Reppy's Hornbook on, 1969, 663 pages, by Joseph H. Koffler, Professor of Law, New York Law School and Alison Reppy, Late Dean and Professor of Law, New York Law School.

Conflict of Laws, Scoles and Hay's Hornbook on, 1982, with 1986 Pocket Part, 1085 pages, by Eugene F. Scoles, Professor of Law, University of Illinois and Peter Hay, Dean and Professor of Law, University of Illinois.

HORNBOOKS & BASIC TEXTS

Constitutional Law, Nowak, Rotunda and Young's Hornbook
on, 3rd Ed., 1986, 1191 pages, by John E. Nowak, Professor
of Law, University of Illinois, Ronald D. Rotunda, Professor
of Law, University of Illinois, and J. Nelson Young, Late
Professor of Law, University of North Carolina.

Contracts, Calamari and Perillo's Hornbook on, 3rd Ed., 1987,
1049 pages, by John D. Calamari, Professor of Law, Fordham
University and Joseph M. Perillo, Professor of Law, Fordham
University.

Contracts, Corbin's One Volume Student Ed., 1952, 1224 pages,
by Arthur L. Corbin, Late Professor of Law, Yale University.

Corporations, Henn and Alexander's Hornbook on, 3rd Ed.,
1983, with 1986 Pocket Part, 1371 pages, by Harry G. Henn,
Professor of Law Emeritus, Cornell University and John R.
Alexander.

Criminal Law, LaFave and Scott's Hornbook on, 2nd Ed., 1986,
918 pages, by Wayne R. LaFave, Professor of Law, University of Illinois, and Austin Scott, Jr., Late Professor of Law,
University of Colorado.

Criminal Procedure, LaFave and Israel's Hornbook on, 1985
with 1986 pocket part, 1142 pages, by Wayne R. LaFave,
Professor of Law, University of Illinois and Jerold H. Israel,
Professor of Law University of Michigan.

Damages, McCormick's Hornbook on, 1935, 811 pages, by
Charles T. McCormick, Late Dean and Professor of Law,
University of Texas.

Domestic Relations, Clark's Hornbook on, 2nd Ed., 1988, about
1100 pages, by Homer H. Clark, Jr., Professor of Law,
University of Colorado.

Economics and Federal Antitrust Law, Hovenkamp's Hornbook
on, 1985, 414 pages, by Herbert Hovenkamp, Professor of
Law, University of Iowa.

Employment Discrimination Law, Player's Hornbook on, about
650 pages, 1988, by Mack A. Player, Professor of Law,
University of Georgia.

X

Environmental Law, Rodgers' Hornbook on, 1977 with 1984 Pocket Part, 956 pages, by William H. Rodgers, Jr., Professor of Law, University of Washington.

Evidence, Lilly's Introduction to, 2nd Ed., 1987, 585 pages, by Graham C. Lilly, Professor of Law, University of Virginia.

Evidence, McCormick's Hornbook on, 3rd Ed., 1984 with 1987 Pocket Part, 1156 pages, General Editor, Edward W. Cleary, Professor of Law Emeritus, Arizona State University.

Federal Courts, Wright's Hornbook on, 4th Ed., 1983, 870 pages, by Charles Alan Wright, Professor of Law, University of Texas.

Federal Income Taxation, Rose and Chommie's Hornbook on, 3rd Ed., 1988, about 875 pages, by Michael D. Rose, Professor of Law, Ohio State University and John C. Chommie, Late Professor of Law, University of Miami.

Federal Income Taxation of Individuals, Posin's Hornbook on, 1983 with 1987 Pocket Part, 491 pages, by Daniel Q. Posin, Jr., Professor of Law, Catholic University.

Future Interest, Simes' Hornbook on, 2nd Ed., 1966, 355 pages, by Lewis M. Simes, Late Professor of Law, University of Michigan.

Insurance, Keeton and Widiss' Basic Text on, 1988, about 1000 pages, by Robert E. Keeton, Professor of Law Emeritus, Harvard University and Alan I. Widiss, Professor of Law, University of Iowa.

Labor Law, Gorman's Basic Text on, 1976, 914 pages, by Robert A. Gorman, Professor of Law, University of Pennsylvania.

Law Problems, Ballentine's, 5th Ed., 1975, 767 pages, General Editor, William E. Burby, Late Professor of Law, University of Southern California.

Legal Ethics, Wolfram's Hornbook on, 1986, 1120 pages, by Charles W. Wolfram, Professor of Law, Cornell University.

Legal Writing Style, Weihofen's, 2nd Ed., 1980, 332 pages, by Henry Weihofen, Professor of Law Emeritus, University of New Mexico.

Local Government Law, Reynolds' Hornbook on, 1982 with 1987 Pocket Part, 860 pages, by Osborne M. Reynolds, Professor of Law, University of Oklahoma.

New York Estate Administration, Turano and Radigan's Hornbook on, 1986, 676 pages, by Margaret V. Turano, Professor of Law, St. John's University and Raymond Radigan.

New York Practice, Siegel's Hornbook on, 1978 with 1987 Pocket Part, 1011 pages, by David D. Siegel, Professor of Law, St. John's University.

Oil and Gas Law, Hemingway's Hornbook on, 2nd Ed., 1983, with 1986 Pocket Part, 543 pages, by Richard W. Hemingway, Professor of Law, University of Oklahoma.

Property, Boyer's Survey of, 3rd Ed., 1981, 766 pages, by Ralph E. Boyer, Professor of Law Emeritus, University of Miami.

Property, Law of, Cunningham, Whitman and Stoebuck's Hornbook on, 1984, with 1987 Pocket Part, 916 pages, by Roger A. Cunningham, Professor of Law, University of Michigan, Dale A. Whitman, Dean and Professor of Law, University of Missouri, Columbia and William B. Stoebuck, Professor of Law, University of Washington.

Real Estate Finance Law, Nelson and Whitman's Hornbook on, 2nd Ed., 1985, 941 pages, by Grant S. Nelson, Professor of Law, University of Missouri, Columbia and Dale A. Whitman, Dean and Professor of Law, University of Missouri, Columbia.

Real Property, Moynihan's Introduction to, 2nd Ed., 1987, 239 pages, by Cornelius J. Moynihan, Late Professor of Law, Suffolk University.

Remedies, Dobbs' Hornbook on, 1973, 1067 pages, by Dan B. Dobbs, Professor of Law, University of Arizona.

Secured Transactions under the U.C.C., Henson's Hornbook on, 2nd Ed., 1979 with 1979 Pocket Part, 504 pages, by Ray D. Henson, Professor of Law, University of California, Hastings College of the Law.

Securities Regulation, Hazen's Hornbook on the Law of, 1985, with 1988 Pocket Part, 739 pages, by Thomas Lee Hazen, Professor of Law, University of North Carolina.

Sports Law, Schubert, Smith and Trentadue's, 1986, 395 pages, by George W. Schubert, Dean of University College, University of North Dakota, Rodney K. Smith, Professor of Law, Delaware Law School, Widener University, and Jesse C. Trentadue, Former Professor of Law, University of North Dakota.

Torts, Prosser and Keeton's Hornbook on, 5th Ed., 1984 with 1988 Pocket Part, 1286 pages, by William L. Prosser, Late Dean and Professor of Law, University of California, Berkeley, Page Keeton, Professor of Law Emeritus, University of Texas, Dan B. Dobbs, Professor of Law, University of Arizona, Robert E. Keeton, Professor of Law Emeritus, Harvard University and David G. Owen, Professor of Law, University of South Carolina.

Trial Advocacy, Jeans' Handbook on, Soft cover, 1975, 473 pages, by James W. Jeans, Professor of Law, University of Missouri, Kansas City.

Trusts, Bogert's Hornbook on, 6th Ed., 1987, 794 pages, by George T. Bogert.

Uniform Commercial Code, White and Summers' Hornbook on, 3rd Ed., 1988, about 1250 pages, by James J. White, Professor of Law, University of Michigan and Robert S. Summers, Professor of Law, Cornell University.

Urban Planning and Land Development Control Law, Hagman and Juergensmeyer's Hornbook on, 2nd Ed., 1986, 680 pages, by Donald G. Hagman, Late Professor of Law, University of California, Los Angeles and Julian C. Juergensmeyer, Professor of Law, University of Florida.

Wills, Atkinson's Hornbook on, 2nd Ed., 1953, 975 pages, by Thomas E. Atkinson, Late Professor of Law, New York University.

Wills, Trusts and Estates, McGovern, Rein and Kurtz' Hornbook on, 1988, by William M. McGovern, Professor of Law, University of California, Los Angeles, Jan Ellen Rein, Professor of Law, Gonzaga University, and Sheldon F. Kurtz, Professor of Law, University of Iowa.

Advisory Board

XIV

DEBTOR–CREDITOR LAW
IN A NUTSHELL

By

DAVID G. EPSTEIN
Dean, Emory University Law School
(Formerly, Professor of Law,
University of Texas)

THIRD EDITION

ST. PAUL, MINN.
WEST PUBLISHING CO.
1986

Library of Congress Cataloging in Publication Data

Epstein, David G., 1943–
    Debtor creditor law in a nutshell.
    (Nutshell series)
    Includes index.
    1. Debtor and creditor—United States. I. Title.
KF1501.Z9E67 1985   346.73'077   85–22451
                          347.30677

ISBN 0–314–94999–2

Epstein Debt.-Cred.Law 3d Ed. NS
2nd Reprint—1988

To Charles, Daniel, and Isaac Epstein.
I Hope That I Will Be As "Special" to My Sons
as My Father Is to Me.

*

PREFACE

As the title page indicates, this is the third edition of Debtor-Creditor Law in a Nutshell. I prepared a second edition in 1979 because Congress enacted a new bankruptcy code in 1978.* I have prepared this edition in 1985 because Congress enacted significant amendments to the 1978 legislation in 1984.**

Like the first two editions, this book attempts to summarize debtor-creditor law, a/k/a creditors' rights. It sets out the rules, the problems, and the answers to those problems that I can answer. It does not attempt to develop the history of the law, to evaluate the law critically or to propose reform of the law. In short, I have attempted to follow West Publishing Company's suggestion that a nutshell "be a succinct exposition of the law usually covered in one law school course to which a troubled student can turn for reliable guidance." This, of course, does not preclude beneficial use of this nutshell by people studying for a bar examination, lawyers unfamiliar with debtor-creditor law, or even *untroubled* students taking a course in creditors' rights (if any such people exist).

* And because I had moved to Fayetteville, Arkansas, and bought an old house that needed a lot of remodeling work.

** And because I have moved to Atlanta and bought an old house that needs a lot of remodeling work.

Relatively few cases are mentioned by name. Essentially, this book contains citations only to leading, recent or illustrative cases. Virtually no secondary sources are cited. There are, however, numerous references to statutory provisions—particularly the Uniform Commercial Code and the Bankruptcy Code. Provisions in both the Bankruptcy Code and the Uniform Commercial Code are generally referred to as "section _____"; however, the different numbering schemes of the two acts should prevent your confusing the two.

I hope this book will prove helpful in reviewing or learning debtor-creditor law. Creditors' rights is not a very easy course, and this is not a very easy book. However, a course in debtor-creditor law is—or at least should be—challenging, interesting and even enjoyable. Writing this nutshell has been all of these things.† I hope that, to at least some extent, reading it is.

DGE

Atlanta, Georgia
September, 1985

---

† Karen Stevens deserves a lot of the credit for that; she deserves a lot of the credit for this book. She has been an exceptional student research assistant; she is going to be an exceptional lawyer.

OUTLINE

Chapter I. Introductory Material

Chapter II. Extrajudicial Collection Devices

Chapter III. Judicial Debt Collection

Chapter IV. Creditors With Special Rights

Chapter V. Debtor's State Law Remedies, a/k/a Collective Creditor Action

Chapter VI. Bankruptcy: An Overview

Chapter VII. Commencement and Dismissal of a Bankruptcy Case

Chapter VIII. Stay of Collection Actions and Acts

Chapter IX. Property of the Estate

Chapter X. Exemptions

Chapter XI. Avoidance of Pre–Bankruptcy Transfers

Chapter XII. Post–Bankruptcy Transfers (Page 241)

Chapter XIII. Effect of Bankruptcy on Secured Claims

Chapter XVIII. Chapter 13

Chapter XIX. Allocation of Judicial Power Over Bankruptcy Matters

*

TABLE OF CASES

References are to Pages

TABLE OF CASES

TABLE OF CASES

*

CITATIONS
OF THE
BANKRUPTCY CODE

BANKRUPTCY ACT OF 1898

BANKRUPTCY REFORM ACT OF 1978

BANKRUPTCY ACT

BANKRUPTCY ACT

BANKRUPTCY RULES

BANKRUPTCY ACT

*

DEBTOR–CREDITOR LAW

LAW

IN A NUTSHELL

*

CHAPTER I

INTRODUCTORY MATERIAL

A. DISCLAIMER OF ANY IMPLIED WARRANTIES AS TO "FITNESS OF TITLE"

First, it should be noted that the order of appearance of the words "debtor" and "creditor" in the title is of no legal significance. It does not mean that debtors are more important than creditors. It does not mean that this book cannot be used as a study aid in a course in creditors' rights. All that it does mean is that I find it easier to say "debtor-creditor" than "creditor-debtor."

Secondly, it must be confessed that the title is probably misleading. It is misleading in the sense that use of the term "nutshell" implies that a complex and confusing area of the law is completely synthesized and translated into a few pages of relatively readable everyday English. I have attempted to discuss as succinctly and clearly as possible the topics covered in most law school debtor-creditor or creditors' rights courses, to consider the questions that are most commonly raised, and to answer those questions that are answerable. Nevertheless, this brief text should not be viewed as a substitute for study of the cases and the statutes in this area. Particularly the statutes. Particularly the Bankruptcy Code.

B. LIENS AND PRIORITIES [1]

The title is also misleading in that it indicates that there are only two separate identifiable interests to consider: the debtor's and the creditor's. There are at least three identifiable categories of creditors: (1) creditors with a "lien," (2) creditors with a "priority," and (3) creditors with neither a lien nor a priority. While each of these three classes of creditors has the same basic interest—prompt and complete payment of all debts—the law affords each distinctive rights and remedies.

A "lien" is a charge on the debtor's property that must be satisfied before the property or its proceeds is available for satisfaction of the claims of general creditors. A lien thus affects not only the lienor and the debtor but other creditors as well, because it withdraws some of the debtor's re-

1. Unfortunately, the word "priority" has two different meanings in debtor-creditor law:

1. rights of a lien creditor *vis-a-vis* another creditor with a lien on the same property

E.g., on January 10, S lends D $10,000 and obtains and perfects a security interest in D's equipment;

February 2, X lends D $20,000 and obtains and perfects a security interest in D's equipment;

March 3, D defaults on both loans. The equipment is only worth $8,000. Both S and X are lien creditors. The property subject to the two liens is not sufficient to satisfy both liens. It is necessary to determine which lien has PRIORITY.

2. rights of a creditor without a lien in an insolvency proceeding.

sources that would otherwise be available for distribution to other creditors.

The lienor may resort to the encumbered property for the purpose of collecting its claim, yielding only to certain creditors with competing liens. To illustrate, assume that *D* has property worth $1,000 and owes *A* $300, *B* $400 and *C* $500. Assume further that *D*'s property includes a 1951 Henry J worth $400 on which *B* has a lien. In the event that *D* defaulted on his debts, *B* would have first right to the Henry J or the proceeds from the sale thereof. If, however, *D*'s Henry J was worth only $300, *B*'s claim for the other $100 would be treated no differently from the claims of *A* and *C*. A creditor is a lien creditor only to the extent of the value of its collateral.

A lien may be created by agreement, common law, statute, or judicial proceeding.[2] Consensual liens on personalty are governed by Article 9 of the Uniform Commercial Code and are commonly referred to as security interests; consensual liens on realty are generally called mortgages. The creation and perfection of consensual liens is treated in the commercial law course in most law schools and

2. The term "lien creditor" is given an artificial meaning by the Uniform Commercial Code. Section 9–301(3) limits "lien creditor" to a creditor who has obtained through judicial proceedings a lien that reaches the same property as the unperfected security interest in question. If the creditor obtained his lien by reason of statute or through agreement, he is not a "lien creditor" as the term is used in the UCC, and section 9–301(3) does not apply. Cf. section 9–310 (statutory liens); section 9–312 (consensual liens).

is beyond the scope of this nutshell. Judicial liens result from prejudgment collection efforts such as attachment or garnishment, from the judgment itself or recordation thereof, and from post-judgment efforts to enforce the judgment such as execution and garnishment. Statutory liens are more difficult to describe and more difficult to identify. Common statutory liens include landlords' liens, mechanics' liens, and tax liens.

Not all devices that are called liens are liens, however. Some are merely "priorities."

The major distinction between liens and priorities is drawn on the basis of when the interest arises. A priority does not arise until distribution of a debtor's assets on insolvency. Liens normally arise before and are enforceable without regard to insolvency of the debtor. There are, as the following chart indicates, other differences.

Liens	Priorities
1. Consensual, judicial, or statutory	1. Almost always created by statute
2. Interest in particular property of the debtor	2. Satisfied from the general assets of the debtor
3. In a distribution governed by state law, lien creditors are paid first. Some lien creditors have "priority" over other lien creditors	3. Priorities generally affect only the rights of one general creditor (or group of general creditors) *vis-a-vis* other general creditors. Accordingly, in a distribution governed by state

[*4*]

| | law, creditors with a priority usually are paid after lien creditors and before general creditors without any priority |
| 4. In a distribution governed by the Bankruptcy Code, liens that meet certain statutory standards are paid first | 4. All state-created priorities are invalid in a bankruptcy case. Bankruptcy law contains its own priority provision, section 507 |

C. SOURCES OF DEBTOR–CREDITOR LAW

This nutshell considers both bankruptcy and nonbankruptcy debtor-creditor law. The nonbankruptcy part of debtor-creditor law is primarily state collection law. Much of the state law is codification of early English common law doctrine. These codifications and the judicial interpretations thereof vary considerably from state to state. Rather than attempting to set out a fifty-state survey on each topic, I have tried to explore the principal issues and the common resolutions of such issues. There is no recent treatise dealing with state debtor-creditor law.

Bankruptcy law is federal law. The Constitution in article 1, section 8, clause 4 empowers Congress to establish "uniform laws on the subject of Bankruptcies throughout the United States." Congress has acted pursuant to this grant of power and so states are preempted from enacting bankruptcy laws.

Bankruptcy laws can be found in Title 11 of the United States Code. If you look at a copy of Title 11 published prior to 1979, you will find the Bankruptcy Act of 1898, as amended.

In 1970, Congress established the Commission on the Bankruptcy Laws of the United States to evaluate the Bankruptcy Act of 1898 and propose a concrete statutory alternative. The Commission issued a report in 1973 that contained a statutory proposal entitled the Bankruptcy Act of 1973. After five years of delay and debate, bankruptcy legislation was passed by Congress and sent to the President. On November 6, 1978, the President signed the Bankruptcy Reform Act of 1978. This law was amended by the Bankruptcy Amendments and Federal Judgeship Act of 1984 which the President signed on July 10, 1984.

Most of the case law interpreting these bankruptcy statutes is decisions of bankruptcy judges. In response to the passage of the Bankruptcy Reform Act of 1978, West Publishing Company added a new unit to the National Reporter System—the Bankruptcy Reporter. There are, also, three loose-leaf services that reproduce a number of bankruptcy decisions: Bankruptcy Court Decisions, Collier Bankruptcy Cases, and CCH Bankruptcy Law Reports.[3]

3. These services publish not only decisions by bankruptcy judges but also decisions by district judges and judges on the courts of appeals dealing with bankruptcy law questions.

SOURCES OF DEBTOR–CREDITOR LAW

The bankruptcy portion of this book will focus on the provisions of the Bankruptcy Reform Act of 1978 as amended in 1984.

CHAPTER II

EXTRAJUDICIAL COLLECTION DEVICES

As long as the debtor is making payments when due, debtor-creditor law is of little practical significance. The debtor, of course, does not always make the required payments. The ready availability of consumer credit often leads to over-extension in debt and, subsequently, default. The creditor can proceed to collect the debt by using either extrajudicial or judicial methods. Because of the delay and expense involved in litigation, the creditor is likely initially to employ extrajudicial tactics to obtain payment.

The extrajudicial collection method most generally used is the dunning letter. This letter, containing a request for payment, can be either cordial or hostile depending on the policy of the creditor and the length of time that the debt is outstanding. Debtors often do not respond to a polite request for payment. Consequently, creditors seek other methods to recover the money due and owing, including telephone calls, personal visits, threats of lawsuit, and communications with the debtor's employer. Occasionally the creditor or his agent becomes overzealous, particularly when the debtor is weak and vulnerable.

[8]

A. COMMON LAW LIMITATIONS

Courts have sought to moderate the conduct of creditors by allowing debtors to recover for unreasonable collection activities under the following common law tort concepts: defamation, invasion of the right to privacy, and intentional infliction of mental anguish. Recoveries on these theories, however, are relatively rare. It is difficult to match the facts of debt collection with the elements of these torts.

Defamation is aimed at publication of false material. Truth is thus a defense—in most jurisdictions, an absolute defense. A statement truthfully disclosing that a debt is due, owing, and unpaid is not actionable. A statement that falsely imputes a general unwillingness to pay debts or unworthiness to obtain credit may be the basis of a defamation action.

Another defense to defamation is privilege. A communication will be privileged if it pertains to a matter in which the recipient of the communication has a legitimate interest. Informing an employer that his employee has not paid his debts is a common collection tactic to induce payment through indirect pressure on the employee. Employers want to avoid the bother and costs of wage garnishment. Courts are divided as to whether employers have a sufficient interest to cause the communication to be privileged.

Debtors have also sued on invasion of privacy grounds for injuries resulting from creditors' communications with employers—generally with little success. Public disclosure of private facts is one form of invasion of the right to privacy. However, as a general rule, reasonable oral or written communications to an employer have not been viewed as a sufficient disclosure of private facts; as with defamation, the communication is privileged based on the employer's interest in his employee's debts.

Some courts have granted recovery where the creditor has done more than inform the employer that a debt is overdue—for example, contacting the employer on numerous occasions. Additionally, there are cases finding an invasion of privacy by communications such as calls to the debtor's neighbors, publication of the debtor's name and amount of debt in a newspaper, and posting a notice of the indebtedness at the creditor's place of business.

A second form of violation of the right to privacy is a wrongful intrusion on the solitude of the debtor. Obviously, every creditor contact, every intrusion, is not actionable. The creditor has the right to contact the debtor—has the right to try and collect the debt. The problem is one of balancing the respective interests. Only unreasonable intrusions are actionable. In determining reasonableness, courts generally consider factors such as the content, nature, number, and time of communications.

Where these communications are "extreme and outrageous" and result in emotional distress, the debtor may be able to recover on a theory of intentional infliction of mental distress. Several difficulties inhere in such an action. First, the creditor's actions must be beyond all bounds of decency; as the Restatement puts it, "recitation of the facts to an average member of the community would arouse his resentment against the actor and lead him to exclaim 'Outrageous'." Restatement of Torts 461 (supp.1948). Another difficulty attending this cause of action is the requirement that the emotional stress be severe. The normal strain caused by contact with a collection agency is not sufficient. The debtor has to establish serious mental stress. Most courts also have been hesitant to impose liability for mental distress alone, and have insisted on some form of physical injury.

The following paragraph from an excellent student note summarizes the shortcomings of present judicial remedies for debt collection abuses.

"In short, relief available through present common law remedies is not sufficient for several reasons. Not all conduct that one might wish forbidden affords a basis for relief in court. The economic and social class most in need of protection is precisely the class most alienated from the legal system and therefore least likely to attempt to vindicate its rights through litigation. Relief to one debtor does not necessarily provide any protection to other members of that class.

Finally, a judicial sanction can be somewhat indefinite because of difficulties inherent in the translation of adjudicated results into generalized rules. These shortcomings contrast sharply with the capacity of legislative prohibition and regulation."

Note, Debt Collection Practices: Remedies for Abuse, 10 B.C.Ind. & Com.L.Rev. 698, 702–3 (1969).

B. FAIR DEBT COLLECTION PRACTICES ACT

A number of states statutorily regulate the collection of consumer debts. The Federal Trade Commission has published a *proposed* trade regulation rule relating to the collection of consumer debts. And, in 1977, Congress enacted the Fair Debt Collection Practices Act, FDCPA.

FDCPA does *not* apply to all consumer credit collection efforts. It governs the conduct of "debt collectors," i.e., persons who regularly collect debts owed to someone else. FDCPA does not apply to the lender or credit seller that is attempting to collect its own debts.[1]

The Act severely limits "debt collector" contacts with third parties. A "debt collector" may contact a person other than a consumer, the consumer's spouse (or the consumer's parents if the consumer

---

1. It does apply to a creditor who "in the process of collecting his own debts, uses any name other than his own which would indicate that a third person is collecting or attempting to collect the debts," section 803(6).

is a minor) and the consumer's attorney only for
the purpose of finding the debtor. Section 804 sets
out specific guidelines which a "debt collector"
must follow when contacting third parties to learn
a debtor's whereabouts. The "debtor collector"
may not volunteer that she is a "debt collector";
such information may be furnished only if "expressly requested." Even if expressly requested, a
"debt collector" may not tell a third party that the
debtor owes a debt.

Once the debtor has been located and contacted,
the "debt collector" must give the debtor the opportunity to require verification of the debt. No
later than five days after first communicating with
the debtor, the "debt collector" must send the
debtor a written notice setting out the amount of
the debt, the name of the creditor, the debtor's
right to dispute the accuracy or existence of the
debt, and the debt collector's duty to obtain verification of the debt if it is disputed by the debtor
within thirty days.

FDCPA does not expressly limit the number of
times that a "debt collector" may contact a debtor
in attempting to collect a debt. Section 805, however, governs such contacts. The contact must not
be at a time or place "which should be known to be
inconvenient." All "debt collector" contact with
the debtor must cease when the debt collector
learns that the debtor is represented by an attorney, receives a written refusal to pay, or receives a
written communication from the debtor requesting
that such contacts end.

In addition to the above rules limiting contacts by "debt collectors," FDCPA also generally forbids any conduct by "debt collectors" which is abusive, deceptive, misleading, or unfair. Sections 806 through 808 contain "laundry lists" of illustrative practices which are specifically forbidden.

Section 811 governs venue of collection suits filed by "debt collectors." Actions brought to enforce a lien on real property may be brought only in the county in which the real property is located. Other collection actions may be brought by "debt collectors" only where the debtor resides or where the contract is signed.

A "debt collector" who violates the FDCPA is civilly liable for (1) actual damages, (2) "additional damages" up to $1,000 [In assessing "additional damages," the court is to look to the frequency, persistence, and nature of the violations as well as the extent to which the violations were intentional], and (3) attorneys' fees and costs. The court may grant attorneys' fees *to* the "debt collector" if the action against the "debt collector" was brought in "bad faith and for the purpose of harassment."

A violation of FDCPA is also considered an unfair or deceptive act or practice, in violation of the Federal Trade Commission Act, section 814. The Federal Trade Commission may thus seek a variety of remedies against a "debt collector" that violates the FDCPA, including a fine of up to $10,000 per violation.

[*14*]

CHAPTER III

JUDICIAL DEBT COLLECTION

A. EXEMPT PROPERTY

Today all states constitutionally or statutorily restrict creditor recourse to certain property. Property designated in these exemption provisions can *not* be reached by creditors through judicial collection efforts. A three-pronged purpose is commonly attributed to exemption statutes: protection of the debtor, protection of the family of the debtor, and protection of society. By allowing the debtor to retain certain property free from appropriation by creditors, exemption statutes extend to a debtor an opportunity for self-support so that he will not become a burden upon the public.

In looking at exemption statutes, a lawyer or law student should look for the answers to three different questions:

(1) what property can a debtor claim as exempt

(2) what does a debtor have to do to claim the exemptions

(3) what creditors are not affected by a claim that property is exempt.

The exemption statutes of the different states answer these questions differently.

[*15*]

There are two notable characteristics of state exemption statutes: (1) obsolescence and (2) extreme variety.[1] Nevertheless, certain generalizations are possible. All states exempt certain personal property from creditor process. In some jurisdictions, the exempt property is identified by type (e.g., the family bible, the family rifle); in others, by value (e.g., personal property of a value of $5,000); in still others, by both type and value (e.g., an automobile with a value of not more than $1,500). In most states, some specific provision is made for the exemption of life insurance (both the proceeds of the policy and the cash surrender value thereof) and wages.

The procedure for asserting rights under an exemption statute also varies from state to state. The burden usually is on the debtor to claim the exemption, and usually the statute sets a time limit on assertion of an exemption. Where the statute is of a "value" type—e.g., personal property of a value of $5,000—the statute generally provides for the appointment of appraisers who value property selected as exempt by the debtor. Where the statute specifies items of property that are exempt, courts are often confronted with the problem of applying a 19th century statute to 20th century

1. In 1976, the National Conference of Commissioners on Uniform State Laws promulgated a Uniform Exemption Statute. To date, no state has adopted this uniform act. Section 522 of the Bankruptcy Reform Act of 1978, considered infra at pages 177–182 is markedly similar to the Uniform Exemption Statute.

property—e.g., whether a television set is a "musical instrument" or whether an automobile is a salesman's "tool of trade."

Almost all states also have homestead laws designed to protect the family home from the reach of certain classes of creditors. Homestead laws only protect real property interests of the debtor and so are of no aid to the urban apartment dweller. Moreover, not all real property interests of the debtor may be the subject of a homestead claim. Common statutory limitations include the requirements that the debtor have a family, that the property be occupied and used as a residence (an almost universal limitation), that the owner have a specified (usually present, possessory) interest in the property, and (in a few states) that there be a formal declaration that the property is a homestead.

The protection afforded by an exemption statute is not absolute. The federal tax lien reaches and may be satisfied from "exempt property." A number of states make similar exceptions for state taxes, claims for alimony and child support, materialmen and mechanics' liens. By statute in most states, case law in others, mortgages and security interests are generally not affected by an exemption statute. Thus, the bank that finances the purchase of a home or car will be able to seize and sell the property notwithstanding the fact that the property is covered by an exemption statute. Or, if D gives C a second lien on her car to secure a

Christmas loan, C can, on D's default, foreclose on
D's car. On the other hand, an executory agreement to waive the benefit of an exemption has
generally been held to be invalid as against the
public policy, notwithstanding some obvious similarities between such a waiver and a nonpurchase
money mortgage.

There are also federal statutes that exempt property from the reach of creditors in either federal
court or state court. Most of the federal provisions
relate to the benefits of federal social legislation
such as money paid under social security and veterans' benefits. Title III of the Consumer Credit
Protection Act provides a statutory minimum exemption of wages from garnishments.[2] Under Title III, creditors may garnish in the aggregate only
25% of a person's weekly "disposable earnings" or
the amount by which his "disposable earnings"
exceed thirty times the minimum hourly wage,
whichever is less.[3]

2. Title III is not really an exemption provision. It does not
exempt all or part of the debtor's wages. It merely protects the
wages from garnishment. Once the wages have been paid to
the debtor, creditors can look to the money to satisfy their
claims.

3. Title III of the Consumer Credit Protection Act also
affords protection to a debtor from discharge because of garnishment. The Act prohibits the discharge of any employee "by
reason of the fact that his earnings have been subjected to
garnishment for any *one indebtedness.*" Thus if D is indebted
to C, and C garnishes D's wages several times in an attempt to
satisfy his claim, D's employer cannot discharge him because of
these garnishments. Only "one indebtedness." On the other
hand, if D is indebted to both C and E and both garnish D's

"Disposable earnings" is defined in Title III as salary less deductions "required by law." The following hypothetical illustrates the operation of Title III. X's salary is $10,800 a year. X does not, however, receive $900 a month. Rather, X's "take-home pay" is only $700 a month because of the following deductions: $130 for taxes, $50 for social security, $20 for Blue Cross. Only the $130 for taxes and the $50 for social security are deductions "required by law." X's "disposable earnings" is thus $720 a month or $180 a week. Title III limits the amount that X's creditors can garnish to $45 a week.

Title III does not preempt state statutes "prohibiting garnishments or providing for more limited garnishments than are allowed under [Title III]." Where state restrictions are stronger, it will be state law which regulates. Title III also makes provision for state law to apply in lieu of the wage garnishment provisions of Title III where the Secretary of Labor determines that the laws of that state provide restrictions on garnishment which are "substantially similar" to those provided in the Act.

wages, D's employer can discharge him because of the garnishments. More than "one indebtedness." The prohibition against discharge is probably of limited practical significance in light of the difficulty of establishing the reason for dismissal and the absence of any express private remedy for wrongful discharge. The Act provides for enforcement by the Secretary of Labor. Courts are divided as to whether to imply a private right of action.

B. PREJUDGMENT REMEDIES

A creditor trying to collect a claim through the judicial process is not always going to be able to obtain a judgment immediately. Litigation is costly and time-consuming. While the collection lawsuit is pending, the debtor may dispose of his assets or other creditors may seize the debtor's property to satisfy their claims. While the collection action is pending, the creditor may want to try to pressure the debtor to settle. Accordingly, it is necessary to consider prejudgment remedies.

1. Attachment

At early common law, attachment was a form of process to compel the defendant to appear and answer if he failed to appear in response to the summons or original writ. The writ commanded the sheriff to attach the property of the defendant to compel his appearance. If he appeared the property was returned to him; if he failed to appear, the property was forfeited. In the 17th century, the nature of attachment changed from a means of compelling the defendant's appearance to a prejudgment (provisional) collection remedy: attached property was no longer released upon the appearance of the defendant but remained attached until after judgment and collection of same. No longer is the main objective of attachment to coerce the defendant debtor to appear by seizure of his property; today the writ of attachment seizes

[20]

the debtor's property in order to secure the debt or claim of the creditor in the event that a judgment is obtained.

Today attachment is purely statutory. The statutes vary considerably as to when attachment is available. [Federal courts follow the local rules relating to attachment, Fed.Civ.Proc. Rule 64.]

In no state is attachment available to every creditor in every collection action. Rather, the use of attachment is generally limited in the following ways:

(1) The statutes providing for attachment commonly spell out specific kinds of actions that may be the basis for the issuance of an attachment. Attachment statutes in many states distinguish between claims *ex contractu* and claims *ex delicto,* sometimes establishing different requirements with respect to attachment for each type of claim, and sometimes providing for attachment only upon claims *ex contractu.*

(2) Attachment is usually to be had only on a showing of special statutory grounds. In general the statutory grounds deal with one of three situations: (i) where the plaintiff is unable to obtain personal service upon a defendant because the defendant is absent from the state, concealing himself, or a nonresident; (ii) where the nature of the plaintiff's underlying claim entitles it to special treatment such as a claim based on fraud or a claim for "the necessaries of life"; (iii) where the defendant has assigned, disposed of, or secreted, or

is about to assign, dispose of, or secrete property with the intent to defraud creditors.

(3) A bond is commonly required. The usual condition of the bond is that the plaintiff shall pay all costs that may be awarded to the defendant and all damages that defendant may sustain by reason of the attachment, if the order of attachment is dissolved or if the plaintiff fails to obtain judgment against the defendant.

(4) As a result of *Sniadach v. Family Finance Corp., Fuentes v. Shevin,* and *North Georgia Finishing, Inc. v. Di-Chem, Inc.* (all of which are discussed infra on pages 36–40,) an increasing number of states now require that the debtor be provided notice and an opportunity for a hearing before the debtor's property may be attached.

Attachment procedure varies considerably from state to state. In most states, a creditor seeking attachment must first file a complaint. The creditor then files an affidavit stating that a ground for attachment exists, a bond, and a writ of attachment.

Originally, the clerk of the court in which the action had been or was being commenced was authorized to issue writs of attachment ex parte. Since *Sniadach* and its progeny, most states require the opportunity for some form of hearing before a judge. The writ of attachment is directed to the sheriff of a county in which property of the defendant is located. The order instructs the sheriff to attach and safely keep all non-exempt property of the defendant within the sheriff's county, or so much thereof as is sufficient to satisfy the plaintiff's demand together with costs and expenses. It also directs the sheriff to make a written return to the clerk of the court in which the action is pending showing all property attached and the date of seizure.

The act of the sheriff in taking custody over the property of the defendant is commonly referred to as "levy." What "levy" entails depends on the nature of the property. Levy on real property generally involves some act giving notice to the defendant of the lien and some act giving public notice that the debtor's realty is encumbered, such as filing in the real estate record system. A levy of attachment upon tangible personal property generally requires a seizure or taking possession or control of the property. If the chattels are capable of manual delivery, most jurisdictions require the sheriff to take the chattels into his actual custody by either removing them or appointing an independent keeper. Where the property to be attached is of a bulky or cumbersome nature and removal would be very difficult and expensive, levy does not require removal or seizure. For example, in Brunswick Corp. v. Haerter, 182 N.W.2d 852 (N.D.1971), removing a part from each pinsetter making the bowling alley inoperative constituted an effective levy.

Levy on property creates a lien thereon. In most states this lien of attachment dates from the time of the levy although in some states the date of the lien relates back to the date of the issuance of the writ.

A creditor with an attachment lien enjoys a number of advantages:

(1) *Security*

While a collection action is pending, a debtor may try to dispose of his assets. An attachment lien is effective against subsequent purchasers from the debtor. To illustrate, D is in default on its loan obligations to C. C files a lawsuit and obtains an attachment lien on D's collection of Franklin Mint coins by having the sheriff seize the coins pursuant to a writ of attachment. While C's lawsuit against D is pending, D sells the coins to B. C then obtains its judgment against D. C will be able to sell the Franklin Mint coins to satisfy its judgment. C's attachment lien is effective against B, a subsequent purchaser from the debtor, D.

To obtain its attachment lien, C had to levy on, i.e., seize, the Franklin Mint coins. D's lack of possession put third parties such as B on notice of possible creditor's claims.

(2) *Priority*

Often, a debtor lacks sufficient assets to pay all of his creditors. In such instances, state law does *not* provide for pro rata distributions. Rather, state law provides a series of priority rules. Most of the rules are "first-in-time" rules: the earlier the creditor obtains its lien, the greater its priority. For example, a creditor with an attachment lien takes priority over a creditor who subsequently obtains a judgment lien on the same property. To illustrate, D owes A $10,000 and B $20,000. D is in default on both debts, and D's only significant non-exempt asset is Greenacre. A sues D and obtains an attachment lien on Greenacre. Subsequently, B sues D, obtains a $20,000 judgment against D, and obtains a judgment lien on Greenacre. Then, A obtains a $10,000 judgment against D. If a sale of Greenacre only yields $17,000, A will receive $10,000 of the sale proceeds and B will receive the remaining $7,000.

(3) *Jurisdiction*

The priority and security afforded by the lien are not the only advantages to a creditor of obtaining a writ of attachment. Attachment can also be used as a basis for jurisdiction. State courts can take jurisdiction over nonresidents who have property in the state if that property is brought within the court's jurisdiction by attachment and if substituted service (such as service by publication) is made. Such jurisdiction, called "quasi-in-rem" jurisdiction is generally less valuable to plaintiffs than personal jurisdiction: a judgment quasi-in-rem binds only the parties to the action and not the entire world, and it imposes no personal liability on the defendant, the award being limited to the property seized.

The importance of quasi-in-rem jurisdiction—and hence of attachment as a jurisdictional mechanism—has declined over the years.

Long-arm statutes have increased the availability of in personam jurisdiction. Shaffer v. Heitner, 433 U.S. 186 (1977), has decreased the availability of quasi-in-rem jurisdiction.

Prior to *Shaffer,* presence of property in a state was itself sufficient basis for quasi-in-rem jurisdiction of the courts of that state. In *Shaffer,* however, the Court held that the "minimum contacts" standard of International Shoe Co. v. Washington, 326 U.S. 310 (1945), governs not only *in personam* jurisdiction but also *in rem* jurisdiction.

(4) *Leverage*

A more important advantage of attachment is the leverage that it gives the plaintiff. By directing the sheriff to levy on property essential to the defendant/debtor, the creditor greatly strengthens its bargaining position. Deprivation of property used daily or essential to a business may induce the debtor to pay even if the claim is of questionable validity.

Notwithstanding the advantages of attachment discussed above, plaintiff/creditors do not always and should not always obtain a writ of attachment.[4] There are at least three distinct hazards in attachment:

(a) *Fees*

As indicated above, a bond is generally required of the creditor. And, the sheriff will usually require an indemnity bond before levying on property to protect him from liability should he attach the wrong property and incur liability for conversion. The sheriff is also entitled to reimbursement of expenses incurred in levying on the property and in preserving the attached property. Last, but not least, an attaching creditor must pay its attorney for the legal work involved in obtaining an attachment lien.

(b) *Liability for wrongful attachment*

Attachment of personal property deprives the debtor of the use of the property for the duration of the litigation. Attachment of real property makes it difficult if not impossible for the debtor to sell the property for the duration of the litigation. If the debt collection action ends in a judgment for the debtor, the debtor can recover any actual damages she has suffered as a result of the attachment. Additionally, if the creditor attached the debtor's property maliciously and without probable cause, the debtor can recover punitive damages.

---

4. Remember, attachment is not always available to a creditor. Limitations on the availability of attachment are discussed on pages 21–22, supra.

Tort liability has even been imposed on a creditor who prevails in the debt collection action. If the creditor has directed the sheriff as to which property to seize, the creditor is liable to the debtor if excessive property is seized, and is liable to third parties if their property is wrongfully seized.

(c) *Bankruptcy of the debtor*

Attachment benefits a single creditor at the expense of the debtor and other creditors. A debtor deprived by attachment of the use of important property may decide to file a bankruptcy petition. Moreover, attachment may motivate the debtor's other creditors to initiate involuntary bankruptcy proceedings. Under section 547 of the Bankruptcy Code, an attachment lien obtained within 90 days of the filing of the bankruptcy petition is invalid if the debtor was insolvent when the lien was obtained.

Failure to obtain a judgment will result in the attachment being dissolved. A debtor may also terminate the attachment and obtain the attached property by posting a "discharging" or "dissolution" bond; these bonds are conditioned that the defendant in the attachment suit will perform whatever judgment will be entered against him and that, in the event of his default thereof, the surety will pay the amount of the judgment. A second class of bond available in most jurisdictions are "forthcoming" or "delivery" bonds. These are conditioned that if judgment in the attachment suit is rendered against the defendant, the property shall be forthcoming to satisfy such judgment, otherwise the surety will be liable to the extent of the value of the property. Such bonds release the property only from the custody of the levying officer; they do not release the attached property from the lien of attachment.

2. Prejudgment Garnishment

Garnishment (or, in most New England states, trustee process) is a collection remedy directed not at the defendant but rather at some third person, the garnishee, who owes a debt to the principal debtor, has property of the principal debtor, or has property in which the principal debtor has an interest. Prejudgment garnishment is a warning or notice to the garnishee that the plaintiff/creditor claims the right to have such debt or property applied in satisfaction of his claim, and that the garnishee should hold such property until the creditor's suit has been tried and any judgment satisfied. For example, if C brought an action against D to collect a debt that was due and owing and C learned that G held property of D, C might garnish this property. Then, if C was successful in her action against D, C's judgment could be satisfied by the property of D held by G, and, if G no longer had such property, C could recover from G personally. The most common examples of garnishees are the employer of the principal debtor and the bank in which the principal debtor has a savings or checking account.

Garnishment is frequently referred to as a form of attachment. The two remedies are similar in many respects. In a number of states, garnishment is not an independent remedy but rather is a proceeding ancillary to attachment. In other states, however, garnishment is an independent action available for grounds other than those required for the issuance of an attachment and subject to different provisions for bond. In all states, there are some differences between attachment and garnishment. The following chart compares attachment and garnishment.

Attachment	Garnishment
1. Statutory	1. Statutory
2. Federal courts follow state rules as to availability Fed.Civ.Proc. Rule 64	2. Federal courts follow state rules as to availability Fed.Civ.Proc. Rule 64
3. Device for obtaining quasi-in-rem jurisdiction over a nonresident [5]	3. Device for obtaining quasi-in-rem jurisdiction over a nonresident [5]
4. Directed to property in the possession of the principal debtor	4. Directed to property of the debtor held by the garnishee
5. Prejudgment remedy	5. Both a prejudgment and a post-judgment remedy

5. Remember that Shaffer v. Heitner, supra at page 26, limits the availability of quasi-in-rem jurisdiction.

Attachment	Garnishment
6. Seizure of the property pending judgment	6. Property left in the care and custody of the garnishee
7. Lien on attached property, generally dating from time of levy	7. In a few states, no lien; generally held to create a lien that dates from the service of process on the garnishee

3. Replevin

At early common law, a landlord could enforce its rights to rent by the self-help remedy of distraint, i.e., seizing the personal property of the tenant. If the tenant disputed the landlord's claim of unpaid rent, he could, upon giving the sheriff security, obtain a writ of replevin directing the sheriff to recover possession of the seized personal property, pending litigation of the tenant's rent liability.

In this country, replevin has developed into a more general remedy. Today replevin (and sequestration and claim and delivery) is a proceeding to recover possession of any personal property. At the commencement of the action, the sheriff seizes, i.e., replevies the property and turns it over to the plaintiff, pending outcome of the litigation over possession. If the defendant wishes to regain possession of the goods replevied, he may give a delivery or forthcoming bond.

Replevin may not be used by all creditors. Replevin can only be maintained by one who has title or the right to possession of the property sought to be recovered. Unpaid unsecured creditors do not have a right to possession of their debtors' property. Unpaid secured creditors do have a right to possession of the property encumbered by their liens.

To illustrate, assume that Pizza Inc. owes U $1,000 and S $2,000. U is an unsecured creditor. S has a security interest in Pizza Inc.'s oven. Pizza Inc. defaults on both debts. The remedy of replevin is not available to U; S can *possibly replevy* the pizza oven. Either U or S *possibly* can *attach* the pizza oven and/or other property of Pizza Inc.

The following chart compares attachment and replevin.

Attachment	Replevin
1. Statutory	1. Statutory
2. Federal courts follow state rules as to availability Fed.Civ.Proc. Rule 64	2. Federal courts follow state rules as to availability Fed.Civ.Proc. Rule 64
3. Any non-exempt property in the possession of the debtor	3. Limited to personal property which the creditor has a lien on and/or the right to possess
4. Prejudgment remedy	4. Both a prejudgment remedy and a form of action

Attachment	Replevin
5. Seizure of the property by sheriff who retains custody thereof pending judgment	5. Seizure of property by sheriff who turns property over to plaintiff pending judgment
6. Lien on attached property, generally dating from the time of levy	6. Generally thought to create a lien that dates from the time of seizure

4. Receivership

Receivership, like garnishment, is both a prejudgment and a post-judgment collection remedy. A prejudgment receiver is a disinterested party, appointed by the court to administer, care for, collect and dispose of the property or the fruits of the property of another brought under the orders of the court by litigation.

The power to appoint a receiver is inherent in a court of equity. The appointment of a receiver is to a considerable extent a matter resting in the discretion of the court to which the application is made. Courts are very reluctant to appoint receivers prior to judgment, i.e., receivers *pendente lite*. There is a wealth of dictum to the effect that the appointment of a receiver is a harsh remedy and is to be used sparingly—only when the securing of ultimate justice seems to require it. And, since receivership is an equitable remedy, a court will not appoint a receiver when there is an adequate legal remedy such as attachment. Reported cases in which a receiver *pendente lite* has been ap-

[*33*]

pointed generally involve allegations of danger of loss, deterioration, or other impairment of the value of property that is the subject matter of the action or that will be necessary to satisfy any judgment in the action.

In 1844 New York adopted a civil code uniting the practice of law and equity; the Field Code provided in what cases a receiver should be appointed. Numerous other jurisdictions have followed New York's lead. Most such provisions are little more than a codification of the rules of equity except with regard to corporations. Many states have provisions for the appointment of receivers of corporations both before and after dissolution.

The receiver has only such powers as are specifically conferred upon him by the court or by the statute under which he was appointed. Absent a statutory provision to the contrary, the appointment of a receiver works a change in possession of, but not title to, the property over which the receiver is appointed; statutes governing the appointment of a receiver prior to judgment generally contain no provision to the contrary. The powers of receivers *pendente lite* are generally quite limited. The receiver is usually required to take possession of the property as soon as possible after the order appointing him has been entered. The order may contemplate the mere holding of the property for the purpose of preserving it or it may direct some active duties such as the continuance of a business, collecting rents and profits, or the sale of property.

The preceding paragraphs indicate one of the primary reasons that a creditor petitions for the appointment of a receiver *pendente lite*—preservation of property of the defendant/debtor pending determination of the creditor's claim. Receivership is similar to provisional remedies already discussed in that it is also used as leverage to obtain a favorable settlement. Receivership, however, differs from attachment and garnishment in that no advantage *vis-a-vis* other creditors accrues to the creditor who secures the appointment of a receiver. The petitioning creditor does not gain a lien on the property over which the receiver is appointed. And, since the appointment of a receiver *pendente lite* generally does not affect title to the property, existing liens on the property remain valid, and creditors can continue to obtain liens on property held by a receiver *pendente lite*. To illustrate, C sues D; prior to judgment C obtains the appointment of a receiver to hold and manage Greenacre Farms, a tract of land owned by D in Orange County. Prior to C's obtaining a judgment, E obtains a judgment against D. E dockets this judgment in the county in which Greenacre Farms is located. Under the applicable state law, the docketing of a judgment creates a lien on all real property held by the judgment debtor in the county of docketing. [Judgment liens are considered infra at pages 44–49]. This judgment lien would reach Greenacre Farms.

The appointment of a receiver does in a limited way affect the rights of other creditors. While the appointment does not divest existing liens or prevent the creation of new liens, lien creditors cannot enforce their claims and thus disturb the receiver's possession without the permission of the court. Consent of the court that appointed the receiver is also generally regarded as necessary in order to garnish property held by a receiver.

5. Limitations on Prejudgment Remedies

Commencing in the late 1960's, prejudgment remedies came under attack by both the courts and the legislatures. In Sniadach v. Family Finance Corp., 395 U.S. 337 (1969) the Court held that the Wisconsin statute providing for prejudgment garnishment of wages was unconstitutional. Justice Douglas' opinion emphasizes the hardship that results from wage garnishment and suggests that due process requires notice and hearing prior to the issuance of a writ, except in "extraordinary situations."

Sniadach, however, gives little guidance as to what constitutes "extraordinary situations" or whether "extraordinary situations" coincide with the typical statutory grounds for prejudgment garnishment. Justice Douglas cites four cases as instances where summary procedure may be used: three involve summary seizure or impounding of property by a governmental agency to protect the public welfare. The only "creditors' rights" case cited involves attachment of property by a nonresident debtor. [Remember that Shaffer v. Heitner, supra at page 26, limited the use of prejudgment remedies to obtain quasi-in-rem jurisdiction.]

Fuentes v. Shevin, 407 U.S. 67 (1972), expands the due process limitations first recognized in *Sniadach* to property other than wages, to prejudgment remedies other than garnishment. *Fuentes* involved replevin of consumer goods. The Court held the Florida and Pennsylvania replevin statutes unconstitutional; the opinion suggests that except in "extraordinary situations," notice and hearing must precede the seizure.

In discussing what constitutes "extraordinary situations," the *Fuentes* decision cites the same decisions as the *Sniadach* opinion cited. In *Sniadach,* the Court spoke of situations "requiring special protection to a state or *creditor* interest." In *Fuentes,* the Court referred to seizures "directly necessary to secure an important governmental or *general public* interest." While *Fuentes* seems to impose a more restrictive "extraordinary situations" test, there is dictum in *Fuentes* that indicates that "a showing of immediate danger that a debtor will destroy or conceal disputed goods" is an "extraordinary situation."

In Mitchell v. W. T. Grant Co., 416 U.S. 600 (1974), the Court held that a Louisiana statute permitting a judge to issue, without prior notice and hearing, a writ of sequestration based on a vendor's lien adequately balanced the property interests of the creditor and the debtor and satisfied due process.

The opinion distinguishes this Louisiana statute from the Florida and Pennsylvania replevin provisions involved in *Fuentes.* The Louisiana statute requires the creditor to allege specific facts supporting its claim, rather than the conclusory allegations of right that were sufficient under the Florida and Pennsylvania provisions. In *Mitchell,* the application for prejudgment relief was made to a judge, not a clerk. And, the Louisiana statute at issue in *Mitchell* gives the debtor the right to an immediate post-seizure hearing.

The majority opinion in *Mitchell* generated confusion (even among the Justices of the Supreme Court) as to whether *Fuentes* had been overruled. The *Mitchell* decision has also created uncertainty as to whether (1) *Mitchell* applies to all prejudgment remedies or is limited to prejudgment remedies such as sequestration that are available only to creditors with an interest in the property to be seized, and (2) whether *all* of the safeguards present in the Louisiana statute are necessary in the absence of a pre-seizure adversary hearing.

North Georgia Finishing, Inc. v. Di-Chem, Inc., 419 U.S. 601 (1975), provides some answers. In finding the Georgia prejudgment garnishment statute in violation of procedural due process, the Court cites and relies on *Fuentes.* The *North Geor-*

gia opinion also relies on *Mitchell* even though the creditor in *North Georgia* had no property interest in the bank account it was trying to garnish. "The Georgia garnishment statute has *none* of the saving characteristics of the Louisiana statute." The Georgia garnishment statute did not require specific factual allegations of entitlement, judicial participation, or provide the opportunity for a prompt post-seizure hearing.

North Georgia's use of both *Fuentes* and *Mitchell* makes it necessary (and difficult) to reconcile these two opinions. Some commentators have suggested that the unusual procedural safeguards in *Mitchell* come within *Fuentes'* "extraordinary situation" exception. (Remember, the *Fuentes* opinion suggests that notice and hearing must precede the seizure except in "extraordinary situations.")

While the relationship between the various cases is somewhat unclear, the following basic propositions seem clear:

1. Prejudgment remedies are not unconstitutional per se.

2. The use of prejudgment remedies is subject to due process limitations.

3. Due process requires notice and an opportunity for an adversary proceeding.

4. In at least some situations, a pre-seizure ex parte hearing coupled with the opportunity for a prompt post-seizure adversary proceeding will satisfy due process.

Since *Sniadach* a number of state legislatures have eliminated prejudgment wage garnishment and restricted the availability of other prejudgment remedies. Congress by Title III of the Consumer Credit Protection Act has restricted both prejudgment and postjudgment garnishment of wages. The Act exempts a minimum of 75% of the debtor's wages from garnishment, and it prohibits an employer from discharging an employee because of garnishment for a single debt. The statute is considered in more detail at pages 18–19 supra.

C. OBTAINING A JUDGMENT

The prejudgment remedies considered in the preceding sections afford a creditor less than complete relief. At best, such remedies pressure the debtor to pay and provide some security of payment. Accordingly, where the debtor does not capitulate after the use of available provisional remedies, it is necessary for the creditor to obtain a judgment.

A creditor, of course, wants to obtain the judgment as quickly and as inexpensively as possible. A default judgment is thus preferable to a judgment resulting from prolonged litigation. Most collection actions result in a default judgment for the creditor. Some creditors increase the chances for judgment by default by never delivering the summons and complaint and executing a false and fraudulent affidavit of personal service. [This is commonly called "sewer service" to indicate the probable resting place of the process papers.] No formal consideration of the legal implications of "sewer service" is necessary; anything labeled "sewer service" has to be illegal.

Filing a collection action in a distant forum also significantly increases the changes of a default judgment. For example, an Arkansas debtor is more likely to default if the collection action is filed in King of Prussia, Pennsylvania, instead of Little Rock, Arkansas.

Spiegel, Inc. v. FTC, 540 F.2d 287 (7th Cir.1976), held that the Federal Trade Commission has the power to prevent creditors from suing consumers in inconvenient forums. Spiegel, a catalog retailer with its principal place of business in Chicago, regularly sued in Illinois courts to collect delinquent accounts of out-of-state consumer customers. The Illinois long-arm statute granted jurisdiction for such suits. Nevertheless, the FTC issued a "cease and desist order." The Seventh Circuit held that the "unfair practice" language of section 5 of the Federal Trade Commission Act empowers the FTC to enjoin distant forum abuse of consumer debtors.

Section 811 of the 1977 Fair Debt Collection Practices Act protects consumers from suits by "*debt collectors*"[6] in inconvenient forums. Actions by "debt collectors" to enforce a lien on real property may be filed only in the county in which the

6. Remember the limited scope of the term "debt collector." See page 12 supra.

real property is located. Other "debt collector" collection actions may be brought only where the debtor resides or where the contract is signed.

Even cheaper and quicker than a default judgment is a cognovit judgment. In cognovit judgments (a/k/a judgments by confession), the parties agree at the time that the debtor-creditor relationship is created that if the debtor defaults on her obligations, the creditor can obtain a judgment against the debtor without any notice to the debtor, without any hearing. An attorney chosen by the creditor appears in court to confess judgment against the debtor for any unpaid portion of the debt along with various fees and charges without the necessity of even service of process on the debtor. A debtor generally does not know when the cognovit judgment is entered. After learning that a judgment has been entered, a debtor is limited to two avenues of relief. The first available remedy is a petition to strike the judgment. This petition is only available in cases where irregularities constituting fatal defects are apparent on the face of the record. The other available remedy is the petition to open judgment; its main disadvantage is that the burden of proof is placed on the debtor.

Most states have enacted legislation eliminating confession of judgment or severely restricting its use.

The Supreme Court considered due process attacks on confession of judgments; in D. H. Overmyer Co., Inc. v. Frick Co., 405 U.S. 174 (1972), the court held that a confession of judgment provision is not per se violative of due process. *Overmyer* presented the most appealing possible fact situation for upholding the constitutionality of cognovit judgments: both the debtor and the creditor were substantial business entities, and the facts revealed that the cognovit provision was included in the contract as a result of good faith bargaining between the parties. The Court in *Overmyer,* indicated by way of dictum that a confession by judgment may well violate due process "where the contract is one of adhesion, where there is great disparity in bargaining power, and where the debtor receives nothing for the cognovit provision. * * *"

In a case decided the same day as *Overmyer,* Swarb v. Lennox, 405 U.S. 191 (1972), the Court held the Pennsylvania cognovit provisions not unconstitutional on their face. In *Swarb,* a three judge district court had held *inter alia* that (1) the action challenging the constitutionality of the Pennsylvania provisions could not be maintained as a class action on behalf of all Pennsylvania residents who signed cognovit notes; (2) the action, however, could be maintained as a class action on behalf of natural persons residing in Pennsylvania who earned less than $10,000 annually and signed such instruments; (3) the Pennsylvania practice of confessing judgment was unconstitutional as applied to the designated class. Swarb v. Lennox, 314 F.Supp. 1091 (E.D.Pa.1970). Only the plaintiffs appealed, claiming that the court should have declared the Pennsylvania rules and statutes unconstitutional on their face. In rejecting this contention and affirming the district court's opinion, the Court said: *"Overmyer* necessarily reveals some discomforture on our part with respect to the present case. However that may be, the impact and effect of *Overmyer* upon the Pennsylvania system are not to be so delineated in the one-sided appeal in this case and we make no attempt to do so." In light of the facts of both *Overmyer* and *Swarb,* the constitutionality of cognovit notes in a *consumer* credit transaction is still in question.

D. POST–JUDGMENT COLLECTION CONCERNS

1. Judgment Liens [7]

The law governing judgment liens is mostly state law. It is mostly state statutory law. The state statutes vary with respect to (i) the mechanics of obtaining a judgment lien, (ii) the scope of the lien, and (iii) the means of enforcing the lien.

Consider first the mechanics of obtaining a judgment lien. What does a creditor with a state court

---

7. Do not confuse the term "judgment lien" with the term "judicial lien." Judicial lien describes any lien obtained through use of a court-related action. A judgment lien is one form of a judicial lien. Attachment liens, garnishment liens, and execution liens are other common examples of judicial liens.

judgment against D in State 1 have to do to obtain a judgment lien on D's property in State 1?

Many states statutorily provide that the rendition of a judgment itself creates a lien; no additional judgment creditor action is required to create a judgment lien. Other states have statutes that provide that a judgment lien arises only after the "docketing" of the judgment in a county in which the debtor has property. (Docketing is usually accomplished by the county clerk's making an entry of the judgment under the last name of the judgment debtor in the appropriate docket book.) In such states, a judgment rendered by a state court in County X, cannot create a lien on property in County Y until the judgment is docketed in County Y.

What if a creditor has obtained *federal* court judgment against D in State 1? How does it obtain a judgment lien on D's property in State 1? 28 USC 1962 deals with enforcement of federal court judgments. It defers to the statutes of the state in which the federal court is situated. Docketing and the other similar steps that are necessary under state law to create a judgment lien apply to federal court judgments if the state statute so provides. State statutes, however, cannot impose conditions or requirements on federal court judgments that are more stringent than those applicable to state court judgments.

Judgments of other state courts generally do not so easily give rise to a lien. A creditor with a

[*45*]

judgment rendered by a state court in state *1* usually must bring an action in state *2* based on the debt created by the judgment in state *1*, obtain a judgment in state *2*, and docket this judgment in order to have a judgment lien on property of the debtor in state *2*. The Conference of Commissioners on Uniform State Laws has recommended a Uniform Enforcement of Foreign Judgments Act that provides a summary procedure for proving a foreign judgment; to date, it has only been adopted in a handful of states.

When a creditor has a judgment lien, what property is subject to the lien?

The judgment lien operates as a general lien on all of the debtor's property subject thereto, not as a specific lien upon particular property. In Alabama, Georgia, and Mississippi, the judgment lien reaches both real and personal property; California now provides for judgment liens on "business personal property." In all other states that recognize the judgment lien, it is limited to real property—not a specific piece of real property, but all real property of the debtor or, in states that require docketing, all real property of the debtor in counties in which the judgment has been docketed. What constitutes "real property" for judgment lien purposes varies somewhat from state to state. For example, there is disagreement as to whether the judgment lien reaches contingent remainders, leasehold estates, or timber that has been severed from the land. A division also exists as to whether equitable interests are subject to a judgment lien.

In most jurisdictions in which a judgment gives rise to a lien, the lien reaches property obtained subsequently thereto. There is a conflict of authority as to the relative priority of judgment liens on after-acquired property. To illustrate, in January, A obtains a judgment against D and dockets his judgment in Orange County; in May, B obtains a judgment against D and she also dockets her judgment in Orange County. It is not, however, until November that D owns any real property in Orange County. Does A's judgment lien on the real property acquired by D in November have priority over B's judgment lien on the same property? Some courts would answer in the affirmative—priority is governed by the order of docketing. A great majority of courts, however, would respond in the negative—while priority of judgment liens is generally determined by date of docketing, judgments attach simultaneously to after-acquired property, and thus the liens are of equal standing.

A judgment, or even a judgment lien, is not the final step in the collection process. As was stated by Justice Story in Conard v. Atlantic Ins. Co., 26 U.S. 386 (1828), a judgment lien "only creates a right to levy on the * * * [property of the judgment debtor], to the exclusion of other adverse interests subsequent to the judgment; and when the levy is actually made on the same, the title of the creditor for this purpose relates back to the time of his judgment so as to cut out intermediate encumbrances. * * * If the debtor should sell the estate, he [the judgment creditor] has no right to follow the proceeds of the sale. * * * The only remedy of the judgment creditor is against the thing itself by making that a specific title which was before a general lien."

To illustrate, C obtains a judgment against D and dockets the judgment in Orange County in the manner statutorily prescribed. D subsequently transfers Orange County real property that she owns—real property that is subject to C's judgment lien—to T for $10,000. C's judgment lien gives it no rights as to the $10,000; the lien only reaches the real property now owned by T, and C's remedy is to enforce the lien as to such property.

The jurisdictions vary considerably with respect to the proper method of enforcement of judgment liens. In some jurisdictions, foreclosure proceedings is the only method; in other states, levy and sale under a writ of execution is required; and some states permit a choice between foreclosure actions and a writ of execution.

Jurisdictions also vary considerably with respect to time limits for enforcement of judgment liens. At common law, a judgment lien was presumed paid and became dormant so as not to support an execution if the judgment creditor failed to take out a writ of execution within a year and a day. A judgment lien that became dormant could be revived at any time by proceeding scire facias.

Today, most states statutorily limit the duration of judgment liens. Ten year periods are common. Additionally, most statutes provide for "revival" or "renewal."

There are two basic differences between "revival" of a judgment lien and "renewal" of a judgment lien:

1. Revival is by scire facias or judicial decree; renewal is by civil action on the prior judgment.

2. Revival continues the judgment and judgment lien; renewal creates a new judgment and a new judgment lien. This is significant when there are intervening conveyances or encumbrances. Assume for example that C obtains a judgment against D and a judgment lien on Greenacre, D's property, in 1980. In 1982, X obtains a judgment lien on Greenacre. If C later revives its judgment, it will still have priority over X. If C later renews its judgment, it will not have priority over X.

2. Execution Liens

By way of review, what is the practical significance of a judgment lien? Does it give a creditor an interest in the debtor's chattels? In his real property? If so, what is the interest? Can the creditor lawfully seize the property? Can the creditor cause the property to be sold in satisfaction of his claim?

The generally negative answers to the above questions reveal the need for some further creditor remedy. At early common law, the "further" remedy generally took one of four permissible forms: *elegit, capias ad satisfaciendum, fieri facias* and *levari facias.* A writ of *elegit* resulted in the transfer of the debtor's personal property to his creditor at an appraised price, and, if this was not sufficient, the assignment of the use of one half of the debtor's land to the creditor as tenant by *elegit* for a term based on an appraisal of its value. *Elegit* is mainly of historical interest today.

Capias ad satisfaciendum required the local sheriff to arrest a judgment debtor and keep him imprisoned until the debt was paid. Today, a majority of states have constitutional provisions prohibiting imprisonment for debt. In most states, however, the prescription is limited to contract debts; many of these states statutorily provide for imprisonment for failure to satisfy liability resulting from tortious conduct, fraud, and breach of fiduciary relationship. Even in the states that absolutely prohibit imprisonment of debtors a judgment debtor may be imprisoned for civil or criminal contempt of court if she fails to satisfy a judgment.

By the writ of *fieri facias* (fi-fa), a creditor with a judgment could have the sheriff seize and sell the debtor's personal property in satisfaction of his claim; by means of *levari facias,* the judgment creditor could similarly reach the debtor's realty.

Today, the law of execution is statutory. Most statutes provide for a single writ of execution by which a judgment creditor can have the judgment debtor's property seized and sold in satisfaction of the judgment. In most states a writ of execution can reach both personalty and realty; in a very few states a writ of execution does not reach realty; in still others, the judgment creditor is statutorily required to look first to the personal property of the debtor.

As execution is statutory, the exact procedure varies somewhat from state to state. A writ of execution is issued by the clerk of the court in which the judgment was rendered. Issuance of the writ is a ministerial act and involves neither a hearing nor discretion on the part of the clerk. The writ is directed to the sheriff or some other statutorily authorized official; it orders the official to levy on the property described in the writ and, usually after appraisal and due notice, to sell such property at public sale. As with attachment, there are problems as to what constitutes an effective levy and problems of liability for an improper levy. The writ specifies a "return date"; by that date, the sheriff or other official must return the writ to the issuing clerk with an endorsement stating the property seized and sold or the impossibility of finding leviable assets. The latter form of return is often referred to as return *nulla bona.* If the return is *nulla bona,* a second (*alias*) and further (*pluries*) writs may issue.

Execution is also similar to attachment in that it creates a lien on the property seized by the sheriff. Most states date the execution lien from the time of levy. In a few states, the execution lien relates back to the date of issuance of the writ by the clerk or delivery of the writ to the sheriff.[8]

Execution is different from attachment in that the property seized pursuant to a writ of execution is to be sold by the sheriff to satisfy the creditor's judgment while property seized pursuant to a writ of attachment is to be held by the sheriff to secure payment of any judgment obtained by the creditor. Delays in holding an execution sale may result in the loss of the execution lien. There are statutory limitations on the life-span of an execution lien. Additionally, a creditor will lose its execution lien if the lien becomes "dormant."

The classic statement of the judicial doctrine of dormancy is Excelsior Needle Co. v. Globe Cycle

8. These minority rules create problems as to the rights of third parties who obtain liens on or purchase property of the debtor after the writ has been issued but before the property has been levied on by the sheriff. Assume for example, that C obtains a writ of execution on January 10 and delivers the writ to the sheriff. On January 11, B, a bona fide purchaser, buys a boat from the judgment debtor. Can the sheriff now levy on the boat? Under the minority rules, C's execution lien predates B's purchase. Most jurisdictions that date execution liens from issuance or delivery of the writ statutorily protect "gap purchasers" such as B.

Works, 48 App.Div. 304, 309–310, 62 N.Y.S. 538, 540–41 (1900):

"The law is quite clear that the object of the execution is to enforce the judgment, and not to convert it into a security upon the property, and still allow the judgment debtor to prosecute his business regardless of the lien of the execution. As was said in Freeman Executions, § 206: 'In other words, it is not the mere issuing or delivery of the writ which creates a lien, but an issuing and delivery for the purpose of execution. The execution of a writ for the purpose of making or keeping it effective as a lien cannot stop with a mere levy upon the property. If the officer is instructed by the plaintiff not to sell till further orders, the lien of the execution and levy becomes subordinate to that of any subsequent writ placed in the officers' hands for service.' * * * The law, therefore, seems to be settled that any direction by the execution creditor to the sheriff which suspends the lien or delays the enforcement of the levy renders the execution dormant against subsequent creditors or bona fide purchasers. However veiled may be the direction, however much it may be founded on a humane desire to protect the debtor, if it is tantamount to a mandate or instruction to the sheriff to withhold the execution of his process, during the interim that he accedes to this demand the levy ceases to be effective."

[*53*]

3. Comparison of Post-Judgment Liens on the Debtor's Real Property With Post-Judgment Liens on the Debtor's Personal Property

	Real Property	**Personal Property**
1. type lien	judgment lien or execution lien	execution lien
2. property encumbered	all real property in county	specific item(s)
3. duration	statutory	case law
	Under most statutes, judgment liens do not become dormant for at least 5 years	Under most cases, execution liens become dormant within a few months
4. method of obtaining	docketing	levying

As the above chart suggests, the laws relating to judicial liens on real property are very different from the laws relating to judicial liens on personal property. Are these differences warranted? Law review writers have long argued for a single judicial lien system. Recently, California statutorily created a judgment lien on business personal property. A judgment creditor in California can obtain a JLPP by filing a notice of judgment lien with the office of the California Secretary of State; it reaches all inventory, accounts, equipment, farm products, chattel paper and negotiable documents of title of the debtor.

4. Creditor's Bill

At early common law, writs of execution were issued by courts of law and so were confined to those estates and interests of the debtor recognized at law. If the debtor had title to land, the writ of *levari facias* could be levied, giving the creditor the right to collect rents and the property. Similarly, if the debtor owned tangible personal property, the writ of *fieri facias* could be levied, giving the creditor the right to have such property seized and sold. But if the debtor had something which was property in a practical sense, something on which he could realize at any time but which was not capable of being the subject matter of a common law possessory action, no writ of execution was available. Thus at early common law the creditor could not reach the debtor's equitable interests such as beneficial interests in property held in trust or the debtor's intangible property such as choses in action.

To provide a remedy for reaching such property, the Court of Chancery developed an equitable counterpart to execution—the creditor's bill (sometimes referred to as creditor's suit). A creditor unable to satisfy its judgment completely through execution could file a bill in the Court of Chancery asking that court to compel the debtor to turn over his equitable assets to be sold to satisfy the creditor's judgment.

By use of a creditor's bill, a judgment creditor can reach any nonexempt property interest of the debtor that is alienable or assignable under state law. While, as with other judicially created liens, there is some division in the case law as to the time the lien arises, "The general rule is that the filing of a judgment creditor's bill and the service of process creates a lien in equity on the judgment debtor's equitable assets." Metcalf v. Barker, 187 U.S. 165 (1902).

The flexibility of equitable procedure allows the creditor's bill to be used in a variety of ways. A creditor's bill can be used as a liquidation device— a substitute for bankruptcy. A judgment creditor can file a bill not only for himself but also on behalf of such other judgment creditors as may choose to join the action. Under this general creditors' bill, the petitioning creditor does not obtain priority over other participating creditors; rather the court makes a *pro rata* distribution to all such creditors. Despite equity's preference for equality, a creditor may file a bill on his behalf alone and thus obtain priority over other creditors. Such judgment creditor's bills are far more common than the general creditors' bill described above. Usually the judgment creditor's bill includes a prayer for discovery of all of the debtor's property; the debtor and third parties holding property of the debtor are then examined in court to locate the assets. A common step after discovery is the issuance of an injunction to prevent the debtor from disposing of or encumbering the property. Sometimes a receiver is appointed for collecting money due to the debtor or taking charge of property requiring management.

The creditor's bill has not only the advantages but also the limitations of an equitable remedy. For example, the notion that jurisdiction in equity will not be entertained where there is an adequate remedy at law requires exhaustion of legal remedies. There is some confusion as to what constitutes exhaustion of legal remedies in this context. There is uniformity of opinion that, subject to limited exceptions, a judgment must be obtained before a party is entitled to institute a suit by creditor's bill. The difficulty arises in determining exactly how far a plaintiff must proceed after he has obtained a judgment. Most authorities indicate that a creditor must have (1) a judgment, (2) execution issued and (3) return unsatisfied before obtaining a creditor's bill. Other courts merely require judgment and the issuance of execution. The question of which rule is preferable would seem to be academic today in federal court and in states that have adopted rules of procedure modeled after the Federal Rules. Rule 2 abolishes the distinction between law and equity; Rule 18(a) authorizes joinder of legal and equitable claims; Rule 18(b) states that "whenever a claim is one heretofore cognizable only after another claim has

[*57*]

been prosecuted to a conclusion, the two claims may be joined in a single action."

5. Supplementary Proceedings

Several statutory developments have limited the need for and use of the creditor's bill. In most states, the writ of execution has been extended to equitable interests in property and intangible property. Garnishment is now available in many states for the collection of judgments from property of the debtor held by third parties. And, a number of states have enacted an additional remedy: as part of his procedural reform in the middle of the nineteenth century, Field created a new remedy—proceedings supplementary to execution (also called supplemental proceedings)—designed to achieve the purposes of a creditor's bill by a more simple and summary process; a number of states followed New York's example. As the name of the remedy implies, supplementary proceedings could be used only after execution had been issued and returned unsatisfied. Subsequently, in a number of jurisdictions the title of the procedure was changed to proceedings supplementary to judgment, and the requirement of return of execution unsatisfied was eliminated.

While a creditor's bill is an independent, quasi-in-rem action, governed by equitable rules, and a supplementary proceeding is a summary, in personam action, administered by the court in which the judgment was obtained and governed by the provisions of the applicable state law, the reach of supplementary proceedings is very similar to that of the creditor's bill. Most supplementary proceedings statutes provide for (1) discovery of assets through the right of examination of the debtor and others; (2) issuance of injunctions to prevent disposition of property; (3) discretionary power to appoint receivers; and (4) orders for the sale of property.

In a few states, the supplementary proceedings provisions expressly abolish the creditor's bill. Absent any such express provision, the existence of supplementary proceedings in other states neither abolishes creditor's bills by implication nor limits the availability of creditor's bills. Supplementary proceedings need not be tried first and found wanting before a creditor's bill action can be brought. This is in accordance with the well-established equitable principle that where new power is conferred upon the law courts by statutory legislation, the former jurisdiction of equity is unaffected unless the statute contains negative words or other language expressly taking away the pre-existing equity jurisdiction, or unless the whole scope of the statute, by its reasonable construction and its operation, shows a clear legislative intent to abolish that jurisdiction.

While supplementary proceedings usually afford a more expeditious remedy than the creditor's bill, there is at least one situation in which the creditor's bill is still used: recovery of property of the debtor that has been transferred to some third party in fraud of creditors. [The concept and elements of a transfer in fraud of creditors are considered infra at pages 66–80]. As noted above, supplementary proceedings are summary in nature without the usual requirements as to pleadings or jury trial. Thus supplementary proceedings generally cannot be employed where a third party asserts an interest in the property. A few states have amended supplementary proceedings statutes so that the court can adjudicate rights and interests in the debt or property which is the subject of the proceeding.

6. Execution Sales

While obtaining a lien, through execution or otherwise, is important to a creditor for reasons previously stated, it is not tantamount to satisfaction of the claim. Execution, like the provisional remedies and judgment, is but one of the steps that a creditor must take to obtain payment. The final step is the sale of the property levied on; the proceeds of the sale, after deduction for fees and costs of the sale and payment to creditors with priority, are distributed to the levying creditor, with any excess going to the judgment debtor.

Most states have detailed statutory provisions governing the sale of property pursuant to execution. These statutes vary from jurisdiction to jurisdiction as to matters such as property subject to sale, notice, mechanics of the sale, and safeguards as to inadequate price.

Most states also have statutory provisions designed to prevent the sale of property at execution sales for unfair prices. One such statutory device is appraisal statutes. Such statutes, generally provide (1) that an appraisal of the subject property must be made before the sale and (2) either that an execution sale must bring not less than a stated percentage of the appraised value or a stated percentage of the appraised value must be credited on the debt.

Another statutory device providing some protection against inadequate bidding is redemption. Generally, the right of redemption is limited to the repurchase by the execution debtor, within a stated time and at a stated price, of real property sold at execution. Some states permit redemption of personal property; some states have extended the right of redemption to junior lienors of the debtor.

An execution sale differs from a judicial sale in that the writ does not designate any specific property to be sold and the court gives no directions and imposes no conditions with respect to an execution sale, as it may do in its order for a judicial sale of specific property. While most statutes do not provide for judicial confirmation of an execution sale, the court from which the execution issued may, for sufficient cause shown, vacate a sale. Courts usually state that mere inadequacy of price is not sufficient to vacate an execution sale. There are cases to the contrary; additionally, a number of decisions have stated that where the price is inadequate, slight additional circumstances justify setting aside the sale.

One reason for the generally low prices realized at execution sales is the limited protection afforded purchasers at such sales. *Caveat emptor* is the answer customarily given to the unhappy execution purchaser who learns that there are other existing liens prior to that of the judgment creditor or that the judgment debtor had defective title to the property sold by the sheriff. The execution purchaser acquires only such interest as the execution debtor has and generally cannot recover for defects in title. Execution sales are made without implied warranties, either on the part of the sheriff or the execution creditor or debtor.

Most courts likewise hold that the doctrine of *caveat emptor* is applicable even where the levy and sale is made on property to which the judgment debtor has no title: a majority of the cases have denied recovery in actions by the purchaser against the sheriff or the judgment creditor for the price paid at the execution sale, where the debtor had no title to the property so sold. The purchaser's only remedy in such cases is usually by way of subrogation to the creditor's claim against the debtor.

The doctrine of *caveat emptor* is generally not applicable where the sale is rendered void because of irregularities in procedure; while the execution purchaser is not entitled to assume that he will obtain good title, he is entitled to assume that he will obtain such interest as the execution debtor has. Thus, where the sale is set aside, the execution purchaser has been given a variety of remedies—recovery from the person benefitted by the sale price, subrogation to the plaintiff's rights under the judgment including any judgment lien, a lien on the property for all amounts paid, and injunctions to protect possession of the property until reimbursement. The execution purchaser, may, however, be required to account to the execution debtor for rents and profits from the use of the property.

7. Garnishment

Many of the comparisons of attachment and pre-judgment garnishment at pages 30–31 supra, are applicable to execution and post-judgment garnishments. Here again garnishment has more of the attributes of a full-fledged lawsuit. The judgment creditor files an affidavit stating that there is a judgment, that the judgment is wholly or partially unsatisfied and that the garnishee holds property of the judgment debtor. The court then issues a writ of garnishment that is served upon the garnishee; many states [more after *Sniadach*] serve the principal debtor with a copy of the writ.

As with prejudgment garnishment, the service of the summons creates a lien, and there is a division in the authorities as to the property subject to the

lien. In some states, the lien reaches only property of the principal debtor and debts owed to the
principal debtor as of the time of service of the
summons. In others, the lien also reaches property of the principal debtor which comes into the
possession of the garnishee and debts of the garnishee which accrue in the interim between service
on the garnishee and answer by the garnishee;
and, in a few states, the date of determination of
the garnishment proceeding is the relevant date, if
the garnishee's answer is controverted.

The garnishee is required to answer within a
stated time. Failure to answer may result in a
default judgment or contempt proceedings. In its
answer, the garnishee must set out what, if any,
funds, property, or earnings of the principal debtor
it holds. Along with this disclosure, the garnishee
may set up any defense to the garnishment action
that it might have. Since the judgment creditor in
effect represents the principal debtor as against
the garnishee and is entitled to whatever the principal debtor might recover, the garnishee may
make any defense which it might make if sued by
the principal debtor. For example, the garnishee
might assert that it has already paid over the
funds or turned over the property to the principal
debtor before it was served with the notice of
garnishment. The garnishee may also plead as a
defense to the garnishment the exemptions [ex-
empt property is discussed at pages 15–19] of the
principal debtor. And, in most states, the garnish-

ee may set off any of its claims against the principal debtor.

If the garnishee's answer is controverted by the plaintiff, the controverted issue is tried as other civil cases. If the answer is not controverted, the answer is taken as true. If the answer admits indebtedness to the principal debtor, the court will render judgment against the garnishee for the admitted amount. Similarly, any property of the principal debtor acknowledged to be held by the garnishee will be ordered turned over to the court for sale to satisfy the creditor's judgment.

The garnishee is protected by statute in some states, case law in others, from double liability.[9] Payment by the garnishee to the judgment creditor of the amount owed by the garnishee to the principal debtor liberates the garnishee *vis-a-vis* the principal debtor. On the other hand, a judgment in the garnishment proceeding limiting or negating the garnishee's liability to the principal debtor is generally held not to bar an action by the principal debtor for the debt. To illustrate:

9. Protection from double liability is not absolute. A garnishee who fails to disclose that property held by him or the indebtedness owed by him is exempt may be subject to double liability. Also, dictum in Harris v. Balk, 198 U.S. 215 (1905), and numerous subsequent decisions indicate that where the garnishment was prior to judgment in a state other than that of the principal debtor's residence, notice of the garnishment proceeding to the principal debtor is required to protect the garnishee from double liability.

(1) C brings an action against D and obtains a judgment for $500. C, believing that G is indebted to D in the amount of $500, garnishes G. G acknowledges the $500 debt to D and pays this sum to C. D could not subsequently maintain an action against G to collect the $500.

(2) Same facts as # 1 except that G denies any liability to D and prevails in the garnishment proceeding. D would not be bound by the judgment in favor of G from bringing an action against G to collect the debt.

(3) Same facts as # 1 except that G acknowledges a debt of only $300 and pays that amount to C. D could maintain an action against G to collect any amounts owed by G in excess of $300 so that if the court in the second proceeding found that G did owe D $500, D could collect $200.

8. Fraudulent Conveyances

A not untypical reaction of a debtor confronted with the possibility of seizure of property to satisfy the claims of creditors is to convey away his property to friends or relatives for little or no consideration or with the understanding that the debtor shall continue to enjoy the use and benefit of the property. Since Roman law, *such* attempts to defraud creditors have been *ineffective*: The italicized language in the last sentence points out the two major fraudulent conveyance issues:

(1) which transfers are fraudulent conveyances, and

(2) what are the consequences of determining that a transfer is a fraudulent conveyance.

a. What Constitutes a Fraudulent Conveyance

The basis of the modern law of fraudulent conveyances is the Statute of 13 Elizabeth, enacted in 1570. It provides that "covinous and fraudulent feoffments, gifts, grants, alienations, conveyances, bonds, suits, judgments and executions, as well of lands and of tenements as of goods and chattels, * * * devised and contrived of malice, fraud, covin, collusion or guile, to the end, purpose and intent, to delay, hinder or defraud creditors and others * * * shall be utterly void, frustrate and of no effect. * * * "

The law of fraudulent conveyances soon became something other than the language of the Statute. The Statute of Elizabeth says that fraudulent conveyances are "void", but void only as to persons "hindered, delayed or defrauded." In other words, a fraudulent conveyance is valid as between the grantor and the grantee; in other words, a fraudulent conveyance is not void but rather is voidable by certain creditors of the grantor. The language of the Statute also indicates that it is a penal statute with the remedy being the delivery of half the fraudulently transferred property to the crown and the other half to the defrauded creditor. Courts, however, since Mannocke's Case, 3 Dyer 293b (1571), have taken the position that the judgment creditor need not rely on the remedy provided in the statute but can ignore the transfer and proceed directly on the property.

Note also that the Statute of Elizabeth requires "intent to delay, hinder or defraud." Since proof of a particular intent is a difficult task, courts soon developed "badges of fraud," i.e., circumstances indicative of intent to defraud. The first such case was Twyne's Case, 3 Coke 80b, 76 Eng.Rep. 809 (1601). There P was indebted to T for 400 pounds and to C for 200 pounds. C sued P and, while the action was pending, P secretly conveyed to T by deed of gift all of his chattels (worth 300 pounds) in satisfaction of T's claim. P, however, remained in possession of some of his property—some sheep— and treated them as his own. C obtained a judgment against P, but when the sheriff sought to levy on the sheep, friends of P prevented him from doing so, asserting that the sheep belonged to T. Thereupon C sued T to set aside the conveyance from P to T as a fraudulent conveyance. The court held that the transfer was fraudulent, noting the following "badges of fraud": (1) the conveyance is general, i.e., of all P's (the debtor's) assets; (2) the debtor continues in possession and deals with the property as his own; (3) the conveyance is made while a suit against the debtor is pending; (4) the transaction is secret; and (5) T (the transferee) takes the property in trust for the debtor.

In virtually every American jurisdiction, the Statute of 13 Elizabeth has been either recognized as part of the inherited common law or expressly

[*68*]

adopted or enacted in more or less similar terms. The concept of "badges of fraud" has also been generally adopted, although what constitutes a "badge of fraud" varies from jurisdiction to jurisdiction. Among the most commonly recognized "badges of fraud" are those mentioned in *Twyne's Case;* intra-family transfers; voluntary transfers, i.e., transfers of property without consideration; and transfers of all or a substantial amount of property immediately prior to anticipated litigation. Not only do states differ as to what facts give rise to a "badge of fraud," there is also no uniformity as to what weight is to be given to a particular "badge": whether it is conclusive of fraud, prima facie evidence of fraud, or merely admissible evidence of fraud.

About the only "badges of fraud rule" that is uniformly recognized is that preferring one creditor over others is not a badge of fraud. It is not a badge of fraud for debtor, D, to pay creditor, X, in full and pay nothing to other creditors, Y and Z. Obviously, D's payment to X hinders and delays the other creditors. If, however, Y or Z were permitted to set aside the payment to X, there would merely be a substitution of one preference for another. "Fraudulent conveyance law is intended to ensure only that some deserving creditor receives the debtor's reachable assets. Allocation of assets among creditors is determined by bankruptcy statutes." Note, *Good Faith and Fraudulent Conveyances,* 97 Harv.L.Rev. 495, 522 (1983).

Because of the "confusion and uncertainties of the existing law," the National Conference of Commissioners on Uniform State Laws proposed the Uniform Fraudulent Conveyances Act (UFCA) in 1919. In the UFCA, the Commissioners sought to shift the focus from the debtor's intent to objective factors. The UFCA has been adopted in 25 states.

Sections 1–3 of the UFCA contain definitions. As in every statute, the definitions are important. As in every statute, some of the definitions are surprising.[10] Sections 4–8 describe various forms of fraudulent conveyances. Section 7 contains intent to hinder, delay, or defraud creditors language that is similar to the language in the Statute of Elizabeth. Sections 4, 5, 6, and 8, however, contain no reference to the debtor's intent. Most UFCA cases involve section 4 and/or section 7. Accordingly this discussion of what is a fraudulent conveyance under the UFCA focuses on section 4 and section 7.

In section 4, a conveyance is fraudulent if made (1) by a person who is or will thereby be rendered "insolvent" (2) for less than "fair consideration."

Understanding section 4's "insolvent" requirement calls for an understanding of section 2's definition of insolvent. In reading section 2, you should note

10. For example, the definition of "assets" in section 1 excludes exempt property. The definition of "fair consideration" includes a "good faith" test.

(1) Insolvency for purposes of the UFCA depends on a comparison of debts and assets, not a present ability to pay debts. D owns Greenacre. D is not paying his debts because he has no cash. If the value of Greenacre is greater than the amount of D's debts, D is not insolvent for purposes of the UFCA even though D is not able to pay his debts.

(2) In valuing the debtor's assets for purposes of section 2, it is necessary to determine the "present salable value" of the assets. It is also necessary to determine the "probable liability" on D's debts. Neither of these phrases has an accepted accounting or business definition, and no reported case considers at length the meaning of the phrases.

(3) Because of the definition of "assets" in section 1, exempt property is not included in determining whether the debtor is insolvent. [Exempt property is considered infra at pages 15–19.] This exclusion of exempt property means that in states that have generous exemptions, most individuals are "insolvent" for purposes of the UFCA.

Remember that section 4 requires both insolvency and the lack of "fair consideration."

"Fair consideration" is defined in section 3. The UFCA definition of "*fair* consideration" differs from the accepted common law contracts definition of "consideration" in that

(1) Antecedent debt can be "fair consideration." If, for example, D borrows $10,000 on ¹/₁₀ from X and transfers Greenacre to X on ⁷/₇ in satisfaction

of that debt, the $\frac{1}{10}$ debt can be "fair consideration" for the $\frac{7}{7}$ transfer.

(2) "Fair consideration" inquires into the adequacy of the consideration. Peppercorns aren't
enough. Section 3 has a comparative value standard. Actually, it has two comparative value standards. If the transfer is a payment, exchange of
property, or other absolute transfer, the test is
"fair equivalent." In the hypothetical in which
Greenacre was transferred on $\frac{7}{7}$ to *pay* a $\frac{1}{10}$ loan
of $10,000, the issue would be whether $10,000 is
the "fair equivalent" of Greenacre. If the transfer
is a security transfer such as a mortgage or an
Article 9 security interest, the test is the less
demanding "not disproportionately small." If, for
example, a mortgage on Greenacre was granted to
secure a $10,000 debt, the issue would be whether
the $10,000 loan is "not disproportionately small"
to the value of Greenacre.

(3) Fair consideration also requires "good faith"
on the part of the transferee. Although it is not
clear from the reported cases, this would seem to
suggest that the adequacy of the amount of consideration is not determinative.

This inclusion of good faith as a part of "fair
consideration" is inconsistent with the UFCA's
stated goal of replacing subjective determinations
of intent with objective factors. The case law
under sections 4, 5, 6, and 8 of the UFCA indicates
that courts still use badges of fraud. For example,
in cases under section 4 of the UFCA involving

transfers to a member of the transferor's family, some courts have used a badges of fraud analysis to presume insolvency or shift the burden of proof and require the transferee to show the solvency of the transferor. These cases seem inconsistent with the language of section 4.

The language of section 7 of the UFCA is similar but not identical to the language of the Statute of Elizabeth. In section 7, the operative language is "made * * * with actual intent as distinguished from intent presumed in law, to hinder, delay, or defraud."

Note that section 7, unlike section 4, focuses on intent—not adequacy of consideration or the financial condition of the transferor. Note also that section 7, unlike the Statute of Elizabeth requires "actual intent"—not presumptions such as badges of fraud.

How do you prove "actual intent"? What kind of evidence of intent will generally be available? Badges of fraud was the answer in cases under the Statute of Elizabeth. The "actual intent" language in section 7 would seem to preclude the same answer in the UFCA.

Notwithstanding this statutory language, cases under section 7 of the UFCA have considered the same factors as considered by Statute of Elizabeth cases and have even used the same "badges of fraud" terminology. In light of these section 7 cases, the cases presuming insolvency under section 4, and the element of good faith brought into section 4 by the definition of fair consideration, it would seem that there is a considerable overlap between sections 4 and 7.[11] While not all section 4 fraudulent conveyances are section 7 fraudulent conveyances and vice versa, most section 4 fraudulent conveyances would also seem to be section 7 fraudulent conveyances. As is pointed out below, there is a possible practical difference between a determination of a section 4 fraudulent conveyance and a section 7 fraudulent conveyance.

While neither the Statute of Elizabeth nor the UFCA expressly so provides, it is well settled under both types of statutes that a transfer of exempt property cannot be a fraudulent conveyance. The rationale is that since exempt property is not available to the creditor, the creditor has no grievance if the debtor should transfer exempt property.

b. What is the Practical Significance of Determining That a Transfer is a Fraudulent Conveyance

The determination that a transfer is a fraudulent conveyance materially affects the rights and remedies of the creditor of the transferor, the transferee, and creditors of the transferee. Under section 9 of the UFCA (and in most Statute of Elizabeth jurisdictions) a creditor as to whom a

11. One case seems to suggest that the primary difference between proceeding under sections 4 and 7 of the UFCA is burden of proof—"substantial evidence" under section 4 and "clear and satisfactory" proof under section 7. Sparkman & McLean Co. v. Derber, 4 Wash.App. 341, 481 P.2d 585 (1971).

conveyance is fraudulent has a choice of remedies: the creditor can either bring an action (usually a creditor's bill) to set the conveyance aside or ignore the transfer and levy on and sell the property fraudulently conveyed. Most practice books recommend setting the fraudulent conveyance aside. The validity of the conveyance is thus determined in advance of the sale of the property and so the sale is likely to be at a higher price. Also, this minimizes possible liability to the transferee in the event that the transfer was not fraudulent. Yet another factor in determining which remedy to use is the statute of limitations. Both the length of the limitation period and the date that the statute begins to run may vary with the remedy used.

Under the Statute of Elizabeth, these remedies were available only to judgment creditors. The rule is now otherwise in most Statute of Elizabeth jurisdictions: a number of these states have adopted rules of practice modeled on the federal rules [Federal Rule of Civil Procedure 18b permits the joinder of a claim for money and a claim to have a fraudulent conveyance set aside]; others have eliminated the judgment requirement through case law or statutory modification. The UFCA does not distinguish between a judgment creditor and general creditors: rather the UFCA's dividing line is whether a creditor's claim has matured. [Claims *ex contractu* can be mature notwithstanding the absence of any judgment.] If a creditor's claim has not matured, the option of ignoring the transfer and levying on the property is not available. See UFCA section 10.

Note that these statutory remedies are available to creditors as to whom the conveyance is fraudulent. As section 7 of the UFCA uses the phrase "both present and future creditors," the above described statutory remedies are available to all creditors of the transferor where the transfer is a section 7 fraudulent conveyance. Section 4, however, speaks only of "creditors." Thus, where the transfer is a section 4 fraudulent conveyance, these statutory remedies are available only to "present creditors"—creditors of the transferor who had extended credit prior to the making of the fraudulent conveyance.

To illustrate, on January 10, X lends D $1,000. On February 2, D transfers property to Y. On March 3, Z extends credit to D. The remedies of the UFCA will be available to X if the February 2nd transfer was a fraudulent conveyance under section 4 or 7. The remedies of the UFCA will be available to Z only if the February 2nd transfer was a fraudulent conveyance under section 7.

These statutory remedies are further restricted by statutory protection of certain transferees. "Purchasers for fair consideration without knowledge" are completely protected. See UFCA section 9(1). Purchasers for "less than fair consideration" and "without fraudulent intent" are protected to the extent of consideration furnished. See UFCA section 9(2). And, if the transferee has conveyed the property to a bona fide purchaser for value, creditors of the transferor will not be able to reach the property. [Bona fide purchasers are similarly protected under the Statute of Elizabeth.] The creditors can, however, recover traceable proceeds of the second conveyance from the transferee or, in the absence of such proceeds, hold a fraudulent transferee personally liable for the value of the property.

For example, D fraudulently conveys her motorcycle to T. T then sells the motorcycle to X, a bona fide purchaser, for $2,000. The creditors of D have no rights to the motorcycle. They can, however, invoke the law of fraudulent conveyances to recover the $2,000 from T.

Creditors of one who makes a fraudulent conveyance also have common law remedies. Generally, a creditor who has a lien on property fraudulently conveyed can recover damages in tort against persons who prevent execution of the lien. General creditors, however, for the most part have not been allowed to bring an action in tort based upon a fraudulent conveyance. The reason given most frequently for denying general creditors a tort recovery for fraudulent conveyances is that the damages cannot be accurately measured. The most difficult measurement of damages problem would occur when the debtor has multiple creditors. If the sum of the debts is greater than the value of the property fraudulently conveyed, it will be difficult to determine to what extent each creditor has been damaged. Obviously if there had been no fraudulent conveyance, all of the creditors could not have satisfied their judgments from the property. On the other hand, there is no way of knowing which creditor might have acted first and thus satisfied his entire judgment from the transferred property.

Fraudulent conveyance cases do not always involve only the transferee and the creditors of the transferor. The effect of a fraudulent conveyance on the transferor or the creditors of the transferee also presents problems.

Consider first the application of fraudulent conveyance law to the transferor.

A fraudulent conveyance does not eliminate the transferor's personal liability to his creditors. In fact, it increases such liability in jurisdictions that recognize tort liability for a fraudulent conveyance—the additional damages being the incidental costs of tracking down the property and attempting to set aside the fraudulent conveyance.

The affirmative rights of one who makes a fraudulent transfer are virtually nil. Generally the transferor cannot recover property fraudulently conveyed even where the transferee has promised to reconvey. Various rationales have been offered for this rule: *pari delicto,* unclean hands, the policy of discouraging fraudulent conveyances. Once the agreement to reconvey has been executed, however, a majority of jurisdictions reach a different result: an executed reconveyance will be enforced against either the transferee or non-lien creditors of the transferee. Here, the expressed rationale is that since the transferee agreed to reconvey, he was under a moral obligation to do so. It is said that moral obligation supplies consideration for the reconveyance and makes it enforceable. [What about *"pari delicto,* unclean hands, the policy of discouraging fraudulent conveyances"?]

Very few cases have considered the relative rights of the creditors of the transferor and the creditors of the transferee to property that has been fraudulently conveyed. To illustrate, A loans R $100. At the time of the loan, R owns a 1952 Hudson; while A does not take a security interest in the Hudson, she to some extent relies on R's ownership of the car in making the loan. R fraudulently conveys the car to E. E borrows $100 from B. B also relies on his debtor's ownership of the car without taking a security interest in the car. Now both R and E are in default. Both A and B are looking to the Hudson to satisfy their claims. Who has priority? Under the language of the UFCA it would seem that A should have priority; section 9 authorizes a creditor of one who transfers his property in fraud of creditors to pursue the statutory remedies against any person except a bona fide *purchaser*; B is not a bona fide purchaser—B is not even a purchaser. Notwithstanding this statutory analysis, the prevailing view in both UFCA and Statute of Elizabeth jurisdictions seems to be that the first creditor to obtain a lien on the property prevails, the reasoning being that the equities are equal. So, if B is the first to obtain an execution lien on the Hudson, B has priority.

The doctrine of fraudulent conveyances is also of considerable practical significance in bankruptcy. Under section 727(a)(2), the debtor's fraudulent conveyance can be used to deprive him of a discharge in a liquidation bankruptcy. Sections 544 and 548 empower the bankruptcy trustee to void pre-bankruptcy fraudulent conveyances of the bankrupt. These bankruptcy concepts and sections of the Bankruptcy Code are discussed at length later in the nutshell.

CHAPTER IV

CREDITORS WITH SPECIAL RIGHTS

A. CONSENSUAL LIENS

The preceding chapter focused on rights available to all creditors—rights afforded by the judicial process. Some creditors have rights in addition to those already discussed. Agreement of the parties is one source of such rights. The debtor and the creditor may agree that the creditor is to have a lien on certain real or personal property of the debtor.

Obtaining a consensual lien does not destroy or limit the creditor's rights. A lien creditor may proceed against the debtor personally, may utilize the various creditors' remedies discussed in the preceding chapter. Additionally, such a creditor has special rights in the property subject to its lien. The special rights include a right of foreclosure—the right to proceed against the security and apply it to the payment of the debt—and the right of priority—the right to take the security free from the claims of general creditors and later secured creditors.

CREDITORS WITH SPECIAL RIGHTS

1. Security Interests

a. Terminology and Organization of Article 9

Today in every state except Louisiana consensual liens are governed by Article 9 of the Uniform Commercial Code. Although the legislature of every state except Louisiana has adopted Article 9 of the Uniform Commercial Code, each state has adopted a different Article 9. Legislators in every state have made their own "improvements." Moreover, there are now two "official versions" of Article 9: the 1962 Official Text and the 1972 Official Text. Textual discussion in this book will be keyed to the 1972 Official Text.

Article 9 of the Code has a language all its own that can best be explained by illustration. Assume that D wants to borrow $5,500 from S to buy a new pick-up truck. S is only willing to make the loan if the truck will be security; D agrees. In "Code talk," D is the debtor; S is the secured party; the pick-up truck is the collateral; S's interest in the truck is a security interest; the agreement creating the security interest is a security agreement. See sections 1–201; 9–105. Since S is loaning D the $5,500 to acquire the collateral, S's security interest is a purchase money security interest. See section 9–107. [Similarly, if D had financed a car with the seller, and the seller had obtained a security interest in the car, the security interest would be a purchase money security interest.]

The creation of a security interest requires more than a security agreement. It is also necessary that the secured party give value and that the debtor acquire rights in the collateral. When these three requirements are satisfied, the security interest is said to have "attached."

To achieve maximum possible priority, it is necessary for the secured party to "perfect" its security interest. Depending on the kind of collateral involved, a security interest may be perfected when it attaches (e.g., a purchase money security interest in consumer goods other than motor vehicles or fixtures, section 9–302(1)(d)), or it may require a transfer of possession from the debtor to the secured party (e.g., stock certificates, section 9–304(1)) or filing (the usual case, section 9–302). Where filing is required, the document filed is called a "financing statement." It need contain only the names, addresses, and signatures of the parties and a description of the types of items of collateral covered, section 9–402.

Article 9 of the Code is divided into five parts: Part 1 is mostly definitions; Part 2 controls disputes between the debtor and the secured party; Part 3 controls disputes between the secured party and third parties; Part 4 contains the mechanics of filing; and Part 5 governs the rights of the secured party on default. Parts 1 through 4 are ordinarily covered in detail in courses in commercial law. Accordingly, only Part 5 will be discussed at any length.

b. Section 9–301

There is, however, one section in Part 3 of Article 9 that merits consideration in a debtor-creditor law primer. Section 9–301 provides that an unperfected security interest is "subordinate" to a judicial lien on the same property.[1] In other words, section 9–301 contemplates a situation where a judicial lien arises in the gap between the creation and perfection of a security interest: if D gave S a security interest in her truck on October 7, and S perfected this security interest on October 21, any creditor who obtained an attachment or execution lien on the truck between October 7 and October 21 would have priority over S.

Section 9–301 is also important for what it does not say. It does not govern priority as between a secured creditor and a creditor with a statutory lien (see section 9–310) or between two secured creditors (see section 9–312). It does not expressly state that a creditor with an unperfected security interest has priority over general creditors although that is certainly implied. Moreover, section 9–301 is silent as to the relative priority when the judicial lien arises before the security interest attaches. In such cases, it would seem that the first in time rule should apply regardless of whether the security interest is perfected immediately.

---

1. The 1962 Official Text of section 9–301 requires that the judicial lienor be without knowledge of the security at the time the judicial lien arose.

c. Part 5 of Article 9

The application of Part 5 of the Uniform Commercial Code is conditioned on default by the debtor. The term "default" is not specifically defined in the Code. The circumstances which constitute default are a matter of agreement between the parties. Because the secured party usually has superior bargaining power, the security agreement will usually define default as broadly as possible. Common events of default include any impairment of the collateral such as failure to insure, impairment of the personal obligation such as bankruptcy of the debtor, and any feeling of insecurity that the prospect for payment is uncertain (section 1–208). In the absence of any definition of "default" in the security agreement, default occurs only on a failure to pay.

When the debtor is in default, Part 5 of Article 9 gives the secured party the following cumulative remedies:

(1) Foreclose its security interest under the state's non-Code foreclosure law—9–501(1)

(2) Use real estate mortgage procedure when both realty and personalty are involved—9–501(4)

(3) Apply any special remedies provided in the security agreement—9–501(1), 9–501(2)

(4) Take judgment and levy execution on any non-exempt property of the debtor—9–501(1), 9–501(5)

(5) Collect accounts and instruments that are collateral—9–501(2), 9–502

(6) Foreclose its security interest under Code procedure—9–503, 9–504, 9–505, 9–506, 9–507.

While the first five alternatives seem fairly self-explanatory, discussion of the sixth and the Code concepts of repossession, redemption, retention and resale is necessary.

Section 9–503 of the Code authorizes a secured party to take possession of the collateral upon default of the debtor and to do so without judicial process if this can be done "without breach of the peace." "Breach of the peace" is another phrase that is not defined in the Code. Most cases in which there has been a finding of breach of peace under section 9–503 involve either self-help repossession by unauthorized entry into the debtor's house or self-help repossession after protests by the debtor or one acting on his behalf. Recent cases are divided as to whether repossession through trickery violates section 9–503's "breach of the peace" standard.

Recent cases are, however, uniform in upholding the constitutionality of section 9–503. While self-help repossession deprives the debtor of property without prior notice and hearing, *Sniadach* and the other due process decisions are inapplicable.

[*86*]

Self-help repossession does not involve "state action."

If self-help repossession cannot be accomplished without a "breach of the peace," the secured party can "proceed by action," section 9–503. This "action" is variously referred to as replevin, claim and delivery, and sequestration. Regardless of the label, the remedy is essentially the same—the sheriff seizes the collateral pursuant to a court order. And, regardless of the label, there are constitutional requirements of notice and hearing. The state is issuing the writ; the state is seizing the property. State action! Due process requirements of notice and hearing must be satisfied. See pages 36–40 supra. Almost every state has amended its replevin, claim and delivery, or sequestration procedures to provide for some kind of probable cause hearing before the writ is issued by the court and the collateral is seized by the sheriff.

In theory, the debtor has a right to redeem repossessed collateral. Section 9–506 provides that a debtor may redeem by "tendering fulfillment of *all obligations* secured by the collateral as well as the expenses reasonably incurred by the secured party in retaking, holding and preparing the collateral for disposition * * *." Most security agreements contain language accelerating the entire balance due on default. Thus, a debtor who was unable to pay a single installment will have to come up with the entire balance plus expenses in order to redeem, Comment to 9–506.

[*87*]

Additionally, this "right of redemption" is terminated by the occurrence of any one of the following events:

(1) debtor's signing a written waiver after default, or

(2) secured party's disposing of the collateral, or entering into a contract for the sale of the collateral

(3) secured party's retaining the collateral pursuant to section 9–505, discussed below.

In short, a debtor seldom redeems repossessed property.

In the event that the repossession is not followed by redemption, the secured party may either retain the collateral or resell it. There are two significant limitations on the retention alternative.

First, section 9–505 provides that retention of repossessed collateral results in complete satisfaction of the debtor's obligation. If, for example, D owes S $5,000 and S repossesses D's car and elects to retain it, D's entire $5,000 debt is extinguished, regardless of the value of D's car. Accordingly, S is likely to elect the retention alternative only if the collateral is worth as much as or more than the debt owed. The second limitation on retention makes it unlikely that S will be permitted to retain collateral worth more than the debt owed: Retention requires debtor acquiescence.[2] If the collater-

2. If the collateral is consumer goods and the debtor has paid 60% of the debt, the debtor must expressly consent to the

al is worth more than the amount of the secured debt, the debtor will generally insist that the secured party resell the collateral. Any surplus from a resale goes to the debtor, section 9–504(2).

Section 9–504 governs the disposition of the collateral by the secured party. The sale may be either public or private; the secured party may bid-in only if the sale is public or if the collateral is of a type "customarily sold in a recognized market or is of a type which is the subject of widely distributed standard price quotations."

Section 9–504(3) requires that reasonable notice of the resale must be given to the debtor unless the collateral is perishable, threatens to decline rapidly in value, or is of a type "customarily sold on a recognized market." Most courts read the Code's definition of "debtor" as including guarantors so notice must also be provided to guarantors. If the collateral is consumer goods, no other notice of the sale must be provided. If the collateral is other than consumer goods, notice also must be sent to other secured parties from whom the repossessing secured party has received written notice.

Additionally, section 9–504(3) requires that every aspect of sale of a repossessed item "including the method, manner, time, place and terms must be commercially reasonable." "Commercially reasonable" is nowhere defined in the Code. Notwithstanding the statement in section 9–507(2) that low

retention. Otherwise, section 9–505 gives the debtor the opportunity to object to the retention.

resale price is not itself sufficient to establish that the sale was not commercially reasonable, both the courts and the commentators seem to regard the price as a major consideration.

If the proceeds of the sale are not sufficient to satisfy the indebtedness, the debtor is liable for any deficiency, absent any agreement to the contrary. In seeking recovery of a deficiency, the creditor has all of the rights of a general creditor. In the unlikely event that the section 9–504 sale yields a sum greater than that owed by the debtor to the secured creditor, the secured party must account to the debtor for any surplus.

The debtor may recover under section 9–507 for any losses caused by the secured party's failure to comply with the provisions of Part 5. Particularly, in consumer credit transactions it is difficult to prove damages resulting from noncompliance with Part 5. Accordingly, if the collateral is consumer goods, the debtor is statutorily assured a minimum recovery regardless of the lack of any provable damages: "the credit service charge plus ten per cent of the principal amount of the debt or the time price differential plus ten per cent of the cash price," section 9–507(1).

Noncompliance with the requirements of Part 5 of Article 9 may also affect the secured party's right to a deficiency judgment. The Uniform Commercial Code nowhere mentions denial of the section 9–504(2) right to recovery of any deficiency as a remedy for noncompliance with the requirements of Part 5 of Article 9. Nevertheless, a number of courts have held that the noncomplying secured party loses its right to a deficiency judgment. More courts hold that the right to a deficiency judgment is *not* lost by a violation of the requirements of Part 5. However, a growing number of the courts that permit recovery of a deficiency judgment limit the deficiency judgment to the difference between the debt and the value of the collateral, with a rebuttable presumption that the value of the collateral equals the amount of the debt.

2. Mortgages

There is no single uniform law governing real property security, and the rights of a mortgagee on default of the mortgagor vary considerably from state to state. There are, however, a number of similarities between Article 9 of the Uniform Commercial Code and the law of mortgages in most jurisdictions.

The mortgagor's equitable redemption rights virtually mirror the debtor's rights under section 9–506. The redeeming party must pay the entire debt; the right to redeem is terminated by the sale of the property or by strict foreclosure. In about one half of the states, however, statutes augment the mortgagor's redemption rights. These statutes extend the period of redemption beyond foreclosure; the additional period varies from several months to several years. This statutory redemption differs from equitable redemption with regard to the sum payable to effect redemption: the basic factor is the sale price (plus interest at specified rate and other costs), not the debt secured by the mortgage.

In only a few states does the mortgagee have both the options that are available to a secured party under Article 9 of the Uniform Commercial Code: retention or resale. Retention of the mortgaged property, i.e., strict foreclosure, is available in certain circumstances in nineteen states, but is commonly used in only three states. In other states, foreclosure results in a sale of the property.

There are two types of foreclosure sales generally used in the United States: judicial sale and sale pursuant to a power of sale. Judicial sale is more commonly used. The mechanics of such a sale are mostly a matter of local law. The legislation ordinarily provides for notice of a hearing, a hearing, judicial determination of default, notice of sale, sale, confirmation of sale, possible redemption (statutory) and entry of a judgment for any deficiency.

Until court confirmation, the judicial sale is not enforceable by the buyer. There are legal rules limiting the court's discretion in confirming the sale. Absent a statutory provision to the contrary, mere inadequacy of price without more does not justify a refusal to confirm—the inadequacy must be so gross as to shock the conscience. Nevertheless, in cases involving confirmation of the sale, as in cases involving section 9–504(3)'s "commercially reasonable" standard, adequacy of the price seems the primary concern. Moreover, in a number of states, there are "statutory provisions to the contrary." For example, in several states an appraisal in advance of the sale is required, and the sale is not confirmed unless the sales price is at least a certain percentage of the appraisal.

Because of the delays and expenses incident to foreclosure by judicial sale, mortgagees included provisions in the mortgage permitting sale without any judicial proceeding in case of default. This approach to foreclosure has only limited recognition in the United States. Several states legislatively exclude this extrajudicial procedure, and in only eighteen states is foreclosure under a power of sale the prevailing practice. The conduct of the sale under a power of sale is determined by the provisions of the instrument creating it and by any statutory regulations governing its exercise. In the majority of jurisdictions using this type of procedure, the sale must be public, and preceded by notice (usually advertisement) specifying the amount of debt due, description of the property, date and location of sale and such other matters as either the mortgage or the applicable statute may provide. The critical attitude of the courts toward powers of sales makes them quick to grant relief against even slight irregularities. This willingness to overturn sales results in uncertainty of title and is probably the chief reason for the power of sale's failure to gain greater acceptance.

B. LIENS BY OPERATION OF LAW

1. Common Law Liens

Some creditors are given additional rights by operation of law. Common law grants to certain creditors a possessory lien on property of their debtors. A common law possessory lien is the right to retain the property of another for some particular claim or charge upon the property so detained.

Common law from very early times gave the innkeeper a lien on the goods of the guest brought by him into the inn. Similarly, a common carrier has a lien for freight charges on all goods delivered by it. And an artisan who, at the request of the owner, performs services on a chattel has a common law possessory lien on such chattels.

A common law possessory lien is either specific or general. The former attaches to specific property as security for some demand which the creditor has with respect to that property. A general lien is one that the holder thereof is entitled to enforce as security for all the obligations which exist in his favor against the owner of the property. Specific liens have been favored by the courts. General liens exist only when (1) contracted for, (2) conferred by statute, or (3) so common and well-established that the parties to the transaction must be taken to have made their contracts in relation to such custom and usage. The burden of establishing the general lien is on the party claiming it, and courts have been reluctant to find the burden sustained. In certain callings, however, such as those of attorney, banker, factor, and innkeeper, the general lien is well-established.

A common law possessory lien is merely a device to coerce the debtor into payment of his debts by the retention of his property from him until he pays. In general, there is no remedy for enforcing the lien; the lienor has no right to sell the subject matter of the lien to satisfy his claim unless such right is expressly conferred by statute or agreement of the parties.

Although possession is essential to the creation of liens under common law and the lien is in essence a right to retain the goods until certain debts are paid, a change of possession does not necessarily destroy the lien. When the lienholder has parted with possession, it is a question for the jury whether he has so far voluntarily parted with possession as to warrant the conclusion that he has waived the lien. For example, if the owner of the property obtains possession thereof without the knowledge or consent of the lienor, the latter is not divested of his lien. A lienor who has voluntarily and unconditionally surrendered possession of the property cannot thereafter assert a lien on the property. Even if such a lienor subsequently regains possession of the property his lien is not

[*95*]

restored. To illustrate, C makes D a dress and unconditionally delivers the dress to D before D pays the $35 charge. Subsequently, D returns the dress to C to have the hem lowered. C only has a lien on the dress for the hemming work.

2. Equitable Liens

Equitable liens do not depend on the possession of the debtor's property by a creditor. Rather, the basis for an equitable lien is one of two equitable maxims.

First, as equity looks upon as done that which is agreed or intended to be done, an agreement that evidences an intention to create a consensual lien but fails to do so, creates an equitable lien. For example, a mortgage which, through some informality or defect in terms or mode of execution, is not valid as a mortgage, will nevertheless generally create an equitable lien on the property described. Similarly, an agreement to give a mortgage creates an equitable lien.

Second, equity regards as done that which ought to be done and so creates equitable liens to avoid unjust enrichment. To illustrate, B enters into a contract to buy Greenacre from S for $10,000. B makes a partial payment of $2,000. S is unable to comply with the covenants of the contract as to the title she is to convey. Under these facts, B would have an equitable lien on Greenacre to secure the repayment of the $2,000, notwithstanding the absence of any agreement to this effect. A buyer under an executory contract for the sale of land has an equitable lien on the land for purchase money advanced, where the contract fails due to the fault of the seller.

Equitable liens also differ from common law liens in terms of rights available to the lienor. A holder of an equitable lien can enforce his lien by having the subject property sold to satisfy his claim.

C. STATE STATUTORY LIENS

Other sources of additional rights for certain creditors are state and federal statutes. Legislation has enlarged many of the liens recognized at common law and many of those asserted in equity. And, statutes have in many instances gone beyond the liens previously recognized in law or equity and created a number of additional liens. It is not feasible within the scope of this nutshell to do more than indicate this source of liens and mention some of the more common statutory liens: employees' liens on the employer's personalty to secure payment of back wages; landlord's lien on tenant's property (codification of a common law possessory lien); materialmen's and mechanics' liens on land and the improvements thereon to secure the compensation of persons who, under contract with the owner or his agent, contributed labor or materials to the improvement of said land; and tax liens.

[*97*]

D. FEDERAL CLAIMS

The largest creditors are, of course, the various governmental entities. A governmental creditor may be either a general creditor or a lien creditor. When its claim is secured, the government has all the rights of a secured creditor; when its claim is not secured, it has all the rights of a general creditor.

Additionally, a number of states statutorily prefer governmental claims against delinquent debtors to those of private creditors. The federal government's claims are given preference over claims of other creditors primarily by two statutory provisions: the federal priority provision, 31 USC section 191, more commonly referred to by its Revised Statute designation, R.S. 3466; and the Federal Tax Lien Act, Internal Revenue Code of 1954, sections 6321–23.

1. Federal Priority Provision

Section 3466 applies to every kind of debt owing to the federal government: tax and non-tax. The statute provides:

"Whenever any person indebted to the United States is insolvent, or whenever the estate of any deceased debtor, in the hands of the executors or administrators, is insufficient to pay all the debts due from the deceased, the debts due to the United States shall be first satisfied; and the priority established shall extend as well to cases

[*98*]

in which a debtor, not having sufficient property to pay all his debts, makes a voluntary assignment thereof, or in which the estate and effects of an absconding, concealed, or absent debtor are attached by process of law, as to cases in which an act of bankruptcy [3] is committed. The priority established under this section does not apply, however, in a case under Title 11 of the United States Code."

When does section 3466 apply? On its face, section 3466 applies any time the following two requirements are satisfied:

(1) a person is indebted to the United States *and*

(2) that person is insolvent.

Case law, however, has significantly limited the scope of application of section 3466.

United States v. Oklahoma, 261 U.S. 253 (1923), judicially limited the applicability of section 3466 through a somewhat artificial interpretation of the word "insolvent" in the second line of section 3466. The Court there indicated that the statute contemplates "insolvent" in the "bankruptcy sense" of

3. The reference to "acts of bankruptcy" is confusing. The present bankruptcy law does not use the term "act of bankruptcy." It was, however, an important concept under the Bankruptcy Act of 1898. Creditors that filed a bankruptcy petition were required to establish one of the six "acts of bankruptcy" listed in section 3 of the 1898 Act. I don't understand why Congress did not delete the reference to "acts of bankruptcy" in section 3466. Title III of the 1978 Bankruptcy Reform Act did amend section 3466 by adding the last sentence as to its inapplicability in bankruptcy.

having debts in excess of assets, rather than in the "equity sense" of inability to pay debts as they mature. While insufficiency of assets is an essential element of "insolvent" for purposes of section 3466, it alone is not sufficient. *United States v. Oklahoma* held that the "insolvency must be manifested in one of the modes pointed out in the latter part of the statute, which defines or explains the meaning of insolvency referred to in the earlier part." 261 U.S. at 260. [4]

Three years later in Bramwell v. United States Fidelity & Guar. Co., 269 U.S. 483, 488 (1926), the Court added, "the priority [under section 3466] does not attach while the debtor continues the owner and in possession of the property" but applies only when "the possession and control of the estate of the insolvent is given to any person charged with the duty of applying it to the payment of the debts of the insolvent."

William T. Plumb, a Washington, D.C. attorney generally regarded as the leading authority on section 3466, summarizes the cases on section 3466 since *Oklahoma* and *Bramwell* as follows: section 3466 is only applicable when there has been a "divestment of the debtor's property for the benefit of his creditors" when there has been a "collective proceeding involving all or substantially all of a debtor's assets," Plumb, *The Federal Priority in*

---

4. It would be more logical to say that the three events mentioned in the second clause of section 3466 were included in the statute as illustrations, rather than limitations. *United States v. Oklahoma,* however, has been consistently followed.

Insolvency: Proposals for Reform, 70 Mich.L.Rev. 1, 13, 14 (1971).

If a person "indebted to the United States" is "insolvent" in the *United States v. Oklahoma* sense of the term so that section 3466 applies, will the federal government's claim always have priority?

Section 3466 seems to confer absolute priority on the United States whenever a person indebted to the United States becomes insolvent. There are no express statutory exceptions for administrative expenses—the costs incurred in collecting, preserving, liquidating, and distributing the debtor's property. There is, however, a case law exception. Cases under section 3466 consistently hold that administrative expenses are paid before federal claims.

Similarly, the statute fails to make any exception for prior liens.[5] Again, cases have recognized an exception to the seemingly absolute priority for

5. Logically, it would seem that private creditors with liens obtained prior to the insolvency *should* be paid before the federal government.

Remember the nature of a lien and the nature of a priority. A lien is a transfer of a present property interest. A lien holder has an interest in the encumbered property from the time a lien is created. Rights under a priority provision such as section 3466 do not arise until the insolvency. If debtor, *D,* owned Orangeacre and sold it to *X* before *D* became insolvent as contemplated by section 3466, the federal government could not claim priority over *X*. Orangeacre was *X*'s property. Similarly if debtor, *D,* owned Whiteacre and *Y* obtained a lien on White- acre before *D* became insolvent as contemplated by section 3466, the government should not have priority over *Y*. The lien was *Y*'s property.

federal claims under section 3466. There are cases that recognize that creditors that have obtained liens that are *specific and perfected* before the debtor becomes insolvent in the section 3466 sense take priority over federal claims. There is, however, considerable confusion as to when a lien is sufficiently specific and perfected or, to use the terminology the courts employ in section 3466 litigation, when the lien is "choate."

The two most commonly cited decisions on the question of when a lien is choate for purposes of section 3466 so that it is paid before the federal claim are the two Supreme Court decisions discussed below. Probably the most comprehensive (and comprehensible) Court consideration of the choateness doctrine is in Illinois ex rel. Gordon v. Campbell, 329 U.S. 362 (1946). In *Campbell,* the Court said that "the lien must be definite * * * in at least three respects * * *: (1) the identity of the lienor; * * * (2) the amount of the lien * * * and (3) the property to which it attaches." The lien there involved was a state statutory lien for unemployment contributions. The Court found the lien "not sufficiently specific or perfected" to take priority over a federal claim under section 3466. The statutory language—"all the personal property * * * used * * * in business"—was too vague and comprehensive. Thus, it would seem that judgment liens [which reach all of the debtor's real property in the county] and any statutory liens reaching all property of the debtor would similarly fall unless some specific property is seized by the lienor before the federal priority arises.

United States v. Gilbert Associates, Inc., 345 U.S. 361 (1953), added yet another factor to be considered in determining whether a lien is choate for purposes of section 3466. Without considering the three elements set out in *Campbell,* the Court found the lien "general" and "unperfected" as the debtor "had not been divested by the Town [the lienor] of either title or possession." Thus, at least a statutory lien on personalty cannot prevail in insolvency even if it satisfied the *Campbell* tests as to certainty of the lienor, amount and property, unless in addition either title or possession has passed to the lienor before the federal priority attaches.

Nesbitt v. United States, 445 F.Supp. 824, aff'd, 622 F.2d 433 (9th Cir.1980), cert. denied 451 U.S. 984 (1981), reads *Gilbert Associates* as imposing an additional, possession requirement applicable in all 3466 litigation. The court there relied on *Gilbert Associates* to find a judgment lien inchoate; the court stated, "it is clear that a lien is sufficiently perfected and specific for purposes of section 3466 only if it has been reduced to possession."

[I get nervous when I see the word "clear" in an opinion or in a bluebook. I think that all that is clear is that only liens that were "choate" before the federal priority arises take priority over federal claims. It is not at all clear to me which liens are choate. There is no Supreme Court 3466 decision holding that a competing lien is choate.[6] While there are some lower court cases under 3466 holding liens choate, the cases are difficult to reconcile.]

Section 3466 did not apply in bankruptcy cases under the Bankruptcy Act of 1898, cf. section 64a(5). And, it does not apply in bankruptcy cases under the Bankruptcy Code. The 1978 legislation amends section 3466 by adding to the end of it: "The priority established under this section does not, however, apply in a case under Title 11 (Bankruptcy) of the United States Code."

Section 507 establishes which claims are entitled to priority treatment in a case under the Bankruptcy Code. Section 507 is considered infra at pages 277–82. The only governmental claims afforded a priority under section 507 are certain tax claims and unpaid custom duties, and these claims are given only a seventh priority. Thus, creditors with inchoate liens that are valid in bankruptcy and creditors with claims that would be given a priority in bankruptcy may receive more from a bankruptcy proceeding where 3466 is inapplicable than from a state insolvency proceeding where 3466 controls.

6. There were six Supreme Court decisions in the first half of the 19th century that permitted consensual liens to take prior to the government. These cases came long before the "choateness" doctrine, and the Court intimated in *Campbell* that the old "mortgage cases" may require re-examination.

Consider the following illustration. Lawyer D has non-exempt property worth $3,000. She owes the following debts:

$2,200 to the federal government for law school loans

$340 to her secretary for salary

$660 to a creditor who has a judgment lien on real property owned by D that is worth more than $600

$800 to general creditors.

In short, D's debts exceed her assets; she is insolvent D makes an assignment for the benefit of creditors. (Assignment for the benefit of creditors is covered infra at pages 126–133). The assignment coupled with her insolvency triggers section 3466. Assuming administrative expenses of $300, the distribution under section 3466 would be as follows:

$300 for administrative expenses

$2,200 for federal government

$500 to the creditor with the judgment lien.

[The judgment lien is inchoate and thus subordinate to the federal claim because it is not sufficiently definite as to the property subject to the lien. In most jurisdictions, the docketing of a judgment creates a general lien on all real property owned by the debtor—the lien is not restricted to any specific property.]

A general assignment for the benefit of creditors is a basis for a creditor-initiated bankruptcy proceeding. See section 303 considered infra at pages 153–56. Thus, creditors of the requisite number with the required amounts of claims may file a bankruptcy petition against D and transfer administration of D's assets to the bankruptcy court. Assuming higher administrative expenses in bankruptcy—$500—the bankruptcy distribution would be as follows:

$660 to the creditor with the judgment lien [Liens not invalidated by some specific provision of the Bankruptcy Code are enforceable against the property to which they attach or the proceeds of the sale of such property. Valid liens must be satisfied in full before any payments are made to general creditors—even general creditors with a section 507 priority.]

$500 to administrative expenses [section 507(a)(1).]

$340 to secretary [section 507(a)(3).]

$1,100 to the federal government and $400 to the private creditors [After liens and priorities are satisfied, the remainder is distributed pro rata. Here, there was $1,500 available to satisfy the $3,000 ($2,200 + $800) of unsecured, nonpriority claims held by the government and by private creditors. Accordingly, each received 50 cents on the dollar.]

2. Federal Tax Lien

Sections 6321–23 of the Internal Revenue Code are commonly referred to as the Federal Tax Lien Act. A lawyer or law student should look to these provisions for answers to the following questions:

(a) When does a federal tax lien arise

(b) What property is covered by a federal tax lien

(c) What are the rights of a third party who buys property from the taxpayer after a federal tax lien arises

(d) What are the rights of the taxpayer's other creditors.

a. When Does the Federal Tax Lien Arise

Section 6321 sets out three requirements for the creation of a federal tax lien:

(1) IRS' assessment of the tax liability; and

(2) IRS' demand for payment of this tax liability;

(3) The taxpayer's failure to pay.

The next section, section 6322, provides that a tax lien dates from the time of assessment. It is thus necessary to know when assessment occurs. Although assessment is only the first of three requirements for creating a tax lien, section 6322 makes the date of assessment important to the

[*107*]

taxpayer, buyers from the taxpayer, and creditors of the taxpayer.

The date of assessment depends on whether the taxpayer acknowledged the liability in his return. When a person files a return acknowledging unpaid taxes, assessment simply involves noting the liability on a list in the office of the district director of the IRS, section 6203. If, for example, D sends the IRS a check for $3,000 along with her return that shows her tax liability is $7,000, assessment of the $4,000 liability would occur almost immediately after the return is received.

If the tax liability is not acknowledged on the return, considerably more time will el pse between the filing the return and assessment. If the tax liability is understated on the return, the deficiency must be discovered through an audit of the return. The taxpayer then must be notified and given the opportunity to respond to the finding of a deficiency. The actual assessment of the tax deficiency cannot be made until the taxpayer either acquiesces in the adjustment of his tax liability or exhausts his opportunities for administrative review.

Section 6303 requires that, after assessment, "as soon as practicable," the taxpayer be given notice, stating the amount of the tax liability and demanding payment. The notice form that the IRS uses gives the taxpayer ten days to make payment.

Remember that while creation of the lien requires (1) assessment, (2) demand, and (3) failure to pay, the lien relates back to the time of the assessment. Remember also that the creation of the lien does not require recordation or other public notice of the lien.

A valid tax lien arises without the federal government filing notice thereof in a public recordation system. It is quite possible that a taxpayer will not know that a tax lien has been imposed upon its property, that buyers from the taxpayer will not know, that other creditors of the taxpayer will not know. An unfiled federal tax lien is valid against the taxpayer and *most* third parties. Pages 110–118 cover which third parties are protected from unfiled federal tax liens.

b. What Property is Covered By a Federal Tax Lien

Section 6321 describes the property covered by a federal tax lien: "All property and rights to property, whether real or personal, belonging to such person." "All" in this context truly means all. The federal tax lien reaches not only all the property that the debtor has an interest in as of the time of assessment but also all property interests later acquired. If the taxes are assessed in June of 1984 and the taxpayer acquires Greenacre in August of 1984, the tax lien would encumber Greenacre. Greenacre would be subject to the tax lien even if Greenacre was the debtor's homestead and exempt under state exemption laws. The tax lien reaches that part of the taxpayer's property that would otherwise be protected by state law from the reach of creditors. The Internal Revenue Code contains its own, nominal exemption provisions in section 6334.

c. What Are the Rights of a Third Party Who Buys Property From the Taxpayer After the Tax Lien Arises

What is the impact of a federal tax lien on a buyer from the taxpayer? For example, X claims that she is entitled to Greenacre because she bought it from D for $10,000. The IRS claims that it is entitled to Greenacre because D owes $10,000 in back taxes and the IRS has a tax lien.

The facts creating such a buyer/IRS priority contest will fit into one of the three patterns:

(1) The sale by the taxpayer occurred before creation of the tax lien, i.e. before tax assessment;

(2) The sale by the taxpayer occurred after creation of the tax lien but before filing of the federal tax lien;

(3) The sale by the taxpayer occurred after creation and filing of the federal tax lien.

Clearly, the purchaser prevails in the first situation. Sections 6321 provides for a tax lien on property of the taxpayer. If X buys Greenacre from the taxpayer before tax assessment, then Greenacre is not "property * * * belonging to such person" at the time the lien arises.

It is equally clear that buyers prevail in the second situation. Section 6323 is in part a recording statute; subsection (f) of section 6323 provides for recording the federal tax lien in the state record systems. Section 6323(a) protects "purchasers" from unrecorded tax liens; an unfiled federal tax lien is not valid as against a "purchaser." If X paid "adequate and full consideration," he is a purchaser, as defined in section 6323(f)(6). If X paid or became legally obligated to pay adequate and full consideration before the federal tax lien was filed, he takes Greenacre free from the federal tax lien. X would be protected by section 6323(a) even if he knew of the unfiled federal tax lien.

Some buyers prevail even over filed federal tax liens. Under section 6323(b) certain third parties take free from a federal tax lien that was filed prior to the sale. For example, section 6323(b)(3) protects purchasers of personal property at retail. If B buys living room furniture from D Furniture Store Inc. the government can not look to this furniture to satisfy its tax claim against D Furniture Store Inc. even though the government filed its federal tax lien.

A filed federal tax lien is, however, effective against most subsequent buyers from the taxpayer. If X buys Greenacre from D after the IRS files its federal tax lien, the IRS will have priority over X.

d. What are the Rights of the Taxpayer's Other Creditors

A person who is not paying his federal taxes is probably not paying his non-governmental creditors and probably lacks sufficient assets to pay all claims against him. Which claims have priority? Remember, under section 6322, the tax lien dates from the time that the taxes were assessed. What if private creditors obtained liens on the debtor's property before the time that the taxes were assessed? Will all such earlier in time liens have priority or will earlier in time liens take priority over the IRS' tax lien only if they are "choate"?

United States v. Security Trust & Sav. Bank, 340 U.S. 47 (1950), was the first case to apply the "choate lien doctrine" to a priority problem under the Federal Tax Lien Act. *Security Trust* involved the relative priority of a federal tax lien and an attachment lien. Since an attachment lien is subject to contingencies that might terminate its enforceability, the lien was deemed inchoate and therefore ineffective against the subsequently arising federal tax lien.

Security Trust relied on section 3466 choateness cases as precedent. Subsequent federal tax lien cases have followed this practice. Nevertheless, the federal tax lien standard of "choateness" seems less stringent than that of the federal priority provisions. As noted previously, the Supreme Court has yet to find a competing lien choate in a case arising under section 3466. There are several Supreme Court federal tax lien cases in which the competing lien was held to be choate.

In Crest Finance Co. v. United States, 368 U.S. 347 (1961), the Supreme Court accepted the government's concession that the competing lien was choate. The lien there involved was an assignment of accounts; the accounts were earned and due prior to the time that the federal tax lien attached.

In both United States v. City of New Britain, 347 U.S. 81 (1954) and United States v. Vermont, 377 U.S. 351, 370 (1964), prior statutory liens on personal property were held choate. The liens involved in these tax lien cases are difficult to distinguish from the liens held *inchoate* in federal priority cases such as *United States v. Gilbert Associates, Inc.,* supra. In neither *New Britain* nor *Vermont* was the taxpayer divested of title or possession. The Court in *Vermont* distinguished *Gilbert* saying "different standards apply where the United States' claim is based on a tax lien arising under §§ 6321 and 6322." 377 U.S. at 358.

To summarize, case law indicates that (1) a private creditor will have priority over the IRS if its lien was choate before the federal taxes were assessed, and (2) the choateness standard in federal tax lien act cases is different from the choateness standard in federal priority cases.

Since 1966, section 6323(a) of the Federal Tax Lien Act indicates that a private creditor will have priority over the IRS if it obtains a security interest, a mechanics lien, or a judgment lien before the federal tax lien is filed.

Like a lot of statutes, the Federal Tax Lien Act uses words differently than you or I ordinarily use them. For example, section 6323(a) gives a "holder of a security interest" priority over an unfiled federal tax lien. Section 6323(h) defines "security interest" so as to limit the protection of section 6323(a) to creditors with *perfected* security interests.[7]

Section 6323(a) also provides that a "judgment lien creditor" takes priority over an unfiled federal tax lien. There is no statutory definition of a "judgment lien creditor." The term is, however, defined in Treasury Regulation section 301.6323(h)–1(g) in a way that includes all post-judgment *judicial* liens—execution liens as well as judgment liens.[8]

---

7. Under section 6323(h), "security interest" includes consensual liens on both personal property or real property. The security interest is deemed to exist only after it is valid under local law against a "judgment lien." This was obviously intended to limit section 6323(a)'s protection to perfected security interests and recorded mortgages.

The use of the term "judgment lien" was unfortunate. Under the laws of most states, a judgment lien does not reach personal property, and therefore even an unperfected UCC security interest would be superior to a judgment lien and thus superior to an unfiled federal tax lien. Such a result would be inconsistent with prior law. There is no indication that Congress intended to change the law and accord priority to unperfected security interests. Instead, it is more likely that Congress did not understand the difference between "judgment lien" and "judicial lien." Most courts read the term "judgment lien" in section 6323(h) as including other types of judicial liens so that only perfected security interests qualify for the protection of section 6323(a). But cf. Major Electrical Supplies, Inc. v. J.W. Pettit Co., 427 F.Supp. 752 (M.D.Fla. 1977).

8. Remember that a "judgment lien" is a particular kind of judicial lien. Under the laws of most states, a judgment lien is

Section 6323(a)'s protection of a judgment lien creditor from an unfiled federal tax lien raises the question of the relationship between section 6323(a) and the choateness doctrine. It should still be clear that a judgment lien is not choate. [A judgment lien reaches all of the debtor's real property in the county, now owned or later acquired; a judgment lien is thus not sufficiently specific as to property to meet the requirements of the common law choateness doctrine.] What is not at all clear is the relationship between section 6323(a) and the choateness doctrine.

The Federal Tax Lien Act nowhere mentions the choateness doctrine. To what extent does section 6323(a) displace the choateness doctrine?

Most authorities suggest that if a creditor comes under section 6323(a), it does not also have to satisfy the choateness requirement. For example, in Aetna Ins. Co. v. Texas Thermal Ind., 591 F.2d 1035 (5th Cir.1979), a security interest v. tax lien case, the court stated, "[W]hatever role the 'choateness' rule of federal common law may play in other contexts, it has been supplanted by the provisions

obtaining by docketing a judgment in the real property record system and only reaches real property. Thus if the term "judgment lien creditor" in section 6323(a) were given its usual meaning, a judgment creditor who obtained a judgment lien on real property by docketing its judgment would take priority over an unfiled federal tax lien while a judgment creditor who obtained an execution lien on personal property by causing the issuance of a writ of execution and the levy on the debtor's property would not take priority over an unfiled federal tax lien.

of section 6323 with respect to tax lien priority questions as to which the statute provides an unambiguous federal law answer." There are, however, cases to the contrary.

The following hypotheticals illustrate the application of section 6323(a):

(1) On January 10, a federal tax lien arises.

February 2, E obtains a judgment against the taxpayer, obtains a writ of execution, and causes the sheriff to levy on personal property of the taxpayer.

March 3, IRS files its federal tax lien in accordance with section 6323(f).

E's execution lien would have priority (assuming that the term "judgment lien creditor" in section 6323(a) is given the meaning suggested in the Treasury Regulation.)

(2) On March 3, a federal tax lien arises.

April 4, J obtains a judgment against the taxpayer and dockets its judgment in a county in which the taxpayer owns real property.

May 5, IRS files its federal tax lien in accordance with section 6323(f).

J's judgment lien would have priority (assuming that a creditor who satisfies the requirements of section 6323(a) does not also have to satisfy a choateness test.)

(3) January 10, a federal tax lien arises.

February 2, S makes a secured loan to the taxpayer and perfects its security interest.

March 3, IRS files its federal tax lien in accordance with section 6323(f).

S's security interest would have priority.

(4) April 4, a federal tax lien arises.

May 5, X makes a secured loan to the taxpayer but neglects to file a financing statement or otherwise perfect its lien.

June 6, IRS files its federal tax lien in accordance with section 6323(f).

IRS would have priority. X did not obtain a security interest AS DEFINED IN THE FEDERAL TAX LIEN ACT prior to federal tax lien filing.

Article 9 security interests are often "floating liens." Security agreements commonly contain after-acquired property clauses such as "This debt is secured by all of the debtor's inventory, now owned or hereafter acquired"—or future advances clauses—"This collateral secures all of the debtor's debts to the secured party, whenever incurred."

Section 6323(c) governs the extent to which the priority enjoyed by a secured party extends to property acquired by the taxpayer after the federal tax lien filing. Section 6323(c) imposes the following limitations:

1. The secured party must have obtained and perfected its security interest prior to the filing of the federal tax lien.

2. The collateral must be commercial financing security, i.e., accounts, chattel paper, or inventory—not equipment.

3. The property must have been acquired within 45 days of the federal tax lien filing.

Assume for example that:

January 10, S lends D $100,000 and obtains and perfects a security interest in all of D's present or future inventory.

February 2, federal tax lien arises.

March 3, federal tax lien is filed.

April 4, D acquires additional inventory.

S's priority extends to the April 4 inventory. S's $100,000 claim must be satisfied in full before IRS has any rights in any of D's inventory.[9]

9. Consider the following variations of the above hypothetical:

(1) January 10, S lends D $100,000 and obtains and perfects a security interest in all of D's present or future inventory;

February 2, federal tax lien arises;

March 3, federal tax lien is filed;

May 5, D acquires additional inventory.

S has priority as to the original inventory; IRS has priority as to the inventory acquired on May 5. It was not acquired within 45 days of the federal tax lien filing.

(2) January 10, S lends D $100,000 and obtains and perfects a security interest in all of D's present or future equipment;

February 2, federal tax lien arises;

Sections 6323(c) and (d) both extend the secured party's priority to future advances in certain situations. Under both,

1. The secured party must have obtained and perfected its security interest prior to the filing of the federal tax lien.

2. The extension of credit must have occurred within 45 days of the federal tax lien filing *or* before the creditor obtained knowledge of the federal tax lien filing, whichever first occurs.[10]

Note, however, that section 6323(c) is limited to "commercial financing security" *but* section 6323(d) is *not*.

Assume for example that:

January 10, S lends D $100,000 and obtains and perfects a security interest in D's *equipment*.

February 2, federal tax lien arises.

March 3, federal tax lien is filed.

April 4, S lends D an additional $40,000.

S's priority would extend to the April 4 loan unless S on April 4 knew of the federal tax lien filing. In

March 3, federal tax lien is filed;

April 4, D acquires additional equipment.

S has priority as to the original equipment; IRS has priority as to the equipment acquired on April 4. Equipment is not "commercial financing security."

10. There is no time limitation on future advances made pursuant to an "obligatory disbursement agreement" as defined in section 6323(c)(4).

other words, S must be paid $140,000 before IRS has rights to D's equipment.

3. Comparison of Federal Priority and Federal Tax Lien

In light of these judicial and statutory limitations on the priority of the federal tax lien and the applicability of section 3466 to federal tax claims, the federal government may fare better asserting a federal priority than a federal tax lien. It should be remembered, however, that the federal priority provision will not always be applicable. Its use is limited to situations in which the debtor is insolvent and one of the three events specified in the second clause of section 3466 has occurred. The following chart compares the federal priority with the federal tax lien:

	Federal Tax Lien Act	**3466**
1. nature of government's right	lien	priority
2. How right is created, a. debt	taxes	any debt to federal government including taxes
b. debtor	fails to pay taxes after assessment and demand	1. deceased and estate insufficient to pay all debts, *or* 2. alive and "insolvent" in the "U.S. v. Oklahoma sense"

FEDERAL CLAIMS

	Federal Tax Lien Act	3466
3. when right arises	at the time of the tax assessment, 6322	at the time when the "possession and control of the estate of the insolvent is given to any person charged with applying it to the payment of the debts of the insolvent." Bramwell v. U.S. Fidelity & Guar. Co., 269 U.S. 483, 490 (1926)
4. role of choateness doctrine a. when applicable	*Unclear* whether courts use choateness doctrine in determining whether federal tax lien has priority over liens of other creditors. Cases are divided as to impact of section 6323(a) on choateness. Does 6323(a) supplement choateness concept or supplant it? Does a section 6323(a) interest have to be choate? What about liens not described in section 6323(a) that were choate before the federal tax lien arose?	*Always applicable* A private creditor can take priority over the federal government only if its lien was choate before the insolvency. [Note that the relevant time is when the federal priority arises, not when the federal claim arose.]

	Federal Tax Lien Act	3466
b. what is choate	The standards for choateness under Federal Tax Lien Act may be different from standards for choateness under 3466.	
5. effect of bankruptcy	recognized in bankruptcy if prior to the taxpayer's filing for bankruptcy the IRS has filed under 6323(f). Cf. section 544(a)	*not* recognized in bankruptcy

4. Circuity of Priority Problems

Both section 3466 and the federal tax lien, by imposing a second priority system on the state priority system, cause circuity of priority (circular priority) problems. Circuity of priority can be best explained by illustration. Assume that D owns property worth $700 and owes A $600, owes B $400 and owes the federal government $500. Both A and B have liens on D's property. A obtained her lien first and under the common law rule of "first in time, first in right" has priority over B under state law. As noted in the previous sections, both the federal priority provision and the Federal Tax Lien Act distinguish between choate and inchoate liens for priority purposes. Thus, if B's lien is choate but A's is not, and either section 3466 or the Federal Tax Lien Act is applicable, the federal claim would be superior to A's claim, but junior to B's.

In summary, A "beats" B under state law; B "beats" U.S. under federal law. U.S. beats A under federal law. It is like the children's game of paper, scissors, and rock.

How should the $700 be distributed? If B is paid before A, state law is ignored. If A is paid before B, it would seem that federal law is being ignored since under federal law B, but not A, is to be paid before the U.S.

The Supreme Court in United States v. City of New Britain, 347 U.S. 81 (1954), adopted a two-step analysis to resolve this dilemma. The federal law of priorities was first applied. An amount equal to the interests that take prior to the federal claim under federal law was set aside to be paid out first. State law was then used to divide the amount so set aside. In the example given in the preceding paragraph only B's lien is prior to the federal government so $400, the amount of B's claim, would be set aside. As A has first priority under state law, the $400 would be paid to A; the remaining $300 would be paid to the federal government. If the value of D's property had been $1000, A would receive the first $400, the government would then receive $500 and the remaining $100 would be paid to A. This seems to be a logical way of resolving the circuity problem, consistent with both federal and state law. The concern of the federal law is what amount is paid prior to the federal claim, not who is paid prior.

5. Other Federal Claims

Most federal claims are governed by neither the federal priority provision nor the Federal Tax Lien Act. Assume, for example, that the SBA guarantees a secured loan to O.K. Supermarkets. The inventory that secures the SBA guaranteed loan is also collateral for an earlier in time loan by Kimbell Foods. If O.K. is unable to pay both debts in full, whose lien has priority: SBA or Kimbell Foods?

Obviously, the Federal Tax Lien Act does not apply. And the federal priority provision does not apply since O.K. is not "insolvent" as defined under section 3466. What law controls a federal claim in a non-tax, "non-insolvent" creditor conflict?

The Supreme Court in United States v. Kimbell Foods, Inc., 440 U.S. 715 (1979), held that:

1. Federal law determines the priority of liens stemming from federal lending programs;

2. Whether federal law incorporates state priority rules or fashions a separate federal rule such as the choateness rule is a matter of judicial policy;

3. A federal rule such as the choateness doctrine is not necessary to protect the governmental interests underlying SBA and FHA programs;

4.   Accordingly, state priority rules and not the federal choateness rule control.

The holding in *Kimbell* is expressly limited to federal claims arising from SBA and FHA loans. The Court carefully leaves open the possibility that in some credit transactions protection of governmental interests may require some special federal rule such as the choateness doctrine.

CHAPTER V

DEBTOR'S STATE LAW REMEDIES, A/K/A COLLECTIVE CREDITOR ACTION

The remedies previously considered are all similar in that (1) all are creditor-initiated and (2) all benefit the specific creditor that invokes the remedy. This chapter will consider a couple of state debtor-creditor remedies—compositions/extensions and assignments for the benefit of creditors—that are at least in theory debtor-initiated. The qualifying words "in theory" are used because people just don't wake up in the morning, and, for the lack of anything else interesting to do, make an assignment for the benefit of creditors or enter into a composition and extension agreement. While these two remedies are debtor-initiated, they are creditor induced.

A. ASSIGNMENTS FOR THE BENEFIT OF CREDITORS

An assignment for the benefit of creditors is a voluntary transfer of assets by the debtor to another person in trust to liquidate the assets and distribute the proceeds to the creditors of the debtor/transferor. The assignee takes legal title to the property transferred.[1] To illustrate, D makes an assignment for the benefit of creditors to A. C, D's creditor, will not be able to attach or execute on the property transferred. Legal title to the property is now in A. A is not indebted to C.

Basically an assignee acquires only the title of the debtor-assignor. The title of the assignee is subject to liens, claims and encumbrances which are valid as against the debtor. Section 9–301 of the Uniform Commercial Code sets out the major exception to this rule. Under Section 9–301(1) of the 1972 Official Text of the UCC, an unperfected security interest is subordinate to the rights of a lien creditor.[2] Section 9–301(3) grants the status of "lien creditor" to the assignee. Accordingly, a security interest that is unperfected at the date of the assignment can be invalidated by the assignee. To illustrate, on January 10, M extends credit to D

---

1. In the absence of a recording statute specifically applicable to assignments for the benefit of creditors, general statutes providing for the recording of transfers of real property will apply to an assignment which includes real property. A general assignment for the benefit of creditors of merchandise, however, is specifically excepted from compliance with the bulk sales law. See section 6–103(2).

2. Under the 1962 Official Text of section 9–301, an unperfected security interest is subordinate to a lien creditor only if the lien creditor was without knowledge of the unperfected security interest. Section 9–301(3) grants the assignee the status of a lien creditor without knowledge unless *all* of the creditors represented by the assignee had knowledge of the unperfected security interest at the time the assignment for the benefit of creditors was made. The assignee's own personal knowledge is irrelevant.

Inc. and takes a mortgage on D Inc.'s building. On February 2, S, another of D Inc.'s creditors, obtains a security interest on D Inc.'s inventory. On March 3, D Inc. makes an assignment for the benefit of creditors. The assignment will not affect M's rights under its mortgage. If, however, S's security interest is unperfected on March 3rd, it will be invalid.

In the absence of special statutes, assignments for the benefit of creditors are regulated according to trust law. The assignee is accountable to creditors as a trustee is accountable to his beneficiaries. The assignee may be removed and may be personally surcharged for any breach of fiduciary duties.

The assignee's duties and responsibilities are those of any trustee. She derives power and authority from the assignment, and, absent any statutory provision, she must be guided by the terms of the assignment. Under the common law, the primary duty of the assignee is to liquidate the assets and distribute the proceeds to creditors as expeditiously as possible. Even where an express power of sale is not contained in the instrument of assignment, the assignee has the power and the obligation to sell the debtor's property to convert it to cash to be distributed to creditors.

Consent of creditors is not a condition precedent to the making of an assignment for the benefit of creditors. The right to make an assignment is regarded as an incident of ownership. The primary common law limitation on use of an assignment for the benefit of creditors is the law of fraudulent conveyances. As an assignment for the benefit of creditors places the debtor's property out of the reach of his creditors—legal title passes to the assignee so that creditors of the assignor can no longer levy on the property—it would seem that creditors would be able to void an assignment for the benefit of creditors under a fraudulent conveyance statute. However, common law early took the position that creditors could not attack an assignment as a fraudulent conveyance if it was truly for their benefit.

An assignment for the benefit of creditors which reserves to the assignor any interest, benefit, or advantage out of the property conveyed to the injury of creditors is a fraudulent conveyance. For example, an assignment is made voidable by the reservation to the assignor of control of the assigned property such as the power to revoke the assignment or to declare the uses and trusts to which the property shall be subject. Similarly, provisions in the assignment which require the assignee to delay liquidation render the assignment voidable as a fraudulent conveyance.

Some jurisdictions consider a partial assignment for the benefit of creditors, i.e., an assignment of less than all of the debtor's property, a fraudulent conveyance. The rationale for this position is that creditors are "hindered" and "delayed" if they are referred to the assignee for satisfaction and then have to come back to the debtor. Some states regard any assignment for the benefit of creditors by a solvent debtor as a fraudulent conveyance: since an immediate sale of the property of a solvent debtor would, theoretically at least, provide funds for the payment of all debts in full, the only result of an assignment by a solvent debtor is to hinder and delay creditors.

A common law assignment for the benefit of the creditors does not discharge the debtor from any deficiencies arising or resulting from the fact that the assigned property is liquidated for less than the amount required to pay creditors in full. [If creditors voluntarily discharge or release the assignor under such circumstances that a composition agreement can be found, the release or discharge will be effective; composition agreements are considered later in this chapter.] This lack of discharge is obviously a major disadvantage of assignments to the debtor and a major reason that assignments for the benefit of creditors are used primarily by corporate debtors.

As the common law permits preferences, a common law assignment for the benefit of creditors which provides for preferential payments to designated creditors is not a fraudulent conveyance. Most courts, however, have held that debtors cannot use preferences to obtain discharges from creditors; assignments that condition preferential treatment on release of the unpaid portion of any claim are generally voided as fraudulent conveyances. To appreciate the reason for this rule, it is

[*130*]

necessary to remember that the assignment places the debtor's property beyond the reach of his creditors. If the debtor could prefer creditors willing to grant a discharge, the creditor would virtually have to accept the debtor's terms. Should the creditor refuse, it would probably receive little if anything from the assignee and would have no rights against the property of the debtor.

Today, assignments for the benefit of creditors are regulated by statute in most states. Some of these state statutes are mandatory; others merely directory. A state statute that is mandatory in its terms must be complied with in order that the assignment be valid. On the other hand, where the state statute is merely directory, the debtor may make a common law assignment or a statutory assignment. If the former is chosen, common law rules apply; if the latter is used, the statute must be complied with.

The state statutes customarily require recording of the assignment, filing schedules of assets and liabilities, giving notice to the creditors and bonding of the assignee, and subject the assignee to court supervision. Virtually all state statutes prohibit the granting of a preference—all creditors except those with liens or statutorily created priorities are to be treated equally. Some statutes, however, expressly provide for the very relief sought by a preferential assignment at common law, i.e., a discharge. Such provisions are, at best, of questionable validity. Article 1, section 8, clause 4 of the Constitution empowers Congress to establish "uniform laws on the subject of Bankruptcies throughout the United States." The exercise by Congress of this power suspends the power of states to enact bankruptcy laws. States may regulate the debtor-creditor relationship, but this regulation may not be a bankruptcy law. In determining whether a state statute is invalid as a bankruptcy law, the Supreme Court has seemed to place primary importance on the presence or absence of discharge provisions. See, e.g., Johnson v. Star, 287 U.S. 527 (1933); International Shoe Co. v. Pinkus, 278 U.S. 261 (1929).

A number of state assignment statutes authorize the assignee to set aside prior fraudulent conveyances, and some empower the assignee to void pre-assignment preferences by the assignor-debtor. Even in these states, however, a bankruptcy trustee has an additional bundle of important rights which are unavailable to an assignee—rights granted by sections 544–549 of the Bankruptcy Code. [These sections are discussed infra in pages 183–246.]

When the debtor has made substantial preferences or fraudulent conveyances or allowed liens, voidable in bankruptcy to attach to his property, creditors may decide that an assignment for the benefit of creditors does not adequately protect their rights. If so, the creditors may be able to force the debtor into bankruptcy. A general assignment for the benefit of creditors is a basis for ordering relief against the debtor in a creditor-commenced bankruptcy. See Bankruptcy Code section 303(h)(2). This means that if creditors of the requisite number with the required amount of claims wish to transfer the administration of the assignor's assets to the bankruptcy court, within the 120 days stipulated by section 303(h)(2) of the Code, it is their privilege to do so. [Section 303(h) (2) requires that the debtor transfer all or substantially all of his property to the assignee. Remember, however, that in at least some states, anything less than a general assignment is a fraudulent conveyance.] Section 543 empowers the bankruptcy court to require an assignee whose administration is superseded by bankruptcy to turn over the debtor's estate to the bankruptcy trustee, and to make an accounting.

An assignment for the benefit of creditors has certain advantages over bankruptcy to creditors. Its flexibility and informality save time and expense, and frequently result in better liquidation prices. Generally, the costs of administration of an assignment will be lower than those of a bankruptcy case. Thus, in the absence of fraudulent conveyances, preferences, or liens voidable in bankruptcy, the dividends to creditors from an efficiently administered assignment will probably be larger than those received from the administration of the same property in bankruptcy.

B. COMPOSITION AND EXTENSION

A composition is a contract between a debtor and two or more creditors in which the creditors agree to take a specified partial payment in full satisfaction of their claims.[3] An extension is a contract between the debtor and two or more creditors in which the creditors agree to extend the time for the payment of their claims against the debtor. An agreement can be both a composition and an extension: an agreement to take less over a longer period of time.

The same rules of law govern compositions and extensions. Both are governed more by principles of contract law than by state debtor-creditor rules. Compositions and extensions encompass all of the essential elements of a simple contract, and the absence of any of these elements renders the agreement invalid. Thus, there must be consideration.

The doctrine of Foakes v. Beer, 9 App.Cas. 605 (1884), that part payment in money of a liquidated

---

3. A number of early cases make mention of "bankruptcy composition." From 1874 to 1938, the Bankruptcy Act provided for a composition in bankruptcy with the added feature that an agreement accepted by the requisite number of creditors was binding on all creditors. The Chandler Act of 1938 repealed these composition provisions and replaced them with Chapter XI (Arrangements), Chapter XII (Real Property Arrangements by Person Other Than Corporations) and Chapter XIII (Wage Earners' Plans). The Bankruptcy Reform Act of 1978 replaced these provisions with Chapters 11 and 13. These federal debtor rehabilitation provisions, similar in nature to a composition, are described infra at page 142.

debt constitutes no consideration for a release of the unpaid balance would seem to invalidate composition agreements. Courts, however, have been able to find consideration in the agreement of creditors each with the other to scale down his claim and accept a lesser sum. Thus, a composition agreement requires the participation of at least two creditors.

While more than one creditor must participate in a composition agreement, there is no requirement that all creditors agree. Creditors who do not agree to the composition are not affected by it. For example, D is indebted to W, X, Y, and Z. D proposes to pay each creditor 10% of its claim each month for the next six months, in full satisfaction of all liability. W, X, and Y agree to this composition/extension. Z does not. As a non-assenting creditor, Z is unaffected by the agreement between W, X, and Y. Z will not receive the monthly payments as provided in the agreement, but Z will be free to attempt to collect the full amount of its claim from D through extrajudicial or judicial means. If W, X, and Y are aware that Z is not taking part in the composition/extension, Z's collection of 100% of its claim from D will not affect the composition/extension agreement.

Similarly, all is well where the other creditors know that one or more of the creditors are being paid more or are being benefited in a way different from the rest. As noted previously, the common law does not condemn preferences; but the law is zealous in seeing that no creditor receives any secret consideration pursuant to a composition and extension agreement. Accordingly, where a creditor is given a secret preference, the other creditors have the right to void the agreement. The creditor with the preference can neither enforce nor void the agreement, and the debtor has a right to recover preferential payments from him. This last "rule" is almost always explained by the presumption of duress: the debtor is presumed to be vulnerable to creditor pressure because of the creditor's *de facto* power to refuse to enter into the composition and therefore to force the debtor to file a bankruptcy petition.

There are a number of reasons that a debtor might prefer a composition to bankruptcy. By making a composition with his creditors, the debtor avoids the stigma that attaches to bankruptcy while he achieves the same result—discharge from all or a substantial portion of his debts. The composition discharge is even broader in scope than that of bankruptcy. A composition releases a surety while a discharge in bankruptcy does not. See Bankruptcy Code section 524(e). A debt discharged by a composition is not revived by a new promise to pay it unless that new promise is supported by new consideration; a promise to pay a debt discharged in bankruptcy need not be supported by consideration in order to be enforceable. Cf. section 524(c). Further a composition does not bar future bankruptcy—a Chapter 7 bankruptcy discharge bars another Chapter 7 discharge for six years. See section 727(a)(8). The main disadvantage of a composition is that it is voluntary. Creditors unwilling to accept its terms are not required to do so. Non-assenting creditors are not affected by the composition.

The following chart compares assignments for the benefit of creditors and compositions:

Assignment for the Benefit of Creditors	Composition
1. Common law; statutory	1. Contractual
2. Affects all general creditors	2. Only affects creditors who enter into the composition
3. Only debts voluntarily released by creditors discharged	3. Discharges all creditors who enter into composition
4. In most jurisdictions, all nonexempt property is delivered to a third person for sale with distribution of proceeds to creditors	4. Debtor retains property except as provided in the agreement
5. Basically liquidation device	5. Basically debtor rehabilitation device
6. General assignment for benefit of creditors basis for involuntary bankruptcy under section 303(h)(2)	6. *Not* a basis for an involuntary bankruptcy proceeding

CHAPTER VI

BANKRUPTCY: AN OVERVIEW

The remainder of the nutshell will focus on bankruptcy. Initially, a couple of basic differences between bankruptcy and state debtor-creditor law should be noted. State law puts a premium on prompt action by creditors. The first creditor to attach the debtor's property, the first creditor to execute on the property, etc. is the one most likely to be paid. Bankruptcy, on the other hand, emphasizes equality of treatment, rather than a race of diligence. While bankruptcy law does not require equal treatment for all creditors, all creditors within a single class are treated the same. After the initiation of bankruptcy proceedings, a creditor cannot improve its position *vis-a-vis* other creditors by seizing the assets of the debtor. Similarly, the debtor's ability to make preferential transfers to creditors before bankruptcy is considerably limited.

Second, the prospects for debtor relief are much greater in bankruptcy. While no debtor is guaranteed a discharge, most debtors do receive a discharge. "One of the primary purposes of the bankruptcy act is to 'relieve the honest debtor from the weight of oppressive indebtedness and permit him to start afresh. * * *'" Local Loan Co. v. Hunt, 292 U.S. 234, 244 (1934).

A. BANKRUPTCY LAW

The law of bankruptcy is federal law. It is primarily statutory law. There are three different federal bankruptcy statutes:

1. Bankruptcy Act of 1898 (commonly referred to as the "Act"). Bankruptcy cases filed *prior* to October 1, 1979, are governed by the Bankruptcy Act of 1898. Of course, most pending bankruptcy cases have been filed since October 1, 1979.

2. Bankruptcy Reform Act of 1978 (commonly referred to as the "Bankruptcy Code"). Bankruptcy cases filed since October 1, 1979, are governed by the Bankruptcy Reform Act of 1978.

3. Bankruptcy Amendments and Federal Judgeship Act of 1984. Bankruptcy cases pending on or filed after July 10, 1984, are subject to most of the 1984 amendments relating to bankruptcy jurisdiction; bankruptcy cases filed after October 7, 1984, are subject to the 1984 changes in the substantive law of bankruptcy.

This book will focus on the Bankruptcy Reform Act of 1978 as amended in 1984.

The Bankruptcy Reform Act of 1978 divides the substantive law of bankruptcy into the following chapters:

[*139*]

Chapter 1, General Provisions, Definitions and Rules of Construction

Chapter 3, Case Administration

Chapter 5, Creditors, the Debtor, and the Estate

Applies to all cases

Chapter 7, Liquidation

Chapter 9, Adjustment of the Debts of a Municipality

Chapter 11, Reorganization

Chapter 13, Adjustment of the Debts of an Individual With Regular Income

Chapter 15, United States Trustees

The provisions in Chapters 1, 3, and 5 apply in every bankruptcy case, unless otherwise specified.

It is also necessary to deal with the Bankruptcy Rules. Pursuant to the authority of 28 USC section 2075, the United States Supreme Court promulgated Bankruptcy Rules. These rules, not the Federal Rules of Civil Procedure, "govern procedure in United States Bankruptcy Courts," Rule 1001. The Bankruptcy Rules are divided into ten parts. Each part governs a different stage of the bankruptcy process.

The Bankruptcy Rules were promulgated in 1983. Since then, Congress has enacted the Bankruptcy Amendments and Federal Judgeship Act of 1984; this legislation significantly changes the judicial role of bankruptcy judges. There will proba-

bly be amendments to the Rules to reflect the
changes in the judicial role of bankruptcy judges.

B. FORMS OF BANKRUPTCY RELIEF

This nutshell will deal with the three basic forms
of bankruptcy relief: Chapter 7, Chapter 11, and
Chapter 13.

Chapter 7 is entitled "Liquidation." The title is
descriptive. In a Chapter 7 case, the trustee col-
lects the non-exempt property of the debtor, converts that property to cash, and distributes the
cash to the creditors. The debtor gives up all of
the non-exempt property she owns at the time of
the filing of the bankruptcy petition in the hope of
obtaining a discharge. A discharge releases the
debtor from any further personal liability for her
pre-bankruptcy debts. Assume, for example, that
B owes C $2,000. B files a bankruptcy petition. C
only receives $300 from the liquidation of B's as-
sets. If B receives a bankruptcy discharge, C will
be precluded from pursuing B for the remaining
$1,700.

As the preceding paragraph implies, every liquidation case under the bankruptcy laws does not
result in a discharge. Section 727(a), considered
infra at pages 293–98, lists a number of grounds for
withholding a discharge. And, even if the debtor
is able to obtain a discharge, she will not necessarily be freed from all creditors' claims. Section 523,
considered infra at pages 303–10, sets out exceptions to discharge.

The vast majority of bankruptcy cases are Chapter 7 cases. The term "bankruptcy" is often used to describe liquidation proceedings under the bankruptcy laws. References to "bankruptcy" in this nutshell should generally be regarded as references to liquidation cases.[1]

Chapters 11 and 13 generally deal with debtor rehabilitation, not liquidation, of the debtor's assets. In a rehabilitation case under the bankruptcy laws, creditors usually look to future earnings of the debtor, not the property of the debtor at the time of the initiation of the bankruptcy proceeding, to satisfy their claims. The debtor retains its assets and makes payments to creditors, usually from post-petition earnings, pursuant to a court-approved plan.

Chapter 11, like Chapter 7, is available to all forms of debtors—individuals, partnerships and corporations. Chapter 11 is considered infra at pages 319-43. Chapter 13 can be used only by individuals with a "regular income" (as defined in section 101(27)) who have unsecured debts of less than $100,000 and secured debts of less than $350,000. Chapter 13 is considered infra at pages 344-61.

1. Liquidation proceedings under the Bankruptcy Act of 1898 are commonly referred to as "straight bankruptcy" cases. Rehabilitation proceedings under the Bankruptcy Act of 1898 are commonly referred to as "chapter proceedings."

C. BANKRUPTCY COURTS AND BANKRUPTCY JUDGES

1. Under the Bankruptcy Act of 1898

The Bankruptcy Act of 1898 provided for "bankruptcy referees." Originally, the judicial role of bankruptcy referees was relatively minor. The referee was primarily an administrator and supervisor of bankruptcy cases, not a judicial officer. Amendments to the Bankruptcy Act of 1898 made the bankruptcy referee more of a judicial officer. In 1973, the Bankruptcy Rules changed the title of the office from "bankruptcy referee" to "bankruptcy judge."

The 1898 Act used the term "courts of bankruptcy." A court of bankruptcy could be either the court of a federal district judge or the court of a bankruptcy judge. Any federal district court could be a "court of bankruptcy." Any judicial power conferred by the Bankruptcy Act of 1898 on the "court" could be exercised by either a federal district judge or a bankruptcy judge; any judicial power conferred by the Bankruptcy Act of 1898 on the "judge" could be exercised only by the federal district judge.

2. Under the 1978 Bankruptcy Law, as Amended in 1984

Both the 1978 enactment and the 1984 amendments deal with the bankruptcy court system separately from the substantive law of bankruptcy.

The substantive law of bankruptcy is now in Title 11 of the United States Code; the law relating to bankruptcy judges is in Title 28.

Title 28 nowhere uses the term "bankruptcy referee." Section 152 of Title 28 provides for "bankruptcy judges" to be appointed by the United States courts of appeals. Section 151 of Title 28 states that these bankruptcy judges "shall constitute a unit of the district court to be known as the bankruptcy court." Note that under Title 28 as amended in 1984, the bankruptcy court is not really a separate court; rather, it is a part of the district court.

Accordingly, the grant of jurisdiction over bankruptcy matters is to the district court, 28 USC section 1334. The federal district judges then refer bankruptcy matters to the bankruptcy judges pursuant to 28 USC section 157.[2]

2. It is important to understand the differences between 28 USC 1334 and 28 USC 157. Section 1334 grants jurisdiction over bankruptcy cases and proceedings; all grants of jurisdiction are to the district court. Neither the phrase "bankruptcy court" nor the phrase "bankruptcy judge" appears in section 1334. Remember, however, that the bankruptcy judge is a unit of the district court under section 151. Accordingly, a grant of jurisdiction to the "district court" does not preclude the bankruptcy judge from playing a role in bankruptcy litigation.

Section 157 spells out the role that the bankruptcy judge is to play in bankruptcy litigation. Section 157 is entitled "Procedures" and deals with referral of matters from the "district court" to the bankruptcy judge. Section 157 is not a jurisdictional provision; it does not grant jurisdiction to the bankruptcy judges.

[*144*]

The allocation of judicial power and responsibility over bankruptcy matters is one of the most controversial and complex areas of bankruptcy law and practice. I believe that you will find it easier to deal with the bankruptcy jurisdiction issues after you have gained some understanding of the substantive law of bankruptcy. Accordingly, bankruptcy jurisdiction issues will not be dealt with until later in this book.

D. TRUSTEES

In every Chapter 7 case, every Chapter 13, and some Chapter 11 cases,[3] there will be not only a bankruptcy judge but also a bankruptcy trustee. Generally, the bankruptcy trustee will be a private citizen, not an employee of the federal government.

A bankruptcy trustee is an active trustee. According to section 323 of the Bankruptcy Code, the bankruptcy trustee is "the representative of the *estate*." The filing of a bankruptcy petition is said to create an estate consisting generally of the property of the debtor as of the time of the bankruptcy filing. This estate is treated as a separate legal entity, distinct from the debtor. The bankruptcy trustee is the person who sues on behalf of or may be sued on behalf of the estate.

In summary, section 1334 speaks to what district courts can do and is jurisdictional. Section 157 deals with what the bankruptcy judges can do and is procedural.

3. In Chapter 11, the bankruptcy court decides whether it is necessary to appoint a trustee, section 1104.

The powers and duties of a bankruptcy trustee vary from chapter to chapter. As noted on page 141, Chapter 7 bankruptcy is liquidation in nature. The duties of a bankruptcy trustee in a Chapter 7 case include:

1. collecting the "property of the estate," i.e., debtor's property as of the time of the filing of the bankruptcy petition

2. challenging certain pre-bankruptcy and post-bankruptcy transfers of the property of the estate

3. selling the property of the estate

4. objecting to creditors' claims that are improper

5. in appropriate cases, objecting to the debtor's discharge, section 704.

Remember that there will be a bankruptcy trustee in every Chapter 7 case. Promptly after the "order for relief" in a Chapter 7 case, the bankruptcy judge must appoint an "interim trustee," section 701. In selecting an interim trustee, the bankruptcy judge is limited to private citizens who are members of a "panel" of private trustees established and maintained by the Director of the Administrative Office of the United States Courts. This interim trustee will serve at least until the first meeting of creditors.

At the first meeting of creditors, the creditors may elect a new trustee to replace the interim trustee if creditors holding at least 20% in amount of certain, unsecured claims vote in the election, section 702(c). This percentage requirement is designed to insure that trustees are elected only in cases in which there is significant creditor interest and to discourage election of trustees by attorneys for creditors who hope to be attorneys for the trustee, as was often the practice under the Bankruptcy Act of 1898. If the creditor interest in the case is sufficient to permit election of a trustee, the creditors are not required to select a trustee who is a member of the panel of private trustees.

If the creditors do not elect a trustee, the interim trustee becomes the trustee and serves in that capacity for the duration of the case.

There will also be a bankruptcy trustee in every Chapter 13 case. Creditors do not have the right to elect a trustee in Chapter 13. The bankruptcy judge always appoints the trustee in Chapter 13 cases. Generally, the bankruptcy judge will appoint one or more individuals to serve as trustee for all Chapter 13 cases in his or her district. Such trustees are generally referred to as "standing trustees."

Remember that Chapter 13 contemplates rehabilitation, not liquidation. In the typical Chapter 13 case, the debtor retains his or her assets and makes payments to creditors from post-petition earnings pursuant to a court-approved plan. The bankruptcy trustee in a Chapter 13 case is in part a disbursing agent—responsible for the supervision of the debtor's performance of the plan. The duties of a Chapter 13 trustee are set out in section 1302: essentially the duties of a Chapter 13 trustee are the same as a Chapter 7 trustee except of course that a Chapter 13 trustee does not collect and liquidate the property of the estate.

While there is a bankruptcy trustee in every Chapter 7 case and every Chapter 13 case, there is rarely a bankruptcy trustee in a Chapter 11 case. In Chapter 11, a bankruptcy trustee will be appointed by the bankruptcy judge only if the bankruptcy judge decides, after notice and hearing, that there is "cause" or the "appointment is in the interests of creditors, any equity security holders, and other interests of the estate."

Remember also that Chapter 11, like Chapter 13, contemplates rehabilitation, not liquidation, and that Chapter 11, unlike Chapter 13, is available to corporations and partnerships as well as individuals. The typical Chapter 11 case involves a business that continues to operate after the bankruptcy petition is filed. If a bankruptcy trustee is named in such a case, he or she will take over the operation of the business. As noted above, generally there will not be a trustee in a Chapter 11 case. The debtor will usually remain in control of the business after the filing of a Chapter 11 petition; such a debtor is referred to as a "debtor in possession." Chapter XVII of this book will deal with Chapter 11 trustees and debtors in possession in more detail.

E. UNITED STATES TRUSTEES

There was no such thing as a United States
Trustee until the 1978 bankruptcy legislation.
During the debate on bankruptcy legislation, considerable concern was expressed over the bankruptcy judges' involvement in the administration
of bankruptcy cases. While both the House and
the Senate seemed to agree that the bankruptcy
judge should not perform administrative functions,
there was disagreement over who should. The
compromise was an experimental United States
Trustee program involving parts of 17 states and
the District of Columbia. These pilot programs
will continue until September 30, 1986.

The United States Trustee is a government official, appointed by the Attorney General. Chapter
15 of the Bankruptcy Code details the duties and
powers of the United States Trustee. Essentially,
the United States Trustee performs appointing and
other administrative tasks that the bankruptcy
judge would otherwise have to perform. For example, in a "pilot" district, the United States Trustee,
not the bankruptcy judge, appoints and supervises
the bankruptcy trustees. Although the United
States Trustee can act as trustee in a Chapter 7
case or a Chapter 13 case (but not a Chapter 11
case), he or she is not intended as a substitute for
private bankruptcy trustees. The United States
Trustee is more of a substitute for the bankruptcy
judge.

CHAPTER VII

COMMENCEMENT AND DISMISSAL OF A BANKRUPTCY CASE

A bankruptcy case begins with the filing of a petition with the bankruptcy court, section 301. Generally, the debtor files the petition. Such debtor-initiated cases are often referred to as "voluntary." Creditors have a limited right to initiate "involuntary" bankruptcy cases against the debtor under Chapters 7 and 11.

A. VOLUNTARY CASES

Section 301 deals with the commencement of voluntary cases under Chapter 7, 11, or 13. It provides that a bankruptcy petition may be filed by any "entity that may be a debtor under such chapter." Section 109 sets out who is eligible to be a debtor under each chapter. Accordingly it is necessary to consider paragraphs (b), (d), (e), and (f) of section 109.

Section 109(b) contains two limitations on the availability of *Chapter 7* (liquidation) relief to a debtor:

1. The debtor must be a "person." "Person" is defined in section 101(35) as including partnerships and corporations. A sole proprietorship would not be a "person."

2. The debtor may not be a railroad, insurance company, or banking institution. Railroads are eligible for bankruptcy relief only under subchapter IV of Chapter 11; insurance companies and banking institutions are excluded from relief under the Bankruptcy Code because their liquidations are governed by other state and federal regulatory laws.

With two exceptions, any person who is eligible to file a petition under *Chapter 7* is also eligible to file a petition under *Chapter 11,* section 109(d). The first exception is railroads. As noted above, railroads are eligible for Chapter 11, but not Chapter 7. The second exception is stockbrokers and commodity brokers; they are eligible for Chapter 7, but not Chapter 11.

There are three significant limitations in section 109(e) on the availability of Chapter 13:

1. The debtor must be an individual. A Chapter 13 petition may not be filed by a corporation or a partnership.

2. The individual must have "income sufficiently stable and regular to enable such individual to make payments under a (Chapter 13 plan)," sections 101(27), 109(e). This includes not only wage earners, but also self-employed individuals, and individuals on welfare, pensions, or investment income.

3. The debtor must have "non-contingent, liquidated" unsecured debts totalling less than

$100,000 and "non-contingent, liquidated" secured debts of less than $350,000.[1]

While too much debt makes a debtor ineligible for Chapter 13, too much assets does *not* make a debtor ineligible for Chapter 7, 11, or 13. Please note that insolvency is not a condition precedent to any form of voluntary bankruptcy action. A debtor may file a petition under Chapter 7, 11, or 13 even though solvent.

A husband and a wife may file a single joint petition for voluntary relief under any chapter that is available to each spouse. If a husband and a wife jointly file under Chapter 13, their aggregate debts are subject to the $100,000/$350,000 limits.[2]

As the preceding pages examining paragraphs (b), (d), and (e) of section 109 indicate, there are debtors that are eligible for some chapters of bankruptcy relief but not eligible for others. Additionally, there are *individual* debtors who are not eligible for relief under any chapter.

New section 109(f) adds what could be roughly called a "frequent filing" limitation. Under section 109(f), an *individual* debtor is not eligible to be a debtor under either 7, 11, or 13, if he or she was a debtor in a bankruptcy case within the last 180 days that was:

1. These debt limitations are considered again on page 345.

2. Joint filing also may affect the property that can be claimed as exempt. See section 522(b), considered infra at pages 177–178.

(i) dismissed by the court for failure of the debtor to abide by court orders or appear before the court, or

(ii) dismissed on motion of the debtor following the filing of a request for relief from the automatic stay. Note that section 109(f) does not bar an individual who has completed a Chapter 7, 11, or 13 case from immediately filing for bankruptcy again.

A debtor who files a bankruptcy petition must pay a filing fee—$60 for Chapter 7 or 13, $200 for Chapter 11, 28 USC § 1930(a). The court may dismiss the bankruptcy case for non-payment of fees, sections 707, and 1307. No provision is made for *in forma pauperis* bankruptcy.

A voluntary bankruptcy case is commenced when an eligible debtor files a petition. No formal adjudication is necessary; the filing operates as an "order for relief," section 301.

B. INVOLUNTARY CASES

Section 303 deals with bankruptcy petitions filed by creditors. It contains a number of significant limitations on involuntary petitions:

1. Creditors may file involuntary petitions under Chapter 7 or 11 but not Chapter 13.

2. Certain debtors are protected from involuntary petitions. Insurance companies, banking institutions, farmers, and charitable corporations may not be subjected to involuntary petitions.

3. The petition must be filed by the requisite number of creditors. Generally, three creditors with unsecured claims totalling at least $5,000 must join in the petition. If, however, the debtor has less than twelve unsecured creditors, a single creditor with an unsecured claim of $5,000 is sufficient.

While the filing of an involuntary petition effects a commencement of the case, it does not operate as an adjudication, as an order for relief.[3] The debtor has the right to file an answer. If the debtor does not timely answer the petition, "the court shall order relief," section 303(h). If the debtor does timely answer the petition, the court "shall order relief against the debtor" only if one of the two grounds for involuntary relief are established.

The first basis for involuntary relief is that the debtor is generally not paying debts as they come due. This is sometimes referred to as "equitable insolvency"; it is different from the definition of insolvency in section 101(29).

The alternative basis for involuntary relief is that within 120 days before the petition was filed, a general receiver, assignee, or custodian took possession of substantially all of the debtor's property or was appointed to take charge of substantially all

3. To review, all bankruptcy cases—voluntary and involuntary—commence when the petition is filed. Numerous Bankruptcy Code provisions refer to and focus on this event. In voluntary cases, the order for relief also dates from the time when the petition is filed. In involuntary cases, the order for relief occurs at a later time. See Rules 1011, 1013.

of the debtor's property. The appointment of a receiver in a mortgage foreclosure action to take possession of Greenacre, less than substantially all of the debtor's property, would not be a basis for involuntary relief.

Usually there will be an interval of at least several weeks between the filing of an involuntary petition and the order of relief against the debtor. During this period, the debtor may continue to buy, use, or sell property and to operate its business, section 303(f).[4] The bankruptcy court may appoint an interim trustee to take possession of the debtor's property or operate the debtor's business "if necessary to preserve the property of the estate or to prevent loss to the estate," section 303(g). If an interim trustee is appointed, the debtor may regain possession by posting a bond.

Notwithstanding the protection of section 303(f), the filing of an involuntary petition adversely affects the debtor's financial reputation and business operations. Section 303(i) attempts to protect debtors from ill-founded petitions by setting out the following remedies in cases in which an involuntary petition is dismissed after litigation:

1. The court *may* grant judgment for the debtor against the petitioning creditors for costs and a reasonable attorney's fee.

---

4. Sections 502(f) and 507(a)(2) protect third parties who deal with a debtor after an involuntary petition has been filed. These provisions are considered infra at pages 274, 279.

2.   If an interim trustee took possession of the debtor's property, the court *may* grant judgment for "any damages proximately caused by the taking."

3.   If the petition was filed in "bad faith," the court *may* award "any damages proximately caused by such filing," such as loss of business, and also punitive damages.

C.   DISMISSAL

The bankruptcy court may dismiss or suspend a voluntary bankruptcy case even though it was filed by an eligible debtor.   And, the bankruptcy court may dismiss or suspend an involuntary bankruptcy case even though all of the requirements are satisfied.

Each bankruptcy relief chapter has its own dismissal provision.   Section 707 governs dismissal of Chapter 7 cases.   Under section 707(a), the standard a bankruptcy court is to apply in ruling on a motion to dismiss is "for cause"; section 707(a) gives two examples of "cause."   This "cause" standard applies to motions to dismiss filed by the debtor as well as motions to dismiss filed by creditors.   A debtor who files a Chapter 7 petition does not have an absolute right to have the bankruptcy case dismissed.

Under section 707(b), a bankruptcy court can act sua sponte and dismiss a Chapter 7 case if

(1) the debtor is an individual

(2) the debts are "primarily consumer debts"

(3) "granting relief would be a substantial abuse of the provisions of this chapter." [5]

In Chapter 11, like Chapter 7, the standard a bankruptcy court is to apply to a motion to dismiss is "for cause." Again, the statute sets out examples of cause, section 1112(b). Again, the "cause" standard applies to both debtor and creditor motions. Section 1112 does not expressly provide for a court to act sua sponte in dismissing a Chapter 11 case.

In Chapter 13, unlike Chapters 7 and 11, a debtor is given an absolute right to have his or her Chapter 13 case dismissed, section 1307(b). Motions to dismiss filed by creditors in a Chapter 13 case are subject to the "for cause" standard. Section 1307(c) sets out examples of "cause."

In Chapter 7, 11, and 13 cases, a debtor or creditors can also base a motion to dismiss on section 305. Section 305 empowers the bankruptcy court to dismiss or suspend a case if there is a foreign bankruptcy proceeding pending concerning the debtor or if "the interests of creditors and the

---

5. Section 707(b) was added in 1984. It is not yet clear from the cases what "substantial abuse" means. Nor is it clear when and how the judge will learn of the abuse. Note the phrase "on its own motion."

debtor would be better served by such dismissal or suspension." [6]

To illustrate, D, Inc., is generally not paying its debts as they come due. D, Inc. is trying to negotiate a workout with its creditors. Three of D, Inc.'s creditors are dissatisfied with the terms proposed in the workout and file an involuntary Chapter 11 petition against D, Inc. The bankruptcy court may decide to dismiss this petition if D, Inc. is making progress in negotiating a workout with its creditors.

A section 305 dismissal must be preceded by "notice and a hearing." The decision to dismiss (or not to dismiss) is not appealable. If an involuntary petition is dismissed under section 305, the petitioning creditors are *not* liable for costs, attorneys' fees or damages under section 303(i).

6. The bankruptcy court may also dismiss a bankruptcy case for failure to pay filing fees.

CHAPTER VIII

STAY OF COLLECTION ACTIONS AND ACTS

After the filing of a bankruptcy petition, a debtor needs immediate protection from the collection efforts of creditors. If the petition is a voluntary Chapter 7, the bankruptcy trustee needs time to collect the "property of the estate" and make pro rata distributions to creditors. If the petition is a voluntary Chapter 11 or Chapter 13, the debtor needs time to prepare a plan. And, if the petition is an involuntary Chapter 7 or Chapter 11, the debtor needs time to controvert the petition. Moreover, since creditors will receive payment through the bankruptcy process or the plan of rehabilitation and some claims will be discharged, continued creditor actions would interfere with orderly bankruptcy administration.

Accordingly, the filing of a voluntary petition under Chapter 7, Chapter 11, or Chapter 13, or the filing of an involuntary petition under Chapter 7 or Chapter 11 automatically "stays", i.e., restrains, creditors from taking further action against the debtor, the property of the debtor, or the property of the estate to collect their claims or enforce their liens, section 362.

There are four stay questions that lawyers (and law students) are asked

    1. when does the automatic stay become effective

    2. what is covered by the automatic stay

    3. when does the automatic stay end

    4. how can a creditor obtain relief from the stay.

A. TIME STAY ARISES

The automatic stay is triggered by the filing of a bankruptcy petition. It dates from the time of the filing, not from the time that a creditor receives notice of or learns of the bankruptcy. If D files a bankruptcy petition on April 5, the stay becomes effective April 5. The stay dates from April 5 even if creditors do not learn of the bankruptcy until much later. If C, not knowing of D's bankruptcy, obtains a default judgment against D on April 29, the default judgment violates the automatic stay and is invalid.

B. SCOPE OF THE STAY

1. Section 362

Paragraph (a) of section 362 defines the scope of the automatic stay by listing all of the acts and actions that are stayed by the commencement of a bankruptcy case. It is comprehensive and includes virtually all creditor collection activity.

Subparagraphs (1) and (2) of section 362(a) cover
most litigation efforts of creditors directed at collecting pre-bankruptcy debts. Section 362(a)(1)
stays creditors from filing collection suits after the
bankruptcy petition is filed or from continuing
collection suits that were commenced prior to
bankruptcy. Section 362(a)(2) bars creditors from
enforcing judgments obtained prior to bankruptcy.

Section 362(a)(6) stays "any *act* to collect
* * *." This has been read as barring informal
collection actions such as telephone calls demanding payments and dunning letters.

Subparagraphs (3), (4), and (5) of section 362(a)
stay virtually all types of secured creditor action
against the property of the estate or property of
the debtor.[1] Creditors are barred from obtaining
liens, perfecting liens, or enforcing liens after the
bankruptcy petition is filed.

While paragraph (a) of section 362 indicates
what is stayed, paragraph (b) lists eleven kinds of
actions that are not stayed. For example, section
362(b)(2) provides a limited exception for alimony
and child support claims. Such claims can be
collected from property that is not "property of the
estate."

There is an important limitation on the scope of
section 362 that is not dealt with in paragraph (b)
of section 362. The automatic stay of section
362(a) only covers the debtor, property of the debt-

1. Property of the estate is considered infra at 173–176.

or, and property of the estate. It does not protect third parties. Assume, for example, that D borrows $3,000 from C and G guarantees repayment. If D files for bankruptcy, section 362(a) will stay C from attempting to collect from D. Section 362(a) will not, however, protect G.

2. Section 1301

While section 362(a) will not protect G, section 1301 might. By reason of section 1301, the filing of a Chapter 13 petition automatically stays collection action against guarantors and other codebtors if

(1) the debt is a consumer debt and

(2) the codebtor is not in the credit business.

Section 1301's automatic stay of actions against codebtors applies only in Chapter 13 cases; it is discussed in the chapter of this book dealing with Chapter 13 cases on pages 345–347.

3. Section 105

Section 105 grants to bankruptcy courts the power to issue orders "necessary or appropriate to carry out the provisions of this title." Courts have used this section 105 power to stay or restrain creditor action.

There is an important procedural difference between section 105 and sections 362 or 1301. An injunction or stay under section 105 will not be automatic. Rather, it will be granted according to the usual rules for injunctive relief.

There is also an important substantive difference between section 105 and sections 362 or 1301. In acting under section 105, the bankruptcy court is not expressly limited by the restrictions in section 362 or section 1301.

If D, Inc. files for bankruptcy, can a court use section 105 to enjoin creditors from proceeding against P who personally guaranteed D, Inc.'s debts? There is *dicta* in numerous cases that a court has the power under section 105 to protect third parties but very few such holdings.[2]

C. TERMINATION OF THE STAY

Paragraph (c) of section 362 describes two situations in which the automatic stay terminates automatically.

Section 362(c)(1) provides that the automatic stay ends as to particular property when the property ceases to be property of the estate. Assume for example that C has a mortgage on D Corp.'s build-

---

2. Most of the cases refer to and quote from In re Otero Mills, Inc., 21 B.R. 777 (Bkrtcy.N.M.1982), which sets out three requirements that must be satisfied before a court enjoins a creditor's actions against a codebtor:

(1) "irreparable harm to the bankruptcy estate if the injunction does not issue;

(2) Strong likelihood of success on the merits; and

(3) No harm or minimal harm to the other party or parties." 21 B.R. at 779.

ing. D Corp. files a bankruptcy petition. C is stayed from foreclosing its mortgage. The bankruptcy trustee sells D Corp.'s office building to X. C is no longer stayed from foreclosing its lien.[3]

Section 362(c)(2) provides that the automatic stay ends when the bankruptcy case is closed or dismissed or the debtor receives a discharge. The typical Chapter 7 bankruptcy can be completed in a matter of months. In Chapter 11 cases and Chapter 13 cases, however, there can be a gap of several years between the filing of the petition and discharge. Accordingly, unless some action is taken, the stay can last several years.

D. RELIEF FROM THE STAY

A bankruptcy court may grant *relief* from the automatic stay on *request* of a *"party in interest,"* section 362(d). The relief will not always take the form of termination of the stay. Section 362(d) provides for *"relief"* "such as by terminating, annulling, modifying, or conditioning such stay." The Rules provide that the *"request"* in section 362 takes the form of a motion, Rules 4001(a), 9014. The facts of the reported cases make clear that the *"party in interest"* in section 362 is usually a creditor, usually a secured creditor.

---

3. Property also ceases to be property of the estate when it is abandoned to the debtor under section 554. Notwithstanding the language of section 362(c)(1), abandonment does not terminate the stay. The stay continues by reason of section 362(a)(5). See In re Cruseturner, 8 B.R. 581, 7 B.C.D. 235 (Bkrtcy.Utah 1981).

What does a creditor have to allege in its motion and establish in its proof in order to obtain relief from the stay? The grounds for relief from stay are set out in section 362(d).

1. Section 362(d)(1)

The most general statutory ground for relief from the stay is "for cause," section 362(d)(1). There is very little case law on what constitutes "cause" for purposes of section 362(d)(1). Most of the reported section 362(d)(1) cases involve the specific example of cause set out in the statute— "lack of adequate protection of an interest in property of such party in interest."

The quoted language raises four questions: (1) who is "the party in interest" (2) what is "the interest in property" (3) from what is it being protected and (4) how much protection is "adequate protection."

The party in interest is the person seeking relief from the stay. Again, typically, the party in interest under section 362(d)(1) will be a secured creditor.

Note that what is to be protected is the secured creditor's interest in property, not the secured party's claim. If, for example, D owes C $100,000 and C has a mortgage on land worth $60,000, section 362(d)(1) contemplates adequate protection of C's lien position, rather than C's right to the payment of $100,000.

The questions of from what the interest in property is to be protected and how much protection is adequate protection are closely related. There is a split of authority in the answers to these questions.

In re Alyucan Interstate Corp., 12 B.R. 803 (Bkrtcy.Utah 1981), for example, reads section 362(d)(1) as protecting the secured creditor from a loss in value of the collateral. There a $1,297,226 debt was secured by realty with a value of $1,425,000. The collateral was not losing value. Because the collateral was not declining in value, Judge Mabey concluded that the creditor had not established a basis for relief from the stay under section 362(d)(1).

More recently, In re American Mariner Industries, Inc., 734 F.2d 426 (9th Cir.1984), read section 362(d)(1) as contemplating not only protection from loss in value of the collateral but also compensation for any delay in enforcing its rights. There a $370,000 debt was secured by $110,000 of collateral. The collateral was declining in value but the bankruptcy judge had already conditioned the continuation of the stay on the debtor making monthly payments to the secured creditor of $1,770, an amount equal to the monthly depreciation. The secured creditor in *American Mariner* argued that:

(i) the debtor was in default;

(ii) under state law, it could take possession of the $110,000 of collateral, sell it, and loan the sale proceeds out at interest;

(iii) "adequate protection" under section 362(d)
(1) contemplates compensation to the secured
creditor for what it might have earned on the
reinvestment of its liquidated interest in the
collateral.

The Ninth Circuit adopted this argument, concluding, "The secured party's right to take possession of and sell collateral on the debtor's default
has substantial, measurable value. * * * This
right constitutes an 'interest in property' * * *
and we are aware of no federal interest that requires this right of the secured party to go unpro-
tected simply because an interested party is involved in a bankruptcy proceeding." 734 F.2d at
435. In so holding the Ninth Circuit relied in part
on section 361 which is entitled "Adequate protection."

Section 361 does not define "adequate protection"; rather, section 361 specifies three non-exclusive methods of providing adequate protection.
The first method of adequate protection specified is
periodic cash payments to the lien creditor equal to
the decrease in value of the creditor's interest in
the collateral. If C has a security interest in D's
car and D files a bankruptcy petition, D can meet
the adequate protection burden of section 362 by
making cash payments equal to the depreciation
on the car, section 361(1).

Section 361(2) indicates that adequate protection
may take the form of an additional lien or substitute lien on other property. Assume, for example,

that P files a Chapter 11 petition. C has a perfected security in P's equipment. P needs to use the encumbered equipment to continue operation of its business, to accomplish a successful Chapter 11 reorganization. Such use will, however, decrease the value of the equipment and C's lien in the equipment. Under section 361(2) adequate protection may take the form of a lien on other property owned by P; the new collateral does not necessarily have to be equipment.

Section 361(3) grants the debtor in possession or trustee considerable flexibility in providing adequate protection. Section 361(3) recognizes such other protection, other than providing an administrative expense claim, that will result in the secured party's realizing the "indubitable equivalent" of the value of its interest in the collateral.

The term "indubitable equivalent" is not statutorily defined. Again, there is a split in the case authority as to the meaning and importance of the phrase. The *American Mariner* decision bases its holding that section 362(d)(1) requires compensation on the words "indubitable equivalent." The Ninth Circuit finds it significant that the very same phrase is used in section 1129(b)(2). The *Alyucan* case, on the other hand, states that "the phrase 'indubitable equivalent' does not have any substantive content. Indeed, something 'indubitable' is more than 'adequate'; 'equivalent' is more than 'protection'; hence, the illustration may eclipse the concept. At best, it is a semantic sub-

[*168*]

stitute for adequate protection and one with dubious, not indubitable application to the question of relief from the stay," 12 B.R. at 809.

In summary, there is uncertainty as to (1) the importance of the "indubitable equivalent" language in section 361, and (2) the requirements of the "adequate protection" language in section 362(d). This uncertainty is attributable in part to the practice of negotiating rather than litigating section 362(d)(1) issues and in part to what is decided in section 362(d)(1) litigation. Section 362(d)(1) does not contemplate that the bankruptcy judge will decide what is adequate protection and mandate that it be provided. Rather, in section 362(d)(1) litigation the bankruptcy judge merely decides whether what the bankruptcy trustee or debtor in protection has offered is adequate protection.

What if (i) there is section 362(d)(1) litigation, (ii) the bankruptcy judge decides that the debtor is providing adequate protection and (iii) the "adequate protection" proves to be inadequate? To illustrate, X has a perfected security interest in the inventory of Oscar De Lah Rentals Corp., O. O files a Chapter 11 petition. At the time of the petition, O owes X $100,000, and the encumbered inventory has a value of $60,000. X requests relief from the stay. The court concludes that O's offer of a personal guarantee by G was "adequate protection," was the "indubitable equivalent." This conclusion turns out to be wrong. When O's Chapter

11 reorganization fails, G is insolvent. The value of the inventory now securing O's $100,000 claim is worth only $20,000. Obviously, X can not sue the bankruptcy judge. What can X do?

Section 507(b) applies when "adequate protection" proves to be inadequate. It grants an administrative expense priority [4] for the losses. In the Oscar De Lah Rentals hypo, X would have a $40,000 administrative expense priority claim.

2.   Section 362(d)(2)

Under section 362(d)(2) a lien creditor can obtain relief from the stay if

(A) the debtor does not have any equity in the encumbered property, AND

(B) the encumbered property is not necessary to an effective reorganization.

The application of section 362(d)(2)(A) would not seem to present any difficult legal issues: generally equity is measured by the difference between the value of the property and the encumbrances against it. If, for example, property has a value of $100,000 and is subject to a $120,000 lien, "the debtor does not have any equity in such property."

The cases under section 362(d)(2)(A), however, are still wrestling with two difficult legal issues. First, how should property be valued for purposes of section 362(d)(2)(A)? Congress deliberately left

---

4. The significance of an administrative expense priority is considered infra at pages 277–279.

unanswered the question of whether property should be valued at a liquidation value, going concern value, or some other value, section 506. Second, which liens are to be considered for purposes of section 362(d)(2)(A)? Assume, for example, that the debtor's land is valued at $300,000. X has a $250,000 lien on the land. Y has a $75,000 lien on the same land. Only X requests relief from the stay. Most courts would find no equity under these facts; the dominant view is that "equity" in section 362(d)(2)(A) refers to the difference between the value of the property and *all* encumbrances against it. Other courts, however, refuse to include liens junior to the creditor requesting relief.

A creditor cannot obtain relief from the stay merely by establishing no equity. Note the conjunction "and" connecting the no equity test of section 362(d)(2)(A) and section 362(d)(2)(B). The issues under section 362(d)(2)(B) will be whether (1) the encumbered property is necessary to the debtor's reorganization and/or (2) an effective reorganization is possible.

3. Relationship Between Section 362(d)(1) and Section 362(d)(2)

Note that section 362(d)(1) and section 362(d)(2) are connected by the conjunction "or." A creditor is entitled to relief from the stay if it is able to establish grounds for relief under either section 362(d)(1) or section 362(d)(2). If, for example, a creditor is able to establish the lack of adequate

[*171*]

protection, it is entitled to relief from the stay even though the property is necessary to an effective reorganization.

4. Burden of Proof in Section 362(d) Litigation

Section 362(g) allocates the burden of proof in stay litigation. The creditor or other party requesting the relief has the burden on the issue of whether the debtor has an equity in the property. The debtor or bankruptcy trustee has the burden on all other issues.

CHAPTER IX

PROPERTY OF THE ESTATE

A. WHY IS PROPERTY OF THE ESTATE AN IMPORTANT CONCEPT

The filing of a bankruptcy petition automatically creates an "estate," section 541(a). "Property of the estate" is one of the most important, most basic bankruptcy concepts.

A number of the general provisions in Chapters 3 and 5 use the phrase "property of the estate." For example, the automatic stay bars a creditor from collecting a pre-petition or post-petition claim from property of the estate, section 362(a)(3), (4).

In a Chapter 7 case, "property of the estate" is collected by the bankruptcy trustee and sold; the proceeds of the sale of the property of the estate are then distributed to creditors, sections 704, 726. In other words, the loss of property of the estate is the primary cost of Chapter 7 bankruptcy to the debtor; the receipt of the proceeds from the sale of property of the estate is the primary benefit creditors derive from a Chapter 7 bankruptcy.

In a Chapter 11 or Chapter 13 case, the debtor retains the property of the estate. Nevertheless, it is necessary to determine what is property of the estate even in a Chapter 11 or Chapter 13 case. In both Chapter 11 and Chapter 13 cases, the value of the property of the estate determines the minimum amount that must be offered to non-assenting general creditors in the plan of rehabilitation, sections 1129(a)(7), 1325(a)(4).

B. WHAT IS PROPERTY OF THE ESTATE

With only minor exceptions, property of the estate includes all property of the debtor as of the time of the filing of the bankruptcy petition.

The seven numbered subparagraphs of section 541 specify what property becomes property of the estate. Paragraph one is by far the most comprehensive and significant. Section 541(a)(1) provides that property of the estate includes "all legal or equitable interests of the debtor in property as of the commencement of the case." This is a very broad statement. Property of the estate thus includes both real property and personal property, both tangible property and intangible property, both property in the debtor's possession and property in which the debtor has an interest that is held by others.[1]

Section 541(a)(1) contains two significant limitations on what constitutes property of the estate. Please re-read the statutory language in the preceding paragraph. Note the phrase "interests of the debtor in property." If, for example, Mr.

---

1. Third parties are statutorily required to return such property to the bankruptcy trustee or debtor in possession, sections 542 and 543. These provisions are considered infra at pages 253–254.

Rourke and Tatoo own an island as tenants in common and Mr. Rourke files a Chapter 7 petition, only Mr. Rourke's limited interest in the island would be property of the estate.[2]

Note also the phrase "as of the commencement of the case" in section 541(a)(1). "Commencement of the case" is synonymous with filing of the petition, sections 301, 303. Thus, property that the debtor acquired prior to the petition becomes property of the estate; property acquired after the petition generally is not property of the estate. For example, if Ben Walton files a Chapter 7 petition on October 2, the money he earns for playing the piano at the Dew Drop Inn after October 2 is *not* "property of the estate."

There are four significant exceptions to the rule that property acquired after the filing of a bankruptcy petition remains the debtor's property.

1.   Property of the estate includes property that the debtor acquires or becomes entitled to within 180 days after the filing of the petition by:

    a.   bequest, devise, or inheritance

    b.   property settlement or a divorce decree

    c.   as beneficiary of a life insurance policy, section 541(a)(5).

2.   Property of the estate also includes the earnings from property of the estate, section 541(a)(6).

2. While only Mr. Rourke's interest in the island is property of the estate, the entire island can be sold under section 363(h), (i), and (j).

If, for example the Ropers file a Chapter 7 petition, the apartments that they own would be property of the estate, and post-petition rents from the apartments would be property of the estate.

3. In a Chapter 13 case, property of the estate includes wages earned and other property acquired by the debtor after the Chapter 13 filing, section 1306.

4. Property of the estate includes property received from a conversion of property of the estate. Assume that James Rockford files a Chapter 11 petition and that the next day his mobile home is destroyed by a tidal wave. Any insurance proceeds would be property of the estate.

CHAPTER X

EXEMPTIONS

A. WHAT PROPERTY IS EXEMPT

Under non-bankruptcy law, Jim Rockford's mobile home would probably be exempt property.[1] Under the Bankruptcy Code, all pre-bankruptcy property in which the debtor has an interest becomes property of the estate, but an individual debtor is permitted to exempt certain property from property of the estate, section 522(b), (*l*).

In bankruptcy, an individual debtor may assert the exemptions to which she is entitled under the laws of the state of her domicile and under federal laws other than Title 11,[2] section 522(b)(2). Alternatively, individual debtors in a few states may claim the exemptions set out in section 522(d).

Section 522(d) is only available to individual debtors that reside in states that have not enacted "opt out" legislation pursuant to section 522(b)(1). Under section 522(b)(1), a state legislature can enact legislation precluding resident debtors from

1. Non-bankruptcy exemption law is considered supra at pages 15–19.

2. Some of the items that may be exempted under Federal laws other than Title 11 include:

Social security payments, 42 USCA 407

Civil service retirement benefits, 5 USCA 729, 2265

Veterans benefits, 45 USCA 352(E).

electing to utilize section 522(d). Most states have enacted such "opt out" legislation.

Even in states that have not "opted out" there are statutory limitations on the debtor's choice of exemption statutes. A debtor cannot select some exemptions from state law and some exemptions from section 522(d). He or she must choose either the non-bankruptcy exemptions or section 522(d). And, under the 1984 amendments, section 522(b), husbands and wives in joint cases filed under section 302 or in individual cases which are being jointly administered under Bankruptcy Rule 1015(b) must both elect either the non-bankruptcy exemptions or the section 522(d) exemptions.[3] While under section 522(m) each spouse will be entitled to separate exemptions, it will not be possible for one to choose section 522(d) exemptions while the other chooses non-bankruptcy exemptions.

The Bankruptcy Code expressly deals with the effect of a debtor's contracting away his or her exemptions. Such a contract has no effect. Whether an individual debtor elects to claim under non-bankruptcy exemption law or under section 522(d), waivers of exemption are not enforceable, section 522(e).

---

3. In states that have not opted out, it may be disadvantageous for a husband and wife to file a joint petition. By filing two individual petitions and paying two $60 filing fees, a married couple may be able to increase the amount of their property that will be exempt.

The Bankruptcy Code does not expressly deal with the consequences of a debtor converting non-exempt property into exempt property on the eve of bankruptcy. What if, just before filing for bankruptcy, D takes funds from her bank account, non-exempt property under relevant law, and invests the money in a homestead? While the Code does not answer this question, both legislative history and case law suggest that the property will be exempt.[4]

B. WHAT IS THE SIGNIFICANCE IN BANKRUPTCY OF EXEMPT PROPERTY

Generally, an individual debtor is able to retain his or her exempt property. Exempt property is not distributed to creditors in the bankruptcy case and is protected from the claims of most creditors after the bankruptcy case. After bankruptcy, there are only four groups of creditors who have recourse to property set aside as exempt in a bankruptcy case:

4. In re Reed, 700 F.2d 986 (5th Cir.1983), acknowledged the legislative history and sustained the claim of exemption. Reed, however, also acknowledged a state law policy against converting exempt property into non-exempt property and sustained an objection to discharge under section 727(a)(2). [Discharge and objections to discharge are considered infra at pages 293–317.]

In *Reed,* the debtor sold antiques, gold coins, and other personal property not exempt under state law and used the $34,000 he received to wipe out liens on his homestead. In sustaining the objection to discharge, the court carefully limited its ruling to the facts of the case, carefully avoided framing a general rule. See 700 F.2d at 991–92.

1.   creditors with tax claims excepted from discharge by section 523(a)(1);

2.   creditors with domestic claims excepted from discharge by section 523(a)(5);

3.   creditors whose claims arise after the filing of the bankruptcy petition;[5]

4.   creditors with liens on exempt property that are neither avoided nor extinguished through redemption.

As # 4 suggests, some liens on exempt property that are valid outside of bankruptcy can be invalidated because of bankruptcy. The general invalidation provisions, discussed infra at pages 183–240, are applicable to liens on exempt property. More importantly, section 522(f) empowers the debtor to avoid judicial liens on any exempt property and to avoid security interests that are both non-purchase money and nonpossessory on certain household goods, tools of the trade, and health aids.

To illustrate, assume that the list of property that an individual claims as exempt includes a stereo system and an automobile. If a creditor has an attachment or execution lien on the stereo, the debtor may avoid the lien, section 522(f)(1). If a creditor has a security interest in the stereo, the security interest may be avoided unless it is either possessory or purchase money, section 522(f)(2). If a creditor has an attachment lien or execution lien

5.   If the debtor chooses the set of exemptions set out in section 522(d), post-petition creditors will be able to reach items not exempted under relevant state law.

on the automobile, the debtor may avoid the lien. If, on the other hand, a creditor has a security interest in the automobile, the debtor cannot avoid the lien.[6]

As the preceding paragraph illustrates, section 522(f) can be used to void any judicial lien on any exempt property. It reaches only those consensual liens that:

(1) are non-possessory, *and*

(2) are non-purchase money, *and*

(3) encumber exempt personal property of a type mentioned in section 522(f)(2).

Possessory security interests in exempt personal property, purchase money security interests in exempt personal property, and any security interests on exempt personal property not covered by section 522(f) may be extinguished through "redemption." Section 722 authorizes an individual debtor to redeem or extinguish a [7] lien on exempt personal property by paying the lienor the value of the

6. It can perhaps be argued that, for some debtors, an automobile is "implements * * * or tools of the trade" for purposes of section 522(f)(2)(B). There are cases holding that the phrase "tools of the trade" in state exemption statutes includes an automobile used by the debtor in his work. Note, however, that section 522(d) makes separate provisions for motor vehicles, section 522(d)(2), and tools of the trade, section 522(d)(6).

7. Section 722 does not apply to liens on tools of the trade. It is limited to liens on "tangible personal property intended for personal, family or household use." In theory, section 722 applies to all liens "securing a dischargeable consumer debt" on such property. As a practical matter, however, a debtor will property encumbered.[8] To illustrate, assume that D owes C $3,000. C has a security interest in D's Subaru. If D files a bankruptcy petition and the value of the Subaru is only $1,200, D can eliminate C's lien by paying C $1,200.

Section 522(f) applies in every personal bankruptcy. Even if the debtor elects to claim exemptions under non-bankruptcy law instead of section 522(d), section 522(f) can be used to invalidate certain liens on certain exempt property.

There are two non-bankruptcy developments that limit the practical significance of section 522(f). First, the Federal Trade Commission has promulgated a trade regulation that makes obtaining a nonpossessory, nonpurchase money security interest in household goods an unfair trade practice. After much discussion and delay, became effective March 1, 1985. Second, some states have revised their exemption laws by providing that property encumbered by nonpossessory, nonpurchase money security interests cannot be claimed as exempt. If a state has both opted out and adopted such a definition of exempt property, its resident debtors can make no effective use of section 522(f). Under section 522(f), the debtors may avoid only those liens on property that is exempt. See In re Pine, 717 F.2d 281 (6th Cir.1983).

not invoke section 722 to redeem property from liens which can be avoided under section 522(f).

8. It is unclear from the Code whether the payment under section 722 must be a cash payment. The courts consistently read section 722 as requiring cash payment.

CHAPTER XI

AVOIDANCE OF PRE–BANKRUPTCY TRANSFERS

Some transfers that are valid outside of bankruptcy can be invalidated by a bankruptcy trustee. The Bankruptcy Code empowers the bankruptcy trustee to invalidate certain pre-bankruptcy transfers. These invalidation provisions reach both absolute transfers such as payments of money, gifts, and sales, and security transfers such as creation of mortgages and security interests.

Consider first the invalidation of an absolute transfer. When the bankruptcy trustee invalidates a pre-bankruptcy absolute transfer, the property becomes property of the estate, sections 550, 541(a)(3). Assume that D owes C $1,000. D repays $600 of the $1,000 debt. D later files for bankruptcy. At the time of bankruptcy, C has a $400 claim against D, and the $600 is not property of the estate. If the bankruptcy trustee is able to void the payment, the $600 will be property of the estate and C will have a $1,000 claim against D.

Avoidance of a security transfer has the same effect. When the bankruptcy trustee invalidates a security transfer, the encumbered property becomes property of the estate free from encumbrances. Assume for example that D borrows $1,000 from S and grants S a security interest in equipment worth $1,000. At the time of bankruptcy, S has a $1,000 secured claim against D and only D's limited interest in the equipment is property of the estate. If the bankruptcy trustee is able to void the grant of the security interest, the unencumbered equipment will be property of the estate and S will have an unsecured $1,000 claim against D.

The various invalidation provisions reflect certain basic bankruptcy policies. The provisions and underlying policies are considered below.

A. PREFERENCES

Common law [1] does *not* condemn a preference. Under common law, a debtor—even an insolvent debtor—may treat certain creditors more favorably than other similar creditors. Although D owes X, Y, and Z $1,000 each, D may pay X's claim in full before paying any part of Y's claim or Z's claim.

Bankruptcy law *does* condemn *certain* preferences. A House report that accompanied a draft of the Code explained the rationale for such a bankruptcy policy as follows:

"The purpose of the preference section is twofold. First, by permitting the trustee to avoid

---

1. Some state statutes void certain transfers because of their preferential character. The trustee may take advantage of such statutes by virtue of his powers under section 544(b): if the state anti-preference provision protects any actual creditor of the debtor, it protects the bankruptcy trustee. Section 544(b) is considered infra at pages 217–221.

pre-bankruptcy transfers that occur within a
short period before bankruptcy, creditors are dis-
couraged from racing to the courthouse to dis-
member the debtor during his slide into bankruptcy. The protection thus afforded the debtor
often enables him to work his way out of a
difficult financial situation through cooperation
with all of his creditors. Second, and more important, the preference provisions facilitate the
prime bankruptcy policy of equality of distribution among creditors of the debtor. Any creditor
that received a greater payment than others of
his class is required to disgorge so that all may
share equally." House Report 95–595 at 117–78.

1. Elements of a Preference

Section 547(b) sets out the elements of a preference; the bankruptcy trustee may void any transfer of *property of the debtor* if he or she can
establish:

(1) the transfer was "to or for the benefit of a
creditor"; and

(2) the transfer was made for or on account of
an "antecedent debt", i.e., a debt owed prior to
the time of the transfer; and

(3) the debtor was insolvent at the time of the
transfer; and

(4) the transfer was made within 90 days before the date of the filing of the bankruptcy
petition, *or*, was made between 90 days and 1

[*185*]

year before the date of the filing of the petition to an "insider" [2]; and

(5) the transfer has the effect of increasing the amount that the transferee would receive in a Chapter 7 case.

The first three requirements of section 547(b) will usually be easy to apply. To illustrate, a true gift is not a preference—not to or for the benefit of a creditor. A pledge of stock to secure a new loan is not a preferential transfer—not for or account of antecedent debt. The third requirement—insolvency of the debtor at the time of transfer—is made easy by section 547(f)'s creation of a rebuttable presumption of insolvency for the 90 days immediately preceding the filing of the bankruptcy petition.

In determining whether the transfer was made within 90 days of the filing of the petition, look to Bankruptcy Rule 9006 which provides that the day on which the transfer occurred is not included.[3] In determining whether the transfer was made to an "insider" so that the relevant time period is 1 year,

2. "Insider" is defined in section 101. An insider includes relatives of an individual debtor and directors of a corporate debtor.

3. If under state law, a transfer is not fully effective against third parties until public notice of the transfer has been given and such public notice is not timely given, then section 547(e) deems the transfer to have occurred at the time public notice was given. The use of section 547 to invalidate transfers not recorded in a timely fashion is considered infra at pages 227–233.

not merely 90 days, look to the Bankruptcy Code section 101(28)'s definition of insider.

Remember that the presumption of insolvency is limited to the 90 days immediately preceding the bankruptcy petition. Accordingly, in order to invalidate a transfer that occurred more than 90 days before the filing of the bankruptcy petition the trustee must establish that (i) the transferee was an "insider"; and (ii) the debtor was insolvent at the time of the transfer.

The fifth element, which essentially tests whether the transfer improved the creditor's position, will be satisfied unless the creditor was fully secured before the transfer or the property of the estate is sufficiently large to permit 100% payment to all unsecured claims. Assume, for example, that D makes a $1,000 payment to C, a creditor with a $10,000 unsecured claim, on January 10. On February 20, D files a bankruptcy petition. The property of the estate is sufficient to pay each unsecured creditor 50% of its claim. An unsecured creditor with a $10,000 claim will thus receive $5,000. S, however, will receive a total of $5,500 from D and D's bankruptcy unless the January 10th transfer is avoided. ($1,000 + 50% × (10,000 − 1,000)). Accordingly, the bankruptcy trustee may avoid the January 10th transfer under section 547(b) to "facilitate the prime bankruptcy policy of equality of distribution among creditors."

The following hypotheticals illustrate the application of section 547(b).

(1) On February 2, D borrows $7,000 from C and promises to repay the $7,000 on March 2d. D repays C on March 2d as promised. On May 24, D files a bankruptcy petition.

The bankruptcy trustee can recover the $7,000 payment from C. See section 547(b); see also section 550.

(2) On February 2, D borrows $7,000 from C. D repays C on March 2d. On June 6, D files a bankruptcy petition.

The bankruptcy trustee can *not* recover the $7,000 from C under section 547(b). Section 547(b)(4) is not satisfied—more than 90 days.

(3) On February 2, D borrows $7,000 from C. On March 2d, X, a friend of D's, pays C the $7,000 D owed. On May 24, D files a bankruptcy petition.

The bankruptcy trustee can *not* recover the $7,000 from C under section 547(b). The payment was not a "transfer of an interest of the debtor in property."

(4) On January 10, D borrows $10,000 from C and grants C a security interest in its equipment. At all relevant times, the equipment has a value of $20,000. On March 3, D repays C $3,000 of the $10,000. On April 4, D files a bankruptcy petition.

The bankruptcy trustee can not avoid the March 3 payment under section 547(b). Section 547(b)(5) is not satisfied. Note that C had a security interest. Note also that the value of the collateral securing C's claim was greater than the amount of the claim.[4] In a Chapter 7 case, the holder of a secured claim will receive either its collateral or its value up to the amount of the debt. Accordingly, even if the payment had not been made, S as a fully secured creditor would have been paid in full. A pre-bankruptcy payment to a fully secured creditor is not a preference.

(5) On February 2, D borrows $200,000 from S and S records a mortgage on Redacre, real property of D's. At all relevant times, Redacre has a value of $140,000. On April 5, D repays $40,000 of the loan. On May 6, D files a bankruptcy petition. The property of the estate is sufficient to pay each unsecured creditor 10% of its claim.

The trustee may avoid the April 5 payment and recover the $40,000 for the estate. All of the elements of section 547(b) including section 547(b)(5) are satisfied. If the transfer had not been made, S would have received $146,000. If the transfer is not avoided, S will receive $182,000. [$140,000 secured claim + $40,000

---

4. See section 506. Under this provision, the amount of a secured claim is limited by the value of the collateral. Assume for example that D borrows $100,000 from S and grants S a security interest in equipment. One debt, one transaction, one note. D later files for bankruptcy still owing S $100,000. If the bankruptcy court values the equipment at $40,000, S has a $40,000 secured claim and a $60,000 unsecured claim.

payment + $2,000 on remaining $20,000 unsecured claim.]

(6) On March 3, D borrows $300,000 from S.
On April 4, S demands security for the loan and
D gives S a mortgage on Redacre. Redacre has a
fair market value of $400,000. On May 5, D files
a bankruptcy petition. The property of the estate is sufficient to pay each unsecured creditor
20% of its claim.

The trustee may avoid the April 4 mortgage so
that Redacre is property of the estate free and
clear of S's lien. Again all of the elements of
section 547(b) are satisfied. The transfer would
enable S to receive $300,000. If the transfer had
not been made, S would receive only $60,000.
[Section 547(b) invalidates liens to secure past
debts.]

(7) On April 4, D borrows $40,000 from S and
gives S a security interest in equipment. The
equipment has a fair market value of $50,000.
On June 6, D files a bankruptcy petition.

The trustee may not avoid the April 4 security
interest. The April 4 transfer was for present
consideration, not "for or on account of an antecedent debt." Element # 2 is not satisfied.
[Section 547 does not invalidate liens to secure
new debts.]

2. Exceptions (Section 547(c))

Section 547(b) sets out the elements of a voidable preference. Section 547(c) excepts certain pre-petition transfers from the operation of section 547(b). If a transfer comes within one of section 547(c)'s exceptions, the bankruptcy trustee will not be able to invalidate the transfer even though the trustee can establish all of the requirements of section 547(b).

The first exception is for a transfer that

(i) was intended to be for new value, not an antecedent debt

(ii) did in fact occur at a time "substantially contemporaneous" with the time that the debt arose, section 547(c)(1).

For example, D borrows $5,000 from C on April 5th. Both parties then intend the loan to be a secured loan, secured by a pledge of D's X Corp. stock. On April 9th, D pledges her X Corp. stock by delivering the certificates to C. On May 6th, D files a bankruptcy petition. The bankruptcy trustee will not be able to void the April 9th pledge under section 547. The transfer for an antecedent debt is protected by section 547(c)(1).

Note that section 547(c)(1) requires both that the transfer actually be a "substantially contemporaneous exchange" and that the parties so intended. Assume that C makes a loan to D that both C and D intend to be a 180 day loan. Later that same day C first learns that D is in financial difficulty and so demands and obtains repayment. Section 547(c)(1) could not apply to the repayment. While the transfer actually was a "substantially contemporaneous exchange," it was not so intended. If bankruptcy occurs within 90 days, the trustee can avoid the payment under section 547(b).

While section 547(c)(1) can apply to either an absolute or a security transfer, section 547(c)(2) protects only absolute transfers—payments. Section 547(c)(2) looks to both the nature of the debt and the nature of the payment. In order to come under the protection of section 547(c)(2).

(1) the *debt* must be in the ordinary course of business (business debtor) or financial affairs (non-business debtor) of both the debtor and the creditor and

(2) the *payment* must be in the ordinary course of business or financial affairs of both the debtor and the creditor and

(3) the *payment* must be made according to ordinary business terms.

To illustrate, D receives her water bill for January water use on February 2. D and most water customers regularly pay their water bills by check before the end of the month. D pays her water bill by check on February 14. Section 547(c)(2) applies.

The third exception protects "enabling loans." Section 547(c)(3) requires that:

(1) the creditor gives the debtor "new value" to acquire certain real or personal property;

(2) the debtor signs a security agreement giving the creditor a security interest in the property;

(3) the debtor in fact uses the "new value" supplied by the creditor to acquire the property; and

(4) the creditor perfects its security interest no later than ten days after the debtor receives possession.

For example, on April 4, F borrows $14,000 from S to buy a new tractor and signs a security agreement that describes the tractor. S files a financing statement. On April 20, F uses S's $14,000 to buy a new tractor. On May 5, F files a bankruptcy petition.

F's bankruptcy trustee may *not* avoid S's security interest. While all of the elements of section 547(b) are satisfied,[5] all of the elements of section 547(c)(3) are also satisfied.

Section 547(c)(4) provides a measure of protection for a creditor who receives a preference and "after such transfer" extends further unsecured credit.

---

5. The creation of a lien is a transfer of property of the debtor. It was, of course, "to or for the benefit of a creditor." And, it was "for or on account of an antecedent debt." "For purposes of this section, a transfer is not made until the debtor has acquired rights in the property transferred," section 547(e)(3). The other elements of section 547(b) are discussed supra on pages 185–187.

For example, on June 6, C lends D $6,000. On July 7, D repays $4,000. On August 8, C lends D an additional $3,000. On September 9, D files a bankruptcy petition. The bankruptcy trustee can recover only $1,000. The July 7th payment of $4,000 was a preference under section 547(b). The trustee's recovery, however, is reduced by the amount of the August 8th unsecured advance of $3,000, section 547(c)(4).

Note that under section 547(c)(4), the sequence of events is of critical significance. The additional extension of credit must occur after the preferential transfer. If on June 6, C lends D $6,000; on July 7, C lends D an additional $3,000; on August 8, D repays $4,000, and on September 9, D files a bankruptcy petition, the trustee could recover $4,000 under 547.

Section 547(c)(5) creates a limited exception from preference attack for certain Article 9 floating liens. As noted on page 81 et seq., Article 9 provides a mechanism for establishing a "floating lien." Such liens are most commonly used in financing accounts or inventory which normally "turn-over" in the ordinary course of the debtor's business. For example, on January 10 Credit Co., C lends Department Store, D, $100,000 and takes a security interest in the store's inventory. Obviously, C wants D to sell its inventory so that it can repay the loan. It is equally obvious that as inventory is sold, the collateral securing C loan decreases unless C's lien "floats" to cover the proceeds from the sale of the inventory and/or cover new inventory that D later acquires. Accordingly, the security agreement that D signs on January 10 will probably contain an after-acquired property clause—will probably grant C a security interest not only in the inventory that D now owns but also in the inventory that D later acquires.

Even though D only signs this one security agreement, section 547 views D as making numerous different transfers of security interests. Under section 547(e)(3), "For purposes of this section, a transfer is not made until the debtor has acquired rights in the property transferred." This means that every time D acquires additional inventory there is a new transfer for purposes of section 547. Thus, if D acquires new inventory on March 3 and files for bankruptcy within the next 90 days, it would *seem* that the trustee can invalidate C's security interest in the March 3 inventory because there was

1. a transfer of property of the debtor to a creditor

2. for an antecedent debt

[The debt was incurred on January 10th. As noted above, section 547(e)(3) dates the transfer of the security interest in the March 3d inventory as March 3d.]

3. presumption of insolvency

[Remember section 547(f)]

[*195*]

    4.   transfer made within 90 days of the bankruptcy petition

    5.   transfer increased bankruptcy distribution to C (unless C was already fully secured.)

Section 547(c)(5), however, will usually protect C. Under this provision, a creditor with a security interest in inventory or accounts receivable is subject to a preference attack only to the extent that it improves its position during the 90-day period before bankruptcy. The test is a two-point test and requires determination of the secured creditor's position 90 days before the petition and on the date of the petition. [If new value was first given after 90 days before the case, the date on which it was first given substitutes for the 90-day point.]

There are seven steps involved in applying section 547(c)(5)'s "two-step" test:

    1.   Determine the amount of debt on the date of the bankruptcy petition;

    2.   Determine the value of the debtor's accounts and/or inventory encumbered by the secured creditor's lien on the date of the petition;

    3.   Subtract # 2 from # 1;

    4.   Determine the amount of debt 90 days before the petition;

    5.   Determine the value of the debtor's accounts and/or inventory encumbered by the secured creditor's lien 90 days before the petition;

    6.   Subtract # 5 from # 4;

7. Subtract the answer in # 3 from the answer in # 6. This is the amount of the preference.

The following hypotheticals illustrate the application of section 547(c)(5).

(1) At the time of its bankruptcy petition, D owes C $100,000 and has inventory with a value of $60,000. C has a security interest in all of D's inventory. 90 days before bankruptcy, D owed C $90,000 and had inventory with a value of $70,000. All of D's inventory was acquired within the last 90 days. Under these facts, C has not improved its position. Under these facts, C's security interest will be protected by section 547(c)(5).

(2) At the time of its bankruptcy petition, D owes C $100,000 and has inventory with a value of $75,000. C has a security interest in all of D's inventory. 90 days before bankruptcy, D owed C $90,000 and had inventory with a value of $30,000. All of D's inventory was acquired within the last 90 days. Under these facts, the bankruptcy trustee may reduce C's secured claim from $75,000 to $40,000.[6]

Compare the facts of (1) with (2). Which fact situation is more common? How often in the "real world" will a debtor in financial difficulty acquire additional inventory or generate an increased

6. There was a $35,000 reduction in the amount by which the claim exceeded the collateral. (90–30) – (100–75). The $75,000 security claim is thus reduced by this $35,000 improvement in position.

amount of accounts? It is submitted that in the usual situation section 547(c)(5) completely protects a security interest in after-acquired inventory or accounts—that in the usual situation the "except" language of section 547(c)(5) is inapplicable.

(3) D files a bankruptcy petition on April 22. At the time of the bankruptcy petition, D owes S $200,000. S has a security interest in D's inventory of oriental rugs which then have a value of $200,000. On January 22, 90 days before the bankruptcy petition was filed, D owed S $200,000, and the rugs had a fair market value of $150,000. D did not acquire any additional rugs after January 22; the value of D's rugs increased because of market considerations. The trustee has no section 547 rights against S. There is no transfer to invalidate. S's improvement in position was not "to the prejudice of other creditors holding an unsecured claim."

(4) D Manufacturing Co., D, files a bankruptcy petition on April 4. At the time of the filing of the bankruptcy, D owes C Credit Corp., C, $40,000. C has a valid in bankruptcy security interest in all of D's equipment. The D–C security agreement has an after-acquired property clause. On the date of the filing of the petition, D's equipment has a fair market value of $31,000. On January 4, 90 days before the filing of the bankruptcy petition, D owed C $40,000 and D's equipment had a fair market value of $32,000. On February 2, D sold a piece of equipment for $6,000. (D used the $6,000 to pay

taxes.) On March 3, D bought other equipment for $5,000. The trustee can limit S's security interest to the equipment owned on January 4. The March 3d "transfer" is a preference under section 547(b).[7] The March 3d "transfer" of a security interest in equipment is not protected by section 547(c)(5) because it only applies to security interests in inventory or accounts.

Section 547(c)(6) exempts "statutory liens" from the scope of section 547. Statutory liens are covered by section 545; section 545 is covered infra.

"Statutory lien" is defined in section 101(45) as a lien "arising *solely* by force of statute." Section 101(45) expressly provides that neither a security interest nor a judicial lien is a "statutory lien." While there are statutes providing for security interests and judicial liens, neither a security interest nor a judicial lien arises "*solely* by force of statute." A security interest will always require an agreement; a judicial lien will always require court action.

The following hypothetical illustrates the operation of section 547(c)(6). C Construction Co. is building a warehouse for D. Under relevant state statutes, a builder can obtain a mechanics lien. C takes the steps required by the state law and obtains a mechanics lien on the warehouse to secure payment for the work that it has done. If D files for bankruptcy, the bankruptcy trustee will

7. Remember, that March 3 is the date that the transfer is deemed made for purposes of section 547, section 547(e)(3).

not be able to attack the mechanics lien under section 547.

Section 547(c)(7) was added in 1984. It applies only if

1.   the debtor is an individual and

2.   his or her debts are "primarily" consumer debts and

3.   the aggregate value of all property covered by the transfer is less than $600.

If, for example, D owes C $1,200 and pays her $400 four days before filing for bankruptcy, the bankruptcy trustee will not be able to recover the $400 from C under section 547.

B.   SETOFFS (SECTION 553)

At times, a party is both a creditor and a debtor of another party. Assume, for example, that Stephen Weed, W, has a checking account at Kane Citizens Bank, B, with a $1,000 balance. W borrows $4,000 from B to buy a new car. B is in the position of a creditor of W's on the car loan; B, however, is in the position of a debtor of W's on the checking account. B is thus both W's creditor and W's debtor.

In attempting to collect the $4,000 loan from W, B may assert its right of setoff. Professor Zubrow defines "setoff" as follows: "Set-off is the cancellation of cross demands between two parties. The term is commonly used to cover both judicially supervised set-offs and automatic extinction of cross-demands." Zubrow, *Integration of Deposit Account Financing Into Article 9 of the Uniform Commercial Code: A Proposal for Legislative Reform,* 68 Minn.L.Rev. 899, 901, n. 3 (1984).

The use of setoff is not limited to banks. Bank setoff is, however, the most common setoff transaction. Accordingly, this book will deal with setoff primarily in a banking context.

To illustrate, if Kane Citizens Bank, B, asserts its right of setoff against Stephen Weed, W, it will reduce W's checking account balance from $1,000 to 0 and reduce the amount owed by W on the $4,000 loan to $3,000.

What if Stephen Weed files a bankruptcy petition one day after the setoff? Can the bankruptcy trustee recover the $1,000 from Kane Citizens Bank? If one day before the filing of a bankruptcy petition, W withdraws $1,000 from his savings account and uses that $1,000 to reduce his indebtedness to B, the trustee can recover the $1,000 under section 547. Is there any reason to treat B's setoff differently?

Section 547 does not apply to setoffs. Section 553 is the only provision of the Bankruptcy Code that limits pre-petition setoffs. It contains a number of limitations on setoffs:

(1) "Mutual Debt"

The debts must be between the same parties in the same right or capacity. For example, a claim against a "bankrupt" [8] as an administratrix cannot be set off against a debt owed to the "bankrupt" as an individual.

(2) "Arose before the commencement of the case"

Both the debt owed to the "bankrupt" and the claim against the "bankrupt" must have preceded the filing of the bankruptcy petition.

(3) "Disallowed", section 553(a)(1)

Certain claims against a "bankrupt" are disallowed. See section 502 considered infra at pages 270–275. A claim that is disallowed under section 502 may not be used as the basis for a setoff. To illustrate, A owes B $4,000. B files a bankruptcy petition. The debt from A to B is property of the estate. The trustee attempts to collect the $4,000 from A. A only pays the trustee $3,000. A alleges that it had set off a $1,000 claim it had against B prior to the bankruptcy filing. If that $1,000 claim would be barred by the statute of limitations in a state collection action, it would be disallowed under section 502(b)(1) and the setoff would be disallowed under 553(a)(1).

8. The Bankruptcy Code uses the term "debtor", not the term "bankrupt". Nevertheless, in discussing setoffs in which each party is the debtor of the other, it seems less confusing to use the term "bankrupt" to identify the party that filed a voluntary bankruptcy petition (or the party whose creditors filed an involuntary bankruptcy petition).

(4) "Acquired" Claims, section 553(a)(2)

Certain acquired claims cannot be setoff. Assume for example, that B is insolvent; A owes B $4,000; B owes C $1,000. Because B is insolvent, C's $1,000 claim is of little value to C. C would be willing to sell its claim against B to A for less than $1,000. A would be willing to buy C's claim for less than $1,000 if it could then assert that claim as a setoff to reduce its debt to B from $4,000 to $3,000.

Under section 553(a)(2) claims against the "bankrupt" acquired from a third party may *not* be set off against a debt owed to the "bankrupt" if:

a. the claim was acquired within 90 days before the bankruptcy petition or after the bankruptcy petition, *and*

b. the "bankrupt" was insolvent when the claim was acquired. [Section 553(c) creates a rebuttable presumption of insolvency.]

(5) Build-ups, section 553(a)(3)

Section 553(a)(3) precludes a setoff by a bank [9] if:

a. money was deposited by the "bankrupt" within 90 days of the bankruptcy petition,[10] and

b. the "bankrupt" was insolvent at the time of the setoff (Remember section 553(c)'s presumption of insolvency.), and

9. Again, section 553(a)(3) is not limited to bank setoffs.

10. A bank deposit is the most common example of a "debt owed to the debtor by such creditor" for purposes of section 553(a)(3).

c. the purpose of the deposit was to create or increase the right of setoff.

For example, X Bank makes a loan to D Corp. Payment of the loan is guaranteed by P, the president of D Corp. D Corp. suffers financial reverses. X Bank pressures D Corp. and P to increase the balance of the corporation's general bank account. D Corp. moves $100,000 from other banks to its X Bank account before filing its bankruptcy petition. Section 553(a)(3) would preclude X Bank from taking the $100,000 by way of setoff.

(6) Improvement in Position, section 553(b)

Section 553(b) is similar to section 547(c)(5), considered supra at pages 194–199. Both are designed to prevent an improvement in position within 90 days of bankruptcy. Application of section 553(b) requires the following simple computations:

1. Determine amount of claim against the debtor 90 days before the date of the filing of the petition; [11]

2. Determine the "mutual debt" owing to the "bankrupt" by the holder of such claim 90 days before the filing of the petition;

3. Subtract #2 from #1 to determine the "insufficiency."

11. If there is no "insufficiency" (as defined in section 553(b) (2)) 90 days before the petition, examine the 89th day, then the 88th day, etc. until a day is found that has an "insufficiency." Computations 1–3 will then focus on that day.

4. Determine the amount of the debt on the date that the right of setoff was asserted;

5. Determine the amount of the setoff;

6. Subtract #5 from #4 to determine the insufficiency;

7. Subtract the answer in #6 from the answer in #3, to determine what part, if any, of the amount setoff the trustee may recover.

The following problems illustrate the application of section 553(b):

(1) D files a Chapter 13 petition.

90 days before the petition, D owes B Bank $100,000 and has $40,000 on deposit.

10 days before the petition, B exercises its right of setoff. At that time, D owes B Bank $70,000 and the account has $60,000 balance.

The trustee may recover $50,000 from B Bank.[12]

(2) D files a Chapter 7 petition.

90 days before the petition, D owes $200,000 to B Bank and has $200,000 on deposit at B Bank.

88 days before the petition D withdraws $80,000 from the account; 5 days before the petition, B exercises its right of setoff. At that

---

12. There was a $60,000 ($100,000 – $40,000) "insufficiency" 90 days before the bankruptcy petition was filed. At the time of the setoff, the "insufficiency" was only $10,000 ($70,000 – $60,000). There was a $50,000 improvement in position ($60,000 – $10,000). The bankruptcy trustee may recover $50,000 of the amount of offset under section 553(b).

time, D owes B $70,000 and has $60,000 on deposit in B Bank.

The trustee may recover $60,000 from B Bank.[13]

In summary, a bankruptcy trustee will apply the above six tests to any setoff that has occurred *prior* to the filing of the bankruptcy petition.

The filing of a bankruptcy petition automatically stays any further setoffs. Section 553 subjects the right of setoff to limitations provided in sections 362 and 363. Section 362(a)(7) stays setoffs. Thus, in order, to exercise a right of setoff after the filing of the bankruptcy petition it is necessary to obtain relief from the stay. Section 362(d), considered supra at pages 164–172, governs relief from the stay.

If a stay is terminated or modified to permit a post-petition setoff, the setoff will be limited by section 553(a)—requirements 1–5, discussed on pages 201–204. Section 553(b) applies only to pre-petition setoffs.

---

13. On the first date within the 90 day period that there was an "insufficiency," it was an insufficiency of $80,000. At the time of the setoff, the "insufficiency" was only $10,000 ($70,000 – $60,000). There was an improvement in position of $70,000 ($80,000 – $10,000). Nevertheless, the trustee may recover only $60,000 under section 553(b). "The amount so offset" establishes the ceiling for recovery under section 553(b).

C. FRAUDULENT TRANSFERS

1. Section 548

The Bankruptcy Code, like non-bankruptcy law, invalidates fraudulent conveyances. Indeed, the Bankruptcy Code fraudulent conveyance provisions are very much like the non-bankruptcy fraudulent conveyance statutes considered supra at pages 66–80.

Section 548 is based on the Uniform Fraudulent Conveyances Act. Section 548(a)(1) corresponds to section 7 of the UFCA; it empowers the trustee to invalidate transfers made with actual intent to hinder, delay or defraud creditors. Section 548(b) is similar to the partnership provisions of section 8(a) of the UFCA.[14] And section 548(a)(2) resembles UFCA sections 4–7; it provides for avoidance of transfers where the debtor received less than a "reasonably equivalent value" *and* (i) was insolvent or became insolvent as a result of the transaction,[15] *or* (ii) was engaged in business or was about

14. Under section 548(b), the trustee of a bankrupt partnership may avoid a transfer of partnership property to a general partner if the partnership was or thereby became insolvent. The consideration given the partnership by the partner is irrelevant since a general partner is individually liable for the payment of the partnership's debts. Transfers by a partnership to a nonpartner are governed by section 548(a).

15. Memories, memories. You may remember that there is a presumption of insolvency in section 547. If so, I hope that you also remember that the presumption of insolvency in section 547 is limited to section 547: "For purposes of this section," section 547(f).

to engage in a business transaction for which his remaining property was unreasonably small capital; *or* (iii) intended to incur or believed that he would incur debts beyond his ability to pay.

Section 548 differs from the UFCA in several significant respects:

1. Section 548 applies to transfers of both non-exempt and exempt property. The UFCA is limited to transfers of non-exempt property.

2. The test in section 548(a)(2) is "reasonably equivalent value." The test in sections 4–7 of the UFCA is "fair consideration." The "fair consideration" standard requires an inquiry into both the amount of consideration and the parties' good faith. Section 548's use of "reasonably equivalent value" eliminates a good faith requirement from value determination. However, the "good faith" of the *transferee* remains significant under section 548. Section 548(c) protects a transferee who takes "for value and in good faith." Accordingly, the practical significance of the use of "reasonably equivalent value" instead of "fair consideration" is the elimination of any inquiry into the good faith of the *transferor* in

You may also remember that the Bankruptcy Code has its own definition of insolvency in section 101. Section 101 compares the amount of the debtor's debts with the value of her *non-exempt* property. What is the practical significance, if any, of this reminder? In states with liberal exemptions, most individuals are insolvent for purposes of section 548.

Final recollection for now. The UFCA uses essentially the same definition of insolvency.

[*208*]

determining whether a trustee can recover property under section 548(a)(2).[16]

3. Section 548 eliminates the requirement of actual unpaid creditors as to whom the transfer was fraudulent. Under the UFCA a transfer by an insolvent not for fair consideration may be set aside only by creditors who were creditors at the time of the transfer. Under section 548(a)(2), such a transfer may be avoided even though all who were creditors at the time of the transfer have been paid.

4. The UFCA does not have its own statute of limitations. States generally have a three to six year limitations period for actions to invalidate fraudulent conveyances. Under section 548, the bankruptcy trustee may only reach transfers made [17] within one year of the filing of the bankruptcy petition.[18] To illustrate, assume that in

16. The transferor's good faith (or lack of good faith) is, of course, a very important factor in determining whether the trustee may invalidate a transfer under section 548(a)(1): "made such transfer * * * with actual intent to hinder, delay or defraud."

17. For purposes of section 548, a transfer will be *deemed* made when it becomes so far perfected that a bona fide purchaser from the debtor could not acquire an interest in the property transferred superior to the interest of the transferor, section 548(d). The problems of determining the date that a transfer will be *deemed* made are considered at pages 233–235 infra.

18. The one-year period of section 548 is not a true statute of limitations. It does not require that the trustee's action to invalidate the transfer be commenced within one year of the time the transfer was made. If the transfer was made within one year of the date of the filing of the bankruptcy petition, the

June of 1985, Mrs. Lupner gave her daughter Lisa a new piano as a graduation present. Mrs. Lupner was insolvent at the time of the gift. On August 1, 1986, Mrs. Lupner files a bankruptcy petition. By the date of bankruptcy, Mrs. Lupner has repaid all of her June, 1985 creditors except Todd DilaMuca whom she owed $10. Mrs. Lupner's bankruptcy trustee will not be able to recover the piano under section 548. The transfer was a fraudulent conveyance (a transfer for less than "reasonably equivalent value" while insolvent) but it was made more than a year prior to the bankruptcy petition.

2. Section 544(b)

Section 548 is not the only provision in the Bankruptcy Code that invalidates fraudulent conveyances. The trustee may also use section 544(b) to invalidate fraudulent conveyances.

Section 544(b) does not specifically provide for the invalidation of fraudulent conveyances. Rather it empowers the bankruptcy trustee to avoid any pre-bankruptcy transfer that is "voidable under applicable law by a creditor holding an unsecured claim that is allowable." [19]

bankruptcy trustee has up until the closing or dismissal of the case or two years after his or her appointment, whichever first occurs, to commence the invalidation action, section 546.

19. Section 502 governs allowance of claims. Section 502 is considered infra at pages 270–275.

Section 544(b) incorporates state fraudulent conveyance law into the Bankruptcy Code. If, outside of bankruptcy, the transfer would be governed by a Statute of Elizabeth fraudulent conveyance statute, section 544(b) is a Statute of Elizabeth statute; if the state statute is the UFCA, then section 544(b) is UFCA. Section 544(b) reflects not only the state substantive law of fraudulent conveyances but also the state limitations period [20] for fraudulent conveyances.

In the Lupner problem, the June gift of a piano would be a fraudulent conveyance under nonbankruptcy law, Statute of Elizabeth or Uniform Fraudulent Conveyance Act, as to Todd DilaMuca. Todd DilaMuca was a creditor holding an unsecured claim that is allowable. Accordingly, the bankruptcy trustee may use section 544(b) to recover the piano.

While the existence of the trustee's section 544(b) avoiding powers depends upon the existence of an avoiding power held by an actual creditor, the extent of the trustee's section 544(b) avoidance powers is greater than the power of the actual

20. The state limitations period determines which transfers may be challenged, not when the challenge must be made. Section 546 again gives the trustee time after his or her appointment to commence the action. To illustrate, D makes a fraudulent conveyance in January of 1985. State law imposes a five-year limitation period on fraudulent conveyance actions. If D files a bankruptcy petition in December of 1989 that satisfies or tolls the state law limitations period, D's bankruptcy trustee will have the additional section 546 period to commence a fraudulent conveyance action.

creditor. In the Lupner problem, under state fraudulent conveyance law, if Lisa Lupner paid Todd DilaMuca $10, she could keep the piano. Under section 544(b), Lisa is not so fortunate. Legislative history clearly indicates that section 544(b) retains the rule of Moore v. Bay, 284 U.S. 4 (1931).

Under the rule of *Moore v. Bay,* the trustee is not limited in his recovery by the amount of the claim of the actual creditor. A transfer which is voidable by a single, actual creditor, may be avoided entirely by the trustee, regardless of the size of the actual creditor's claim. Thus Lisa may *not* keep the piano by simply paying the bankruptcy trustee $10.

3. Comparison of Sections 548 and 544(b)

The Lupner hypothetical points up the similarities and differences of sections 548 and 544(b).

These provisions are also compared by the following chart:

548	544(b)
1. Essentially UFCA	1. UFCA or Statute of Elizabeth, whichever is the state law

548	544(b)
2. Reaches transfers made within one year of bankruptcy petition [limitations period is measured from the time the transfer is *deemed* made. See pages 233–235 infra]	2. Reaches all transfers made with state limitations period [limitations period is measured from the time the transfer was actually made]
3. Elements of fraudulent conveyance tested as of time that transfer was *deemed* made. See pages 233–235 infra	3. Elements of fraudulent conveyance tested as of time that the fraudulent conveyance was actually made
4. Transferee that takes for value and in good faith protected	4. Transferee that takes for value and in good faith protected
5. No requirement of actual creditor as to whom conveyance is fraudulent	5. Voidable only if transfer is fraudulent as to an actual creditor with an unsecured, allowable claim
6. Complete invalidation	6. Complete invalidation

4. Foreclosure Sales as Fraudulent Transfers

There is currently considerable controversy over fraudulent conveyance challenges in bankruptcy to pre-bankruptcy foreclosure sales. Assume, for example, that D obtains a ten year loan from C and grants C a mortgage on real property that D owns.

C records the mortgage in complete compliance with state law. Several years later, D defaults on the mortgage, and C forecloses on the mortgage in the manner provided by state law. A foreclosure sale is held which also completely complies with state law. Several months later, D files a bankruptcy petition. The bankruptcy trustee brings an action alleging that the foreclosure sale was a fraudulent transfer under section 548(a)(2). Such an action raises three issues:

(1) Is a mortgage foreclosure sale a transfer?

(2) If so, was the debtor insolvent at the time of sale?

(3) If so, was the transfer for "reasonably equivalent value"?

Three circuits have considered the first question. Two have found that a foreclosure sale is a transfer for purposes of section 548. See Durrett v. Washington National Insurance Co., 621 F.2d 201 (5th Cir.1980); In re Hulm, 738 F.2d 323 (8th Cir.1984). In re Madrid, 725 F.2d 1197 (9th Cir.1984), on the other hand, held that a foreclosure sale is not a transfer for purposes of section 548. The majority opinion in *Madrid* relied on section 548(d)(1) which provides that a transfer is made for purposes of section 548 when it becomes so far perfected that no bona fide purchaser could acquire an interest superior to the transferee. The *Madrid* majority opinion concludes that the time of the transfer was when the deed of trust was recorded in 1979, not when the foreclosure sale was conducted in 1981.

Under this reasoning, if the mortgage was perfected more than one year before bankruptcy, a mortgage foreclosure sale within one year of bankruptcy could never be attacked under section 548.

There is a concurring opinion in *Madrid* that suggests an alternative ground for excepting mortgage foreclosure sales from challenge under section 548—that the debtor neither consented to nor participated in the foreclosure sale. According to the concurring opinion in *Madrid,* "One cannot presume fraud by the debtor in a transaction where the debtor was not a party * * *. I would therefore hold that only transfers where the bankrupt was a participant can be set aside for absence of 'reasonably equivalent value.'"

The Ninth Circuit decision in *Madrid* is dated February 13, 1984. The bankruptcy amendments enacted on July 10, 1984, seem to take away both the position of the majority and concurring opinion in *Madrid.* It is now difficult to argue that a mortgage foreclosure sale is not a "transfer" for Bankruptcy Code purposes when the definition of "transfer" in section 101(48) now expressly provides that transfer includes "foreclosure of the debtor's equity of redemption." Similarly the 1984 change to section 548 which makes it clear that it applies to both voluntary and involuntary transfers seems to preclude later courts from concluding that section 548 can not apply to a foreclosure sale because the debtor does not consent or participate.

If a court concludes that a mortgage foreclosure sale is a transfer for purposes of section 548, it must then deal with the fact questions of (1) whether the debtor was insolvent and (2) whether the sale was for "reasonably equivalent value." There is dictum in *Durrett* requiring that the sale be for at least "70% of the market value of the property."

If a mortgage foreclosure sale can be avoided under section 548 because of price, it would seem that a sale of personal property collateral pursuant to section 9–504 could be similarly challenged.

D. TRANSFERS NOT TIMELY RECORDED OR PERFECTED

A bankruptcy trustee may avoid certain prepetition transfers that are not timely recorded or perfected. A failure to record or a delay in recording can adversely affect other creditors. If creditor X does not record its lien on D's property, creditor Y might not know that D's property is encumbered. Relying on the mistaken belief that D holds his property free from liens, Y might extend credit, refrain from obtaining a lien, or forebear from instituting collection proceedings.

State law requires recordation or other public notice of a number of transfers. Real estate recording statutes require the recording of deeds and real property mortgages. Article 6 of the Uniform Commercial Code requires that creditors be notified in advance of any bulk transfer. Section 2–326 of the Code calls for public notice of sales on consignment. And, Article 9 of the Uniform Commercial Code calls for public notice, (perfection) of security interests.

The Bankruptcy Code does not have its own public notice requirements. It does *not* simply invalidate all transfers not recorded within 10 days. Rather, the Bankruptcy Code makes use of the notoriety requirements of state law in the following invalidation provisions: sections 544, 547 and 545.

1. Section 544(b)

Section 544(b) empowers the bankruptcy trustee to invalidate any transfer that under non-bankruptcy law is voidable as to any actual creditor of the debtor with an unsecured, allowable [21] claim. In applying section 544(b), it is thus necessary to determine:

(1) whether non-bankruptcy law public notice requirements have been timely satisfied;

(2) which persons are protected by the non-bankruptcy requirement of public notice;

(3) if any actual creditor of the debtor with an unsecured allowable claim comes within the class of persons protected by such state law.

The following hypotheticals illustrate the application of section 544(b):

---

21. Most creditors' claims are allowable. Section 502, particularly section 502(b), indicates the extent to which claims are disallowed. Section 502 is considered infra at pages 270–275.

(1) On January 10, D makes a bulk transfer to X. X fails to give notice to C, one of D's creditors. Under section 6–104, such failure to notify renders the transfer "ineffective" against C. On March 3, D files a bankruptcy petition. On that date, C is still one of D's unsecured creditors. The bankruptcy trustee will be able to invalidate the January 10 transfer to X.

The applicable public notoriety requirement, section 6–104, was not timely satisfied. Section 6–104 protects all creditors of the transferor whose claims arose before the bulk transfer. C is such a creditor. C is an actual creditor of the debtor/transferor with an unsecured, allowable claim. Since the transfer is ineffective as to C, the bankruptcy trustee can invalidate the transfer.[22]

(2) On January 10, D borrows $10,000 from M and gives M a mortgage on Redacre. On February 2, C lends D $10,000. On March 3, M records its mortgage. On July 7, D files a bankruptcy petition. On the date of the perfection, D still owes $10,000 to M and $10,000 to C. D's bankruptcy trustee will not be able to invalidate M's mortgage.

The public notoriety requirements were not timely satisfied. M delayed in recording its mortgages. Most real property recording statutes only

---

22. Remember that under section 544(b), the bankruptcy trustee is not limited by the amount of the actual creditor's claim. A transaction which is voidable (or ineffective) as to a single actual creditor can be completely avoided by the trustee, regardless of the size of that creditor's claim. See page 212 supra.

protect purchasers, and/or lien creditors. C is not within the class of persons protected by the applicable recording statute. Section 544(b) empowers the trustee to invalidate transfers that are invalid as to actual creditors such as C. Since C cannot invalidate the transfer, the bankruptcy trustee cannot invalidate the transfer *under section 544(b)*.

(3) On January 10, D borrows $10,000 from S and gives S a security interest in equipment. On February 2, C lends D $10,000. On March 3, S perfects its security interest. On July 7, D files a bankruptcy petition. On the date of the petition, D still owes $10,000 to S and $10,000 to C. D's bankruptcy trustee will *not* be able to invalidate S's security interest.

The public notoriety requirements of the UCC were not timely satisfied. S delayed in perfecting its security interest. Article 9's perfection requirements, however, protect only certain gap secured creditors and buyers. C is not within the class of persons protected by the applicable recording statute. Section 544(b) empowers the bankruptcy trustee to avoid transfers that are invalid as to actual creditors. Since no actual creditor can invalidate the transfer, the bankruptcy trustee can not invalidate the transfer.

(4) On January 10, D borrows $10,000 from S and gives S a security interest in equipment. On February 2, L obtains an execution lien on the same equipment. On March 2, S perfects its security interest. On July 7, D files a bankruptcy

petition. On the date of the petition, D is still indebted to S and L. The bankruptcy trustee will not be able to invalidate S's security interest.

Again, the public notoriety requirements of the UCC were not timely satisfied. Article 9's perfection requirements do protect a lien creditor such as L, section 9–301. L is a holder of a secured claim. Section 544(b) only gives the bankruptcy trustee the invalidation powers of any actual holders of *un*secured claims.[23] While L has the power to

---

23. Under section 544(b), the bankruptcy trustee may assert the rights of an actual lien creditor whose lien has been invalidated. Under section 551, all avoided transfers are preserved. The preservation, however, is generally of no practical significance.

Preservation of an invalidated lien benefits only the bankruptcy estate—not the lien creditor. Where an invalidated lien is preserved, the trustee is able to assert the status of that lien creditor in attacking other liens on the property. If there are no other creditors with liens on the same property, or if all such other liens are superior to the lien that the trustee avoids, nothing is gained by preserving the invalidated lien. Preservation of a lien is of practical significance only where there are other liens on the property, subordinate to the lien avoidable by the trustee, that the trustee may not attack in any other manner.

To illustrate, on February 2, S lends D $20,000 and takes a security interest in D's equipment. On March 3, X, another creditor of D, obtains an execution lien on the equipment. On March 13, S perfects its security interest. On March 23, D files a bankruptcy petition. X defeats S, section 9–301. The bankruptcy trustee, T, defeats X if D was insolvent on March 3, section 547, (considered supra at page 185 et seq.). X's lien is preserved under section 551. T may then assert the rights of X to invalidate S's security interest under section 544(b).

invalidate S's security interest, the bankruptcy trustee does not have L's invalidation powers.

As problems # 2, # 3 and # 4 illustrate, the use of section 544(b) to invalidate pre-petition transfers that were not timely recorded is severely limited. Section 544(b) gives the trustee the invalidation powers of any actual unsecured creditors. Most recording statutes protect lien creditors or bona fide purchasers, but not unsecured creditors.

2. Section 544(a)

Section 544(b) looks to the rights of actual creditors of the debtor; section 544(a) focuses on the rights of hypothetical lien creditors and bona fide purchasers of real property. Section 544(a) empowers the bankruptcy trustee to invalidate any transfer that under non-bankruptcy law is voidable as to a creditor who extended credit and obtained a lien on the date of the filing of the bankruptcy petition or is voidable as to a bona fide purchaser of real property whether or not such a creditor or purchaser actually exists. In applying section 544(a), it is thus necessary to determine whether:

(1) non-bankruptcy law public notice requirements have been timely satisfied;

Note that in the hypothetical in the preceding paragraph, the trustee could also use section 547 to invalidate S's lien if D was insolvent on March 13, see page 185 et seq. supra. The rule that, under section 544(b), the trustee may assert the rights of an actual lien creditor whose lien has been invalidated is of very limited practical significance.

AVOIDANCE

(2) a creditor who extended credit and obtained a lien on the date that the bankruptcy petition was filed or a bona fide purchaser of real property on the date of the bankruptcy petition comes within the class of persons protected by such state law.

The following hypotheticals illustrate the application of section 544(a):

(1) On January 10, D borrows $10,000 from M and gives M a mortgage of Redacre. On February 2, D files a bankruptcy petition. As of the date of the petition, M had not recorded its mortgage. D's bankruptcy trustee may invalidate M's mortgage under section 544(a).

The public notice requirements of the state real property recording statutes were not satisfied. Real property recording statutes typically protect bona fide purchasers. Since the mortgage was unrecorded on the date that the bankruptcy petition was filed, M's mortgage would be ineffective as against a bona fide purchaser of Redacre on the date that the petition was filed. Section 544(a) gives the bankruptcy trustee the same powers as a person who was a bona fide purchaser on the date that the bankruptcy petition was filed.

(2) On January 10, D borrows $10,000 from S and gives S a security interest in equipment. On February 2, D files a bankruptcy petition. S fails to perfect its security interest prior to February 2. The bankruptcy trustee will be able to invalidate S's security interest under section 544(a).

[222]

The applicable public notice requirement was not satisfied. Article 9's perfection requirements protect creditors with judicial liens, section 9–301. Since the security interest was unperfected on the date that the bankruptcy petition was filed, S's security interest would be subordinate [24] to the claim of a creditor who obtained a judicial lien on the date that the petition was filed, section 9–301. Section 544(a) gives S the same invalidation powers as a person who extended credit and obtained a judicial lien on the date that the bankruptcy petition was filed.

(3) On January 10, D borrows $10,000 from S to buy equipment and gives S a purchase money security interest in the equipment. On January 18, D files a bankruptcy petition. On January 19, S perfects its security interest.[25] The bankruptcy trustee may not invalidate S's security interest.

Section 544(a) empowers the bankruptcy trustee to invalidate security interests that would be subordinate to the claims of a creditor who obtained a

24. Even though the Uniform Commercial Code uses the term "subordinate" instead of "voidable", a security that would be "subordinate" to a creditor that obtained a judicial lien on the date of the filing of the bankruptcy petition is "voidable" by the bankruptcy trustee.

25. The filing of a bankruptcy petition stays or stops most creditor collection efforts. Section 362(a), considered infra at pages 160–162, defines the scope of the stay, by listing the acts that are stayed by the commencement of the bankruptcy case. Section 362(a)(4) stays lien perfection. Section 362(b) lists exceptions to the automatic stay. Section 362(b)(3) excepts perfection of security interests within ten days of bankruptcy.

judicial lien on the date that the petition was filed. By reason of section 9–301(2),[26] S's *purchase* money security interest would be effective as against a creditor who obtained a lien on January 18, the date that the bankruptcy petition was filed. Accordingly, S's *purchase* money security interest is effective against the bankruptcy trustee.

 (4) On January 10, Dudley Doright, D, borrows $10,000 from Snidely Whiplash, S and gives S a security interest in equipment. On December 29, S properly files his financing statement. On December 30, D files a bankruptcy petition. The bankruptcy trustee may not invalidate S's security interest UNDER SECTION 544(a).[27]

The public notice requirements of Article 9 were not timely satisfied; S delayed in perfecting its security interest for almost a year. Article 9's perfection requirements protect *"gap"* lien creditors and buyers. In this hypothetical, the bankruptcy trustee has the right of a lien creditor, but

26. Section 9–301(2) provides in part: "If the secured party files with respect to a purchase money security interest before or within ten days after the debtor receives possession of the collateral, he takes priority over the rights of * * * a lien creditor which arise between the time the security interest attaches and the time of filing." This "ten-day grace period" is also effective against a bankruptcy trustee, see section 546(b).

27. The bankruptcy trustee will probably be able to invalidate S's security interest under some other provision of the Bankruptcy Code. If D was insolvent on December 29, the bankruptcy trustee may invalidate S's security interest under section 547. The applicability of section 547 to transfers not timely perfected or recorded is considered infra at pages 227–234.

not a gap lien creditor. Section 544(a) gives the bankruptcy trustee the invalidation powers of a creditor who obtained a judicial lien as of the date of the bankruptcy petition. On the date of the bankruptcy petition, December 30, S's security interest was perfected. A perfected security interest is effective against lien creditors, cf. sections 9–201, 9–301. Accordingly, S's security interest may not be invalidated under section 544(a).

The above hypotheticals suggest three general rules for the use of section 544(a) in invalidating transfers:

(1) If the transfer has been recorded or otherwise perfected prior to the date that the bankruptcy petition was filed, the trustee will not be able to invalidate the transfer under section 544(a).

(2) Except as noted in (3) below, if the transfer was not recorded or otherwise perfected by the date that the bankruptcy petition was filed, the bankruptcy trustee will be able to invalidate the transfer under section 544(a).

(3) The bankruptcy trustee will not be able to invalidate a purchase money security interest perfected within ten days after the delivery of the collateral to the debtor even if the debtor files a bankruptcy petition in the gap between the creation of the security interest and perfection.

3. Comparison of Section 544(a) and 544(b)

COMPARISON OF SECTION 544(a) AND SECTION 544(b)

	544(a)	544(b)
I. STATUS (federal law) A. Necessity of protected actual creditor with allowable claim	NOT NECESSARY	NECESSARY
B. Effect of amount of actual creditor's claim	IRRELEVANT	IRRELEVANT
II. PRACTICAL SIGNIFICANCE OF STATUS (non-bankruptcy law) A. Real property transfers	1. Recording statute protects either creditors or purchasers 2. Transfers not recorded at time bankruptcy petition filed may be avoided	1. Recording statute must protect unsecured creditors 2. Transfers not timely recorded may be invalidated if an actual creditor with an unsecured allowable claim extended credit in the gap

	544(a)	544(b)
B. Personal Property transfers governed by UCC	Article 9 security interests not perfected at the date of filing of the bankruptcy petition may be invalidated	Subject to the very limited exception noted on the bottom of p. 220. Section 544(b) may not be used to invalidate Article 9 security interests. Section 544(b) may be used to invalidate a bulk transfer if an actual creditor with unsecured, allowable claim failed to receive the notice required by Article 6

4. Section 547(e)

In the Dudley Doright/Snidely Whiplash hypothetical on page 224, the bankruptcy trustee was not able to invalidate Snidely's security interest under section 544(a) notwithstanding Snidely's long delay in giving public notice of his lien. Should Doright's bankruptcy trustee be able to invalidate Snidely's lien?

As noted earlier, there are a number of reasons for invalidating such "secret liens." Creditors of Doright may have been misled by Snidely's failure to record or a delay in recording. Unaware of this "secret", unrecorded lien, Nell Fenwick might extend credit to Doright she would not extend if aware of the lien. Unaware of a "secret", unrecorded lien, Mr. Peabody might delay in collecting a delinquent debt from Doright he would try to collect if aware of the lien. The Bankruptcy Code should provide for invalidation of transfers that are not timely recorded. And it does. In section 547.

Although it is easy to see the reason for invalidating liens that are not timely perfected, it is difficult to understand why section 547 should be the mechanism for invalidating such liens. The easy way to invalidate such secret liens would be to add a section to the Bankruptcy Code to the effect that any lien that can be recorded or otherwise perfected under state law must be recorded within 10 (30?) days after it is obtained in order to be valid in bankruptcy. While that is the "easy way", it is not the way of the Bankruptcy Code. Basically, the Bankruptcy Code's method is to "deem" that for purposes of applying the requirements of section 547(b) [28] the date of transfers not timely recorded is the date of perfection,[29] not the actual date of transfer.

28. The elements of section 547(b) are considered supra at pages 185–190.

29. Section 547 does not specify the means of perfection. Rather, section 547(e)(1) provides that for purposes of section 547, transfers shall be perfected when effective under non-bankruptcy law against certain specified third parties. In a transfer of real property other than fixtures, the third parties are bona fide purchasers, i.e., the date of perfection is the date that the transfer is effective against bona fide purchasers. Non-bankruptcy law generally requires that transfers of inter-

[*228*]

The Doright/Whiplash hypothetical illustrates the practical significance of the statutory delay of the effective date of the transfer until public notice of the transfer has been given. Remember, Doright borrowed $10,000 from Snidely on January 10 and gave Snidely a security interest in equipment which Snidely perfected on December 29. Doright filed a bankruptcy petition on December 30. At first, it might seem that section 547 is not applicable—that the security transfer from Doright to Snidely was not for an antecedent indebtedness and did not occur within 90 days of the bankruptcy petition. For purposes of section 547, however, the transfer will be *deemed* made on December 29, not January 10. [Under section 9–301, Snidely's security interest would not be effective as against subsequent judicial lien creditors until that date. Ac-

ests in real property other than fixtures be recorded in order to be effective against bona fide purchasers.

A transfer of personal property or fixtures is perfected for purposes of section 547 when it is effective against a creditor with a judicial lien. Absolute transfers of personal property are generally effective against subsequent lien creditors of the transferor without any recording. For example, A pays B $1,000. This transfer is effective against subsequent lien creditors of A without any recording. X delivers 200 widgets to Y. Again, the transfer is effective as against subsequent lien creditors of the transferor without recordation.

Security transfers of liens in personal property or fixtures are not effective against subsequent judicial lien creditors of the transferor without recordation or other perfection. For example, D gives S a security interest in equipment to secure a debt. Under UCC section 9–301(1)(b), S's security interest is not superior to the rights of a subsequent judicial lien creditor of D until S perfects.

cordingly, by reason of section 547(e), the transfer will not be deemed made until that date.] Thus, the "December 29 transfer" would be within 90 days of the bankruptcy petition. Thus, the "December 29 transfer" would be for an antecedent indebtedness, i.e., the $10,000 loaned on January 10. Thus, the trustee would be able to invalidate S's security under section 547 if D was insolvent on December 29. [Remember section 547(f) creates a rebuttable presumption of insolvency.]

The above hypothetical illustrates that a delay in perfection can result in a security interest actually given for present consideration being deemed made for an antecedent indebtedness and thus a section 547 preference.

In the Dudley Doright hypothetical, over eleven months elapsed between the granting of the security interest and the perfecting of the security interest. What if the delay was eleven weeks? Eleven days? Eleven hours? Is there some sort of "grace period" in section 547?

Section 547(e) does not require immediate perfection; it provides a ten-day "grace period" for perfection.

Section 547(e)(2) describes three situations. First, section 547(e)(2)(A) deals with transfers perfected within ten days. Such a transfer will be deemed made at the time of the transfer. A transfer deemed made at the time of the transfer is not vulnerable to attack by the bankruptcy trustee under section 547.

Second, section 547(e)(2)(B) deals with transfers not perfected within ten days. Such a transfer will be deemed made at the time of perfection. A transfer deemed made at a point in time later than the time of the transfer is vulnerable to attack by the bankruptcy trustee under section 547.

Third, section 547(e)(2)(C) deals with the effect of filing a bankruptcy petition during the ten-day "grace period." Under such facts, the transfer will be deemed made at the time of the transfer if it is perfected within ten days of the transfer or will be deemed made at the time of the filing of the bankruptcy petition if it is not perfected within ten days.

The operation of section 547(e) is illustrated in the following five hypotheticals:

(1) On January 10, S lends D $10,000 and obtains a security interest in D's equipment. S perfects this security interest on January 19. For purposes of section 547, the security transfer will be deemed to have occurred on January 10, section 547(e)(2)(A). S perfected within ten days after the transfer so the transfer is deemed made when it was actually made, January 10. Not a transfer for an antecedent debt—January 10 transfer for a January 10 debt. Not a preference.

(2) On January 10, D borrows $10,000 from S and grants S a security interest in its equipment. S perfects its security interest on February 2. S did not perfect within ten days so that for purposes of the elements of section 547(b), the transfer will

be deemed to have occurred when it was finally perfected, February 2. A transfer for an antecedent debt—a February 2 transfer for a January 10 debt. Possibly a preference.

(3) On January 10, S lends D $10,000 and obtains a non-purchase money security interest in D's equipment. D files a bankruptcy petition on January 15. S perfects its security interest on January 19.[30] For purposes of section 547, the security transfer will be deemed to have occurred on January 10, section 547(e)(2)(A), section 547(e)(2)(C)(ii). [Same facts as # 1 except that D filed a bankruptcy petition before the security interest was perfected.]

(4) On January 10, S lends D $10,000 and obtains a security interest in D's equipment. D files a bankruptcy petition on January 15. S perfects

---

30. This hypothetical raises not only section 547(e) issues but also issues under section 362 and section 544. Section 362(a)(4) bars the perfection of liens after the filing of a bankruptcy petition. Section 362(b)(3), however, creates an exception for perfection "accomplished within the period provided under section 547(e)(2)(A)." Accordingly, it would seem that the perfection in problem # 3 did not violate the automatic stay. Accordingly, it would seem that the bankruptcy trustee will not be able to avoid the security interest under section 547.

The bankruptcy trustee, however, will be able to avoid the security interest in problem # 3 under section 544(a). Remember, that under section 544(a), the trustee has the rights and powers of a creditor that had a judicial lien as of the time of the bankruptcy filing. At that time, the security interest was unperfected. An unperfected security interest is subordinate to a judicial lien creditor under section 9–301 and thus avoidable by the bankruptcy trustee under section 544(a).

its security interest on February 2. For purposes of section 547, the security transfer will be deemed to have occurred on January 15, section 547(e)(2) (C). Transfers not perfected within ten days are deemed made at the date of the bankruptcy petition if the filing of the petition preceded perfection. [Same facts as (2) except that D filed a bankruptcy petition before the security interest was filed.]

(5) On January 20, M lends D $10,000 and obtains a mortgage on Redacre. The applicable state recording statute contains a twenty-day grace period. M records its mortgage on February 2. D files a bankruptcy petition on March 3. For purposes of section 547, the security transfer will be deemed to have occurred on February 2. Section 547(e) recognizes only a ten-day grace period. M failed to perfect within that ten-day period. Accordingly, the time of the transfer will be deemed to be the date of perfection.

5. Section 548(d)

Section 548(d) is similar to section 547(e). Section 547(e) fixes the time when a transfer is deemed made for purposes of the preference invalidation provisions of section 547. Section 548(d) fixes the time when a transfer is deemed made for purposes of the fraudulent conveyance invalidation provisions of section 548: when the transfer is so far perfected that no subsequent bona fide purchaser of the property from the debtor can acquire rights in the property superior to those of the transferee.

The purpose of section 548(d) is to prevent a fraudulent conveyance from escaping invalidation by being kept secret for over a year. For example, on January 10, 1984, D, an insolvent, gives Redacre to X. X does not record the deed until November 11, 1985. On December 12, 1985, D files a bankruptcy petition. Remember, section 548 has a one year limitations period.[31] The transfer of Redacre was actually made more than one year before the bankruptcy petition was filed. The transfer, however, was not effective against a subsequent bona fide purchaser until it was recorded on November 11. Accordingly, under section 548(d), the transfer is deemed made on November 11, 1985. Without section 548(d), the bankruptcy trustee could not invalidate the gift by an insolvent under section 548.

The transfer from D to X in the preceding paragraph was a "true" fraudulent conveyance: a transfer by an insolvent without "reasonably equivalent value." Section 548(d), however, also may enable the bankruptcy trustee to invalidate some transfers that are not "true" fraudulent conveyances—transfers in which there has been merely a delay in recordation or perfection. Consider the following illustration.

---

31. This one year limitation period and the other requirements of section 548 are considered supra at pages 207–216.

Wallace Cleaver, W, gives Redacre to his brother Theodore, T, in December of 1984. W is solvent at that time. T, however, does not record the transfer until June of 1986. At that time, W is insolvent. In July of 1986, W files a bankruptcy petition. The bankruptcy trustee will be able to use section 548(a)(2) to invalidate the 1984 gift of Redacre.

Note that T's delay in recordation is crucial to the bankruptcy trustee's section 548 case. At the time that the gift is actually made, the donor, W, is solvent. There are no legal problems with people who are solvent making gifts. This happens every Chanukah and Christmas. Gifts are fraudulent conveyances when made by people who are insolvent.

While the donor, W, was solvent when the gift was actually made, he is insolvent when the gift is deemed made under section 548(d)—at the time the transfer is perfected against bona fide purchasers from the transferor. Section 548(d), like section 547(e), enables the trustee to test all aspects of the transaction as of the time of recordation rather than as of the time of the actual transfer. Since W was insolvent when the transfer is deemed made— at the time of recordation—the transfer was fraudulent as a transfer by an insolvent without reasonably equivalent value.

6. Section 545(2)

Section 545(2) invalidates statutory liens that are not perfected or enforceable on the date of the petition against a hypothetical bona fide purchaser. Section 546(b) recognizes any applicable state law "grace period." If under state law, the statutory lien may still be perfected and that perfection relates back to a pre-bankruptcy petition date, then the bankruptcy trustee will not be able to invalidate the lien.

Section 545(2) is of very limited practical significance. First, most statutory liens satisfy section 545(2)'s bona fide purchaser test. Second, statutory liens are also subject to section 544(a) which can be used to invalidate any statutory lien on real property that is voidable by a hypothetical bona fide purchaser and any statutory lien on personal property that is voidable by a hypothetical lien creditor.

E. LANDLORDS' LIENS

Sections 545(3) and 545(4) are the easiest invalidation provisions to read, understand and apply. "The trustee may avoid the fixing of a statutory lien on the property of the debtor to the extent that such lien * * *

(3) is for rent

(4) is a lien of distress for rent."

Note that the provisions only invalidate STATU-TORY landlord liens, i.e., liens for rent arising "solely by force of a statute." If the lease agreement creates an Article 9 security interest in property of the lessee, this contractual lien is not affected by section 545.[32]

F. DISGUISED PRIORITIES

Section 507 [33] of the Bankruptcy Code is a priority provision; it sets out the order in which the various unsecured claims against the debtor are to be satisfied. It displaces any state priority statutes.

Section 545 protects this federal priority scheme from disruption by state priority provisions that are "disguised" as statutory liens. Section 545 reaches spurious statutory liens which are in reality merely priorities.

When is a statutory lien more like a priority than a lien? As noted on page 4, a priority does not arise until distribution of a debtor's assets on insolvency. Accordingly, section 545(1) provides for invalidation of a statutory lien which first

32. When a landlord requires its tenant to sign a security agreement giving the landlord a security interest in property of the tenant to secure rental payments, the landlord has, of course, obtained a lien. This lien held by the landlord is not, however, a "landlord's lien"; it is a security interest. Not all liens securing claims by landlords are "landlord's liens." Only Chuck Berry would be inclined to call a security interest obtained by Mabel "Mabelline."

33. Section 507 is considered infra at pages 277–282.

become effective on the bankruptcy or insolvency of the debtor.

G.   RECLAMATION UNDER SECTION 2–702

When a buyer fails to pay for goods it accepts, the seller has a legal right to recover the contract price, UCC section 2–709.   This legal right is of limited practical significance if the buyer is insolvent.   Accordingly, the Uniform Commercial Code grants unpaid sellers a right to recover the goods. Section 2–702 of the Uniform Commercial Code empowers a seller to "reclaim" the goods if:

(1) credit sale, *and*

(2) buyer insolvent when goods received, *and*

(3) written misrepresentation of solvency within three months before delivery *or* the demand for reclamation is made within ten days of the buyer's receipt of the goods.

Case law has created a similar right of reclamation for sellers paid with bad checks.[34]

What is the effect of the bankruptcy of the buyer on the seller's right of reclamation?   Sections 546(c) and (d)[35] deal with this question.   Section

34. The right of reclamation of a "cash" seller who has been paid by a check that is subsequently dishonored is based on section 2–507.   See In re Samuels & Co., Inc., 526 F.2d 1238 (5th Cir.1976).

35. Section 546(d) was added in 1984.   It deals with the effect of bankruptcy on the non-bankruptcy reclamation rights of farmers who have sold grain to storage facilities and fishermen who have sold fish to processing facilities.   Section 546(d)

546 does not create a right of reclamation. Instead, it sets out the effect of bankruptcy on a right of reclamation created under non-bankruptcy law.

Section 546(c) has four requirements:

(1) The seller has a right of reclamation under non-bankruptcy law.

(2) The buyer received the goods while insolvent.

(3) The sale was in the ordinary course of the seller's business.

(4) The seller makes a written reclamation demand within ten days of the buyer's receipt of the goods.[36]

has the same general requirements as section 546(c). Accordingly, this nutshell will discuss only section 546(c).

---

36. The requirements of section 546(c) are similar to but not identical to the requirements of section 2–702 of the UCC. The two provisions differ in the following respects:

1. Section 546(c) requires that the sale in question be "in the ordinary course of such seller's business." Section 2–702 does not.

2. While both provisions require insolvency of the buyer at the time of receipt of the goods, the definition of insolvent in section 101(29) of the Bankruptcy Code is significantly different from the definition of insolvent in section 1–201(23) of the UCC.

3. Section 546(c) requires a demand in writing. Section 2–702 does not.

4. Section 546(c) requires that the seller demand reclamation "before ten days after [within?]" receipt. Section 2–702 imposes a similar ten-day limitation unless there has been a written misrepresentation of solvency within three months before delivery.

If a seller has complied with these four requirements, the bankruptcy trustee can *not* invalidate the seller's right of reclamation under section 544(a) (considered supra at page 221), section 545 (considered supra at page 236), section 547 (considered supra at page 185), or section 549 (considered infra at page 241).[37] The bankruptcy court may, however, deny reclamation to a seller who has met the four requirements of section 546(c) if it protects the seller by either granting its claim arising from the sale of goods an administrative expense priority or securing the claim by a lien.[38]

What if a seller with a non-bankruptcy reclamation claim fails to satisfy the four requirements of section 546(c)? While the Bankruptcy Code does not deal with the question directly, there are cases that hold that the bankruptcy trustee can avoid the reclamation rights of a seller who fails to comply with section 546(c).

37. Section 546(c) does not protect the seller's right of reclamation from invalidation based on section 544(b). Section 544(b) is considered supra at pages 217–221. If other unsecured creditors have rights superior to the seller's right of reclamation, the trustee may assert these rights under section 544(b) to defeat the seller's right of reclamation. If a secured creditor has rights superior to the seller's right of reclamation, the trustee may assert these rights only if the trustee is able to avoid the lien of the secured creditor and preserve it for the benefit of the estate.

38. Under section 546(d), the bankruptcy court may only deny reclamation if it secures the farmer or fisherman's reclamation claim by a lien.

CHAPTER XII

POST–BANKRUPTCY TRANSFERS

The prior chapter dealt with avoidance of transfers that occurred prior to the time that the bankruptcy petition was filed. Sections 544, 545, 547 and 548 apply only to pre-bankruptcy transfers. None of these provisions can be used to avoid an unauthorized transfer of property of the estate that occurs after the bankruptcy petition is filed. Section 549 applies to post-bankruptcy transfers.

For most purposes, the date of the filing of the bankruptcy petition is the critical date. Subject to limited exceptions noted on pages 175–176, only the property of the debtor as of the date of the filing of the petition becomes property of the estate. Generally, property acquired by the debtor after the bankruptcy petition has been filed remains property of the debtor.

The date of the filing of the petition is significant not only in determining what property becomes property of the estate but also in determining when the property becomes property of the estate. The filing of a bankruptcy petition—voluntary or involuntary—creates the estate.

The date of the filing of the bankruptcy petition is not, however, the date that the debtor loses possession of her property. Even in Chapter 7 cases. While section 701 provides for the appointment of an interim trustee in Chapter 7 cases "promptly after the order for relief," there will be some delay before the trustee takes possession of the property.

During the hiatus between the filing of the bankruptcy petition and the bankruptcy trustee's taking possession of the property of the estate, the debtor will usually have possession and control of the property of the estate. At times, the debtor will, after the filing of the petition, transfer property of the estate to some third party. Assume, for example, that B files a Chapter 7 petition on January 10. On January 12, B sells her summer home to X. On January 13, B sells her boat to Y. Obviously, B should not have made these post-bankruptcy transfers. Obviously, the trustee has a cause of action against B for conversion. Obviously, the trustee can claim any proceeds from the post-bankruptcy transfers as property of the estate. And, obviously the claim against the debtor and the right to remaining proceeds will usually be of limited practical significance. The significant inquiry is can the trustee recover the summer house from X and/or the boat from Y? Should the bankruptcy laws protect X and/or Y?

Section 549 protects X and Y in certain circumstances. Before considering these circumstances, remember that section 549 protects only the *transferee,* not the debtor-transferor.

Generally, section 549 protects the *transferee* if:

(1) the transfer was authorized by the Bankruptcy Code or by the bankruptcy court; *or*

(2) the transfer was after an involuntary petition for post-bankruptcy consideration; *or*

(3) the transfer was a real property transfer that was recorded before the bankruptcy was noted in the real property records.

The first of the three situations in which a transferee is entitled to retain property of the estate transferred by the debtor after the bankruptcy filing is the easiest to understand and apply. Obviously, a post-bankruptcy transfer will be effective against the bankruptcy trustee if the transfer was authorized by the Bankruptcy Code or the bankruptcy court. See section 549(a)(2)(B). Most of the post-bankruptcy transfers by a Chapter 11 debtor will be authorized under section 363.

Second, section 549(b) validates transfers by the debtor that occur after the filing of an *involuntary* bankruptcy petition and before the order for relief to the extent that the transferee gave value to the debtor after the filing of the bankruptcy petition. To illustrate,

(1) On February 22, D's creditors file an involuntary petition. On February 25, D sells her stove to X for $300. The trustee may *not* recover the stove from X. X is protected by section 549(b).

(2) Same facts as # 1 except that D knew of the involuntary petition. Same result. Section 549(b) protects post-petition transfers "notwithstanding

any notice or knowledge of the case that the transferee has."

(3) On January 10, C lends D $1,000. On February 2, D's creditors file an involuntary petition. On February 15, D transfers his stereo to C in satisfaction of the January 10 debt. The trustee can recover the stereo from C. The stereo was transferred to satisfy a debt that arose before the petition. The transferee did not give value to the debtor after the filing of the bankruptcy petition. The transferee is not protected by section 549(b).

(4) On April 4, the creditors of D file an involuntary petition. On April 14, D sells Greenacre to Y for $40,000. The trustee may not recover Greenacre from Y. Section 549(b) protects transferees of both personalty and realty.

Third, section 549(c) protects post-petition transfers of *realty* from trustee avoidance. A transfer of real property by the debtor after the filing of a voluntary petition or after an order for relief in an involuntary case will be effective against the bankruptcy trustee if:

(1) the transfer occurs and is properly recorded before a copy of the bankruptcy petition is filed in the real estate records for the county where the land is located, *and*

(2) the transferee is a buyer or lienor for fair equivalent value without knowledge of the petition.

Consider the following hypothetical illustrating the operation of section 549(c):

On February 2, B files a voluntary petition. On February 3, B sells land in White County to Y for $10,000, the "fair equivalent value" of the land. Y has no "knowledge of the commencement of the case." Y properly files the transfer in the White County real estate records on February 4. A copy of the bankruptcy petition is filed in the real estate records for White County on February 5. The trustee can *not* avoid the transfer. Y is protected by section 549(c).

There is no personal property counterpart of section 549(c). Personal property of the debtor transferred by the debtor after the filing of a voluntary petition can be recovered from the transferee unless the transfer was authorized by the Bankruptcy Code or by the bankruptcy court.

Some post-petition transfers of property of the estate are made by persons holding property of the debtor, not the debtor. For example, on January 11, D files a voluntary bankruptcy petition. As of that date, D has $1,000 in her checking account at B Bank. This checking account becomes property of the estate on January 11. On January 13, B Bank honors a $300 check issued by D to X on January 7 and charges D's account. Can D's bankruptcy trustee recover the $300 from B Bank? Bank of Marin v. England, 385 U.S. 99 (1966) protected the bank under the Bankruptcy Act of

1898; section 542 protects the bank under the Bankruptcy Code.

Under section 542(c), a third party who in good faith transfers property of the estate after the filing of the petition is protected from the bankruptcy trustee if the third party had "neither notice nor actual knowledge of the commencement of the case." Accordingly, if B Bank has neither actual knowledge or notice of D's petition, it will not be liable to the bankruptcy trustee. Note that section 542(c) only protects B Bank, the party that transfers the property of the estate; it does not protect X, the transferee. The trustee has a right to recover the $300, property of the estate, from X.[1]

1. This is the point of the reference to section 542(c) in section 549(a)(2)(A). Even though section 542(c) protects the person who transfers property of the estate post-petition, section 549 empowers the trustee to recover the property from the transferee.

CHAPTER XIII

EFFECT OF BANKRUPTCY ON SECURED CLAIMS

A. WHAT IS A SECURED CLAIM

The Bankruptcy Code deals with "claims," not creditors. Accordingly, under the Bankruptcy Code there will be creditors with secured claims, not secured creditors.

A creditor has a secured claim if it holds a lien on or has a right of setoff against "property of the estate." The claim is secured only to the extent of the value of "such creditor's interest in the estate's interest in such property," section 506(a). To illustrate,

(1) Suture Self, Inc. (S), a do-it-yourself health care center, owes X $100,000 and Y $200,000.

Both X and Y have mortgages on S's building. X's mortgage has priority over Y's under state law.

S files for bankruptcy. The building has a value of $160,000.[1]

---

1. In law school hypotheticals, the teacher gets to decide what the value of the collateral is. "Real lawyers" do not enjoy that luxury. The question of the value of the collateral is a difficult and important one. The Bankruptcy Code does not provide a method for valuing collateral. Section 506(a) states that value is to be determined by the court on a case by case basis in light of the purpose of the valuation and of the proposed disposition of the property.

Under these facts, X would have a $100,000 secured claim; Y would have a secured claim of $60,000 and an unsecured claim of $140,000.

(2) Sunshine Cab Co. obtains a $2,000 judgment against Bobby Wheeler and causes the sheriff to execute on personal property belonging to Wheeler.

The personal property subject to Sunshine's execution lien has a value of $800.

Sunshine has a $800 secured claim and a $1,200 unsecured claim.

(3) Bates Motel, Inc. owes Fairvale Bank & Trust $30,000 on an unsecured loan.

Bates Motel, Inc. has $9,000 on deposit in the bank.

Fairvale Bank & Trust has a $9,000 secured claim and a $21,000 unsecured claim.

The answer to problem (3) assumes that Fairvale Bank & Trust has a right of setoff under state law. The answers to problems (1) and (2) assume that the liens are valid in bankruptcy.

B. INVALIDATION OF LIENS

Some liens that are valid outside of bankruptcy can be invalidated in a bankruptcy case. Section 522(f) considered supra at pages 180–183, empowers the debtor to invalidate certain liens on certain exempt property. Sections 544, 545, 547, 548, and 549, considered supra at pages 183–246, empower the bankruptcy trustee to invalidate certain transfers that create liens.

To illustrate, assume that S lends D $10,000 and obtains a security interest in D's inventory. S does not file a financing statement or otherwise perfect its security interest. Under section 9–203 of the Uniform Commercial Code, S has a valid security interest. Under section 9–201, this unperfected security interest is effective between S and D and is effective against most third parties. For example, S's right to D's inventory is superior to the rights of any of D's unsecured creditors. If, however, D files a bankruptcy petition, S's unperfected security interest may be invalidated by the trustee under section 544(a)[2] so that S will simply have an unsecured claim for $10,000.

Note the effect of lien invalidation. All that is eliminated is the lien. The creditor's claim remains. Lien invalidation converts a secured claim into an unsecured claim.

---

2. Section 544(a) gives the bankruptcy trustee the rights and powers of a creditor who obtains a judicial lien at the time the bankruptcy petition was filed. At the time the bankruptcy petition was filed, S's security interest was unperfected. An unperfected security interest is ineffective as against a creditor with a judicial lien, UCC section 9–301. Accordingly, S's unperfected security interest is ineffective as against the bankruptcy trustee. Section 544(a) is considered supra at pages 221–227.

C. OVERVIEW OF IMPACT OF BANKRUPTCY ON SECURED CLAIMS

In thinking about the impact of bankruptcy on secured claims, a law student or lawyer should focus on two questions:

1. How can the debtor's bankruptcy filing adversely affect the holder of a secured claim?

2. How can a secured claim be satisfied when the debtor is in bankruptcy?

D. WHAT CAN HAPPEN TO SECURED CLAIMS DURING BANKRUPTCY

Most liens can not be avoided under sections 522(f), 544, 545, 547, 548, or 549. What effect does bankruptcy have on a creditor that holds a valid in bankruptcy lien? [This question is particularly important in Chapter 11 cases and Chapter 13 cases for two reasons:

1. a Chapter 11 or Chapter 13 case often lasts three years or more;

2. in Chapter 13 cases and in most Chapter 11 cases, the debtor remains in possession of encumbered property.]

1. Delay in Realizing on Collateral

Recall that the automatic stay of section 362 prevents a creditor from enforcing its lien against property of the estate or property of the debtor. Accordingly, a creditor will not be able to sell or even seize encumbered property from a debtor who is in bankruptcy without obtaining relief from the automatic stay.

2. Debtor's Use, Lease, or Sale of Collateral

Section 363 provides for continued use, lease, or sale of encumbered property during bankruptcy. The lien holder is protected by section 363's adequate protection requirements. Section 363 is considered infra at pages 326–329.

3. Loss of Priority

Section 364(d) empowers the bankruptcy court to approve the debtor's granting a post-petition creditor a lien on encumbered property that has priority over all pre-petition liens. To illustrate, X makes a $600,000 construction loan to D and obtains and records a first mortgage on the project. D is unable to complete the building with the $600,000 provided by X. D is unable to obtain additional financing. D is able to file for Chapter 11. Y is willing to loan D the $200,000 needed to finish the building if its mortgage has priority over X's. Under section 364(d), the bankruptcy court can authorize D's granting Y, the later-in-time post-petition lender, a lien that has priority over X's.

Section 364(d) imposes three requirements on the granting of such a "super-priority": (i) there must be "notice and a hearing," (ii) the debtor in possession or trustee is unable to obtain credit otherwise, and (iii) the holder of the pre-petition lien is adequately protected.

4. Limitations on Floating Liens

In commercial credit transactions, security agreements usually provide that the collateral includes property that the debtor later acquires. Such after-acquired property clauses are expressly permitted by section 9–204 of the UCC; such after-acquired property clauses are expressly cut off in bankruptcy by section 552(a). The following example illustrates the operation of section 552(a):

On January 10, S extends credit to and obtains and perfects a security interest in all of the inventory of wine, now owned or later acquired, of the Mary Decker Wine Co., D.

On March 3, D acquires additional wine.

On March 4, D files a Chapter 11 petition and continues operating its business.

On April 7, D acquires additional wine. In bankruptcy, S's claim would be secured by the January 10th inventory and by the March 3d inventory. It would not be secured by the April 7th inventory. Section 552(a) states that a security agreement entered into before the commencement of the case does not reach property acquired after the commencement of the case other than proceeds.

Under Article 9, a security interest automatically floats to proceeds, section 9–306(2). The Bankruptcy Code generally recognizes a security interest in post-petition proceeds from pre-petition collateral, section 552(b). If, for example, the Mary Decker Wine Co., D, sold wine on March 5th, the proceeds from this post-petition sale of pre-petition property would be subject to S's security interest.

5. Return of Repossessed Property

Section 542(a) compels the holder of a secured claim that has taken possession of its collateral prior to bankruptcy to return it to the debtor when she files a bankruptcy petition. Assume, for example, that S extended credit to D and obtained and perfected a security interest in D's inventory. D defaulted. S repossessed the inventory. D then filed for Chapter 11 relief. Reading section 362(a) (4) should leave you convinced that S can not sell the inventory without obtaining relief from the stay. Reading section 542 should leave you confused.

Section 542(a) compels the turnover of "property that the trustee may use, sell, or lease under section 363" "unless *such property* is of inconsequential value or benefit to the estate." What is the antecedent of the pronoun "such"? If it is "property that the trustee may use, sell, or lease under section 363," then it is necessary to look at section 363. Section 363 provides for the use, sale, or lease of "property of the estate." [3] It is thus

3. Section 363's use of the term "property of the estate" is probably misleading. Section 363 does more than just authorize the use, sale, or lease of property of the estate, i.e., the debtor's

necessary to look at section 541 which describes property of the estate in terms of the "interest of the debtor in property." What is the interest of the debtor in inventory that has been repossessed? A right of redemption under section 9–506? A right to any surplus produced by a forced sale under 9–504? Are these rights of "inconsequential value" for purposes of section 542?

The Supreme Court worked through these questions in U.S. v. Whiting Pools, Inc., 462 U.S. 1981 (1983), and concluded that section 542 requires that a creditor that seized its collateral prior to bankruptcy turn over the property to a Chapter 11 debtor. *Whiting Pools* involved a seizure by the IRS of property subject to a tax lien. It seems clear from dicta in Whiting Pools that the Court would reach a similar result if a private creditor seized property subject to its security interest.

E. SATISFACTION OF SECURED CLAIMS

1. Overview

a. *Recovery of Collateral*

If the holder of a secured claim recovers its collateral, the secured claim is extinguished. Assume, for example, that D owes S $22,000 and S has a security interest on equipment worth $10,000. D files a Chapter 7 bankruptcy petition. If the trustee turns over the equipment to S, S no

interest in property. Instead, section 363 authorizes the use, sale, or lease of property in which the debtor has an interest.

longer has a secured claim. S still has a $12,000 claim, but the claim is an unsecured claim.

Chapters 7, 11, and 13 all *permit* satisfaction of a secured claim by surrender of the collateral. Neither Chapter 7, nor Chapter 11, nor Chapter 13 *requires* the satisfaction of a secured claim by surrender of the collateral.

b. Payment of Amount Equal to the Value of the Collateral

If the holder of a secured claim does not recover its collateral, it should receive a payment equal to the value of the collateral. In a Chapter 7 case, this payment should be in cash unless the holder of the secured claim agrees to periodic payments pursuant to a section 524 reaffirmation agreement. Chapters 11 and 13 both contemplate periodic payments to holders of secured claims pursuant to the court approved plan.

2. Chapter 7

There are six different ways that a Chapter 7 case can result in the holder of a secured claim obtaining either the collateral or its cash value.

(1) Obtaining Relief from the Automatic Stay. Under state law, a secured creditor can generally realize on its lien by foreclosure. In bankruptcy, a holder of a secured claim can foreclose its lien only after it has obtained relief from the automatic stay of section 362.

(2) Abandonment by the Bankruptcy Trustee. Section 521(4) requires that debtor surrender all property of the estate to the trustee. Assume, for example, that James Kirk, K, files a Chapter 7 petition. Mr. Spock is appointed as trustee. K owes Federation Bank, F, $100,000. F has a properly perfected security interest in K's ship. The ship has a value of $80,000. If K files for Chapter 7 relief, section 521(3) requires that the ship be surrendered to Mr. Spock.

Because the amount of F's secured claim is greater than the value of the ship, the ship is of "inconsequential value" to the estate. Section 554 authorizes a bankruptcy trustee to abandon any property that is burdensome to the estate or of inconsequential value to the estate. Thus, Mr. Spock can abandon the ship. According to the legislative history, "abandonment may be to any party with a possessory interest in the property abandoned," H.R.Rep. 95–595, 377 (1977). Some courts have relied on this language and on the language in section 362(a)(5) to hold that encumbered property must be abandoned to the debtor, not to a creditor with a lien on the property. Even if Spock abandons the ship to K, K can then release the ship to F.

(3) Sale of the Collateral by the Bankruptcy Trustee and Distribution of the Proceeds from This Sale to the Holder of the Secured Claim. In certain, limited situations, the trustee is empowered to sell encumbered property free and clear of all liens, see section 363(f). For example, Mr. Spock can sell K's ship if the sale yields more than F's $100,000 secured claim, section 363(f)(3). The proceeds of any such sale will first be used to cover the costs of the sale, sections 363(j), 506(c). The first $100,000 of net proceeds will be paid to F.

(4) Redemption by Payment by the Debtor. Section 722 empowers Chapter 7 debtors to extinguish liens on certain property by paying the holder of the secured claim an amount equal to the value of the encumbered property. Please read section 722. Note that section 722 would apply to the Federation lien only if (1) the ship was "intended primarily for personal, family, or household use" (i.e. not an enterprise), (2) the debt was a "dischargeable consumer debt," and (3) the ship had been exempted or abandoned.

(5) Payments Pursuant to a Reaffirmation Agreement. A debtor who has filed for bankruptcy relief can agree to continue paying some of his pre-bankruptcy debts after the bankruptcy case. For example, K can agree to pay F $20,000 a year for the next 4 years. Such an agreement is commonly referred to as a reaffirmation agreement. Not all reaffirmation agreements are legally enforceable. Section 524 controls reaffirmation agreements. Section 524 is considered infra at pages 313–314.

(6) Voluntary Return by Trustee. If encumbered property of a Chapter 7 debtor is not foreclosed by a holder of a secured claim after it obtains relief from the stay under section 362(d), or abandoned under section 554, or sold by the trustee under section 363(f), or redeemed under section 722, or covered by a section 524 reaffirmation agreement, then section 725 controls its disposition. Please read section 725. "The purpose of this section is to give the court appropriate authority to ensure that collateral or its proceeds is returned to the proper secured creditor." H.R. Rep., No. 95–595, 382; S.Rep. 95–989, 96. Section 725 contemplates that Mr. Spock release K's ship to F.

3. Chapters 11 and 13

What the holder of a secured claim receives in a Chapter 11 case or a Chapter 13 case depends on the provisions of the plan. A Chapter 11 plan can modify the rights of the holder of any secured claim, section 1123(b)(1). A Chapter 13 plan can modify the rights of the holder of any secured claim other than a claim secured "only by a security interest in real property that is the debtor's principal residence," [4] section 1322(b)(2). There are, however, statutory limits on the modification of the rights of holders of secured claims. Unless the holder is willing to settle for less, the plan must provide for either (1) the surrender of the collateral to the holder of the secured claim, or (2)

---

4. If an individual wants to change the terms of her home mortgage and the creditor is not willing to agree to changes, her attorney should consider Chapter 11, not Chapter 13. See generally In re Gregory, 39 B.R. 405 (Bkrtcy.M.D.Tenn.1984).

payments to the secured creditor that have a present value equal to the value of the collateral, sections 1129(b)(2);[5] 1325(a)(5).

Assume, for example, that D owes S $220,000. S has a mortgage on Blueacre. If Blueacre is worth $180,000, D's Chapter 11 plan or Chapter 13 must either surrender Blueacre to S or propose to pay S an amount that has a present value of $180,000. Obviously, a plan that provides for 36 monthly payments of $5,000 would not meet this standard. $180,000 over 36 months does not have a present value of $180,000. Obviously, Chapters 11 and 13 contemplate that a secured creditor that is being paid in installments will receive interest on its secured claim. What is not obvious from either the statute or cases is what the rate of interest should be. Some cases have looked to the contract rate of interest; some have looked to the current market rate on comparable credit transactions, some have looked to other factors.

To illustrate, in January of 1985, D borrows $10,000 from C and offers to pay 14% interest on the debt until it is repaid. D grants C a mortgage on Blueacre. In February of 1986, D files a Chapter 11 petition. At the time of the bankruptcy filing, D owes C $12,000 in principal and unpaid,

---

5. In Chapter 11, the payments under the plan to a non-assenting secured creditor must also be "totaling at least the allowed amount of such a claim," section 1129(b)(2)(A). Understanding this requirement requires an understanding of section 1111(b). All of this understanding will take place in Chapter XVII, infra.

accrued interest, and Blueacre has a value of $8,000. Accordingly, C has an $8,000 secured claim and a $4,000 unsecured claim, section 506(a).

D's Chapter 11 plan is confirmed in March of 1987. C's $8,000 secured claim does not accrue interest from the date of bankruptcy filing in February of 1986 until the time of confirmation in March of 1987. Only a claim that is fully secured draws interest from the time of the filing of the petition to the date of confirmation of the plan, section 506(b). C's $8,000 secured claim will, however, draw interest from the time of confirmation of the plan until it is fully satisfied. It is not clear whether this interest will be 14% or some other rate.

To summarize, (1) only a claim that is fully secured will draw interest from the time of the bankruptcy filing until the confirmation of a plan; and (2) any claim that is paid in installments will draw interest from the time of the confirmation of the plan until the time of the last plan payment.

F. POSTPONEMENT OF TAX LIENS IN CHAPTER 7 CASES

A government's claim for taxes is usually secured by a statutory lien.[6] Such a statutory lien will not always be valid in bankruptcy. For example, an unfiled federal tax lien can be avoided by

---

6. Federal tax liens are considered supra at pages 107–122.

the trustee under section 544(a).[7] If the government has not obtained a tax lien prior to bankruptcy or if the tax lien has been avoided under section 544, the tax claim will be an unsecured claim. Such an unsecured claim is governed by section 507(a)(7), not section 724.

Section 724 only applies if (1) Chapter 7 bankruptcy and (2) claim for taxes secured by a valid in bankruptcy tax lien. Section 724(b) postpones the payment of such a tax claim until the complete payment of all claims entitled to priority under section 507(a)(1)–(6).[8]

(1) The debtor has property worth $4,000. This property is subject to a properly recorded tax lien for $3,000. The debtor also has $3,000 of debts entitled to priority under section 507(a)(1)–(b) and $5,000 of unsecured debts. The distribution in Chapter 7 would be

$3,000 to the section 507(a)(1)–(6) claimants

$1,000 to the tax lienor.

7. An unfiled federal tax lien is not valid as against a creditor with a judicial lien, IRC 6323(a). Section 544(a) gives the bankruptcy trustee the rights and powers of a creditor that obtained a judicial lien as of the date of the bankruptcy filing. Accordingly, if the federal tax lien had not been filed prior to bankruptcy, the bankruptcy trustee can invalidate the tax lien under section 544(a). Section 544(a) is considered supra at pages 221–227.

8. The priority provisions of section 507 are considered infra at pages 277–282. In 1984, Congress amended section 507 by adding a new sixth priority and postponing taxes to a seventh priority. Congress neglected to amend section 724 to conform to this change.

[See section 724(b)(5).]

(2) Same facts as # 1 except that the property is also subject to a $2,000 security interest. Under non-bankruptcy law, the security interest is junior in right to the nonpossessory tax lien. The distribution in Chapter 7 would be

$3,000 to 507(a)(1)–(6) claimants

$1,000 to the junior security interest.

[See section 724(b)(4). Note that the junior secured creditor is receiving exactly the same amount that it would have received if section 724(b) had not been applicable. Section 724(b) results in different claims being paid prior to the junior, *non-tax* lien, but the amount so paid is not affected by section 724(b).]

(3) Same facts as # 2 except that the amount of the claims entitled to a section 507(a)(1)–(6) priority is $6,000. The distribution in Chapter 7 would be

$3,000 to section 507(a)(1)–(6) claimants

$1,000 to the junior security interest.

(4) Same facts as # 2 except that the amount of the claims entitled to a section 507(a)(1)–(6) priority is only $1,400. The distribution in Chapter 7 would be

$1,400 to section 507(a)(1)–(6) claimants

$1,600 to the tax lienor

$1,000 to the junior security interest.

[See section 724(b)(3).]

(5) Same facts as # 1 except that the property is real property and is also subject to a $3,000 mortgage. Under non-bankruptcy law, this mortgage is senior in right to the tax lien. The distribution in bankruptcy would be

$3,000 for the senior mortgage

$1,000 to section 507(a)(1)–(6) claimants.

[See section 724(b)(1).]

The above combinations do not exhaust all possible section 724(b) problems. In resolving other section 724(b) problems remember that the amount distributed to a claim secured by a *non-tax* lien is neither increased nor decreased by the application of section 724(b); such creditors should receive the same distribution they would receive if section 724(b) were not applicable.

CHAPTER XIV

CHAPTER 7 AND UNSECURED CLAIMS

A. WHAT IS A CLAIM

Generally, the Bankruptcy Code deals with "claims," not creditors. The term "claim" is defined in section 101(4). It is clear from section 101(4)(A) that any right to payment is a "claim." The right to payment can be contingent, unliquidated, unmatured, and disputed and still be a claim. To illustrate,

1. C buys goods from D Corp. The goods are defective. D Corp. files a bankruptcy petition before C files a law suit. C has a claim.

2. D borrows $2,000 from C. X guarantees repayment of the loan. D files for bankruptcy. Both C and X have claims.

Section 101(4)(B) dealing with rights to equitable remedies is less clear. Some, but not all, rights to equitable remedies are claims. The test is whether the right to an equitable remedy "gives rise to a right to payment." What does this mean?

It would seem that an order restraining an individual from seeing his wife or a corporation from polluting the water would not give rise to a right to payment—would not be a "claim." What about an order requiring a business to clean up a waste site?

In Ohio v. Kovacs, 105 S.Ct. 705 (1985), the Court concluded that an injunction order that obligated Kovacs to clean up a dump site was a "claim." In so holding, the Court emphasized that a receiver had been appointed prior to bankruptcy and that after his appointment "the only performance sought from Kovacs was the payment of money." 105 S.Ct. at 710. Lower courts are divided as to whether restitution ordered as part of a criminal sentence gives rise to a section 101(4)(B) "claim."

B. WHAT IS AN UNSECURED CLAIM

A claim is unsecured if the creditor has not obtained a consensual, judicial, or statutory lien or if the value of the property subject to the lien is less than the amount of the creditor's claim. Consider the following examples of unsecured claims:

1. C provides diaper service to D. D files a bankruptcy petition. At the time of the bankruptcy petition, D owes C $100 for diaper service. C has an unsecured claim.

2. D Corp. borrows $2,000,000 from C and grants C a mortgage on Redacre. At the time of D Corp.'s bankruptcy it still owes C $2,000,000 and the encumbered property has a value of $800,000. S is a creditor with a $1,200,000 unsecured claim. [S is also a creditor with a $800,000 secured claim.[1]]

---

1. The rights of holders of secured claims in a Chapter 7 case are considered supra at pages 255–258.

C. COLLECTION OF UNSECURED CLAIMS FROM THE DEBTOR

Under section 362, the filing of a Chapter 7 petition operates as a "stay." This automatic stay prevents a creditor from collecting its unsecured claim from the debtor until the bankruptcy case is closed. The automatic stay and relief therefrom is considered in Chapter VIII.

Under section 727, the bankruptcy court generally grants the debtor a "discharge." This discharge prevents a creditor from collecting its claim from the debtor after the bankruptcy case is closed. The discharge and exceptions thereto is considered in Chapter XVI infra.

The section 362 stay coupled with the section 727 discharge makes it necessary for most holders of unsecured claims to look to the "property of the estate" for the satisfaction of their claims.

D. SATISFACTION OF UNSECURED CLAIMS IN CHAPTER 7 CASES

Now that we know

1. what an unsecured claim is, and

2. that the automatic stay generally precludes collection of unsecured claims from the debtor during the bankruptcy case, and

3. that the discharge generally bars collection of unsecured claims from the debtor after the bankruptcy case, we need to determine how to

collect on unsecured claims in a Chapter 7 bankruptcy case.

It thus becomes necessary to learn

1. what property is distributed to unsecured claims in a Chapter 7 case, and

2. which holders of unsecured claims are eligible to participate in the distribution of this property, and

3. what is the order of distribution, i.e., which claims are paid first.

1. What Property Is Distributed to Holders of Unsecured Claims in Chapter 7 Cases

In a Chapter 7 case, the bankruptcy trustee has a statutory duty to sell the "property of the estate," section 704(1). The net proceeds received from the liquidation of the "property of the estate" is to be distributed to the holders of unsecured claims. Such claimants do not, however, receive the net proceeds from the sale of all of the "property of the estate":

1. Some "property of the estate" will be turned over to the debtor as exempt property, section 522.

2. Some "property of the estate" will be transferred after the filing of the bankruptcy petition to third parties protected by section 549.

3. Some "property of the estate" will be subject to liens that are valid in bankruptcy. Encumbered property or the proceeds thereof must be first used to satisfy the holders of secured claims, section 725.

4. Some "property of the estate" must be used to satisfy the administrative expenses of the bankruptcy proceeding.

Subject to these four exceptions, holders of unsecured claims receive the net proceeds from the bankruptcy trustee's sale of the "property of the estate."

2. Which Holders of Unsecured Claims Participate in the Distribution of Property of the Estate

a. Proof of Claim

In a case under Chapter 7 of the Bankruptcy Code, the debtor will file a list of creditors, section 521. The court will then send notice of the Chapter 7 case to the listed creditors, section 342. The creditors that wish to participate in the distribution of the proceeds of the liquidation of the "property of the estate" must file a proof of claim, sections 501, 726.

Most of the requirements as to form, content, and procedure for proofs of claim are found in the Bankruptcy Rules. For example, there is no statutory language governing the time for filing a proof of claim. Section 501 simply speaks of "timely filing." Rule 3002(c) governs the time for filing a proof of claim in a Chapter 7 case or a Chapter 13 case.[2]

Section 501(c) authorizes the debtor to file a proof of claim for a creditor who does not timely file. This provision is primarily intended to protect the debtor if the claim of the creditor is nondischargeable. When no proof of claim is filed, there will be no bankruptcy distribution to the holder of the claim. If no bankruptcy distribution is made to the holder of a claim excepted from discharge, the debtor will have to pay the claim in full after the bankruptcy case is closed. If, however, the debtor files a proof of claim, the holder of the nondischargeable claim will participate in the bankruptcy distribution and the post-bankruptcy liability of the debtor to the creditor will be reduced by the amount of distribution.

To illustrate, assume that David Lee Roth, D, files a Chapter 7 petition. He owes California Bank, C, $10,000. C made the loan to D because of a false financial statement; its claim against D is excepted from discharge.[3] If no proof of claim is filed by or for C, it will have a $10,000 claim against D after the close of the Chapter 7 case. If, however, D files a proof of claim for C Bank, its post-bankruptcy claim against him will be reduced

2. In Chapter 11 cases, a creditor is required to file a proof of claim only if its claim is scheduled as disputed, contingent, or unliquidated, section 1111(a); Rule 3003(b)(1).

3. Section 523(a)(2) excepts from discharge claims based on credit extended in reliance on a false financial statement. Section 523(a)(2) is considered infra at pages 303–307.

by the amount it receives in the bankruptcy distribution.

b. Allowance

In a Chapter 7 case, the proceeds of the liquidation of the property of the estate is not distributed to all holders of unsecured claims against the debtor. Rather, the distribution is only made to unsecured creditors whose claims are "allowed," section 726.[4]

If a proof of claim has been filed, the claim is deemed allowed "unless a party in interest objects," section 502(a). The statute does not define "party in interest"; clearly, another creditor or the bankruptcy trustee is a "party in interest" for purposes of objections to allowance of a claim.

The statute does set out nine grounds for disallowing claims in section 502(b):

1. If the claim is unenforceable against the debtor or the property of the debtor by reason of any agreement or applicable law, it will not be allowed, section 502(b)(1).

---

4. Under the Bankruptcy Act of 1898, only claims that were both allowable and *provable* were permitted to participate in the bankruptcy distribution. The requirement of provability excluded certain tort claims and certain other contingent and unliquidated claims from sharing in the distribution of the proceeds from the liquidation of the bankrupt estate, section 63. The Bankruptcy Code eliminates the requirement of provability. Tort claims and other contingent and unliquidated claims may participate in the bankruptcy distribution, cf. sections 502(b)(1), 502(c).

[A non-recourse loan is an example of an agreement which makes a claim unenforceable; UCC section 2–302 is an example of a law which makes a claim unenforceable.]

2. A claim for "unmatured" interest will be disallowed, section 502(b)(2).

[Generally, interest stops accruing when a bankruptcy petition is filed.[5] Assume, for example, that D borrows $1,000 from C; the loan agreement provides for 14% interest. At the time of the bankruptcy filing, D owes $1,444. C's allowable claim will be $1,444; it will not draw the 14% interest after the bankruptcy filing.]

3. If a claim is for an ad valorem property tax, it will not be allowed to the extent that the claim exceeds the value of the estate's interest in the property, section 502(b)(3).

4. If the claim is for services of debtor's attorney or an "insider,"[6] it will be disallowed to the extent the claim exceeds the reasonable value of such services, section 502(b)(4).

5. "Insider" is defined in section 101(28). "Insider" includes the relatives of an individual debtor; the partners of a partnership debtor; and the officers, directors, and other control persons of a corporate debtor.

6. Only claims that are secured by collateral that has a value greater than the amount of the claim will accrue interest after the filing of a bankruptcy petition, section 506(b).

5. If the claim is for post-petition alimony or child support, it will not be allowed, section 502(b) (5).[7]

6. If the claim is that of a landlord for future rent, it will be limited to the greater of one year's payments or 15% of the payments for the balance of the lease, not to exceed three years' payments in total, section 502(b)(6).

(Note that section 502(b)(6) only limits the allowance of claims for future rentals by a lessor of *real* property.[8] It does not affect a claim for rentals due on or before the filing of the bankruptcy peti-

7. These claims are excepted from discharge under section 523(a)(5). The following hypothetical illustrates the application of sections 502(b)(5) and 523(a)(5).

H and W are divorced in January of 1979. The divorce decree orders H to pay alimony of $1,000 a month. H files a bankruptcy petition on December 31, 1979. He owes W $2,000 for November and December alimony.

W's claims for $2,000 of unpaid 1979 alimony is allowable. Section 502(b)(5) only disallows a claim for alimony that is "unmatured on the date of the filing of the petition." Accordingly, W's claim for post-petition alimony is disallowed.

If W's claim for $2,000 of unpaid 1979 alimony is not fully satisfied by the bankruptcy distribution, W may attempt to collect any deficiency from H personally. Section 523(a)(5) excepts alimony claims from the bankruptcy discharge. Accordingly, H's bankruptcy discharge will not affect W's right to collect post-petition alimony from H personally.

8. Section 502(b)(6) does not limit the amount of a claim for future rents of personal property. Section 547(e) suggests that the Bankruptcy Code considers "fixtures" to be real property. If so, section 502(b)(6) would apply to a claim by a lessor of equipment that was installed in such a manner as to become a fixture under state law.

tion. It does not affect a claim for rentals under a lease of personal property.

(Note also that section 502(b)(6) does not guarantee an allowable claim for back rent plus a minimum of one year's rent; rather, it places a ceiling on the allowance of rent claims. Assume, for example, that D rents a building from C and signs a 20 year lease at a monthly rental rate of $5,000. At the time that D files her bankruptcy petition, she owes C $10,000 in back rent. If D immediately rejects the lease and C then relets the building to X for $6,000 a month, C's allowable claim will be limited to the $10,000 in back rent.)

7. Section 502(b)(7) imposes a similar limitation on the allowable claim for termination of an employment contract—no more than back wages due at the time of the bankruptcy filing and one year's future compensation.

8. If the claim is a federal tax claim which arises because the state unemployment tax is paid late and so no federal tax credit is allowed, the federal claim will be treated the same as if the credit had been allowed in full in the federal return, which means the federal tax claim would be disallowed, section 502(b)(8).

The fact that a claim is contingent or unliquidated at the time that the bankruptcy petition is filed does not affect its allowance. The court may either delay bankruptcy distribution until the claim is fixed in amount, or, if liquidation of the claim would "unduly delay the administration of the case," estimate the amount of the claim, section 502(c). Assume, for example, that V files a $100,000 tort suit against T. T immediately files a bankruptcy petition. V then files a proof of claim. V's claim is allowable. The court may either delay distribution to T's creditors and the closing of T's bankruptcy case until V's tort claim has been litigated or estimate the amount of V's claim.[9]

Generally, only claims that arise before the bankruptcy petition are allowable. If, for example, D files a voluntary bankruptcy petition on January 11, and C lends D $100 on February 2, C's claim is not allowable.

There are four exceptions to the rule that only claims that predate the bankruptcy petition are allowable in Chapter 7.[10]

1. In an involuntary case, claims arising in the ordinary course of the debtor's business after the commencement of the case but before the earlier of the appointment of a trustee or the order for relief will be allowed as if the claim had arisen before the bankruptcy petition, section 502(f).

9. Section 502(c) does not indicate which judge shall do the estimating for purposes of allowance. 28 USC 157(b)(2)(B) states that "estimation of contingent or unliquidated personal injury tort or wrongful death claims against the estate for the purposes of distribution" is not a "core proceeding." This provision is considered in the chapter on allocation of judicial power over bankruptcy on page 362 et seq.

10. In Chapter 13 cases, certain post-petition taxes and consumer debts are allowable, section 1305(a).

2. Claims arising from the rejection of an executory contract or unexpired lease of the debtor are allowed as if the claim had arisen before the date of the filing of the petition, section 502(g).

3. A claim arising from the recovery of property because of a voidable transfer will be determined and allowed as though it were a pre-petition claim, section 502(h).[11]

4. A claim that does not arise until after the commencement of the case for a tax entitled to the seventh priority shall be treated as if the claim had arisen before the date of the filing of the petition, section 502(i).

Before a case is closed, a claim that has been allowed may be reconsidered for cause and reallowed or disallowed according to the equities of the case, section 502(j).

3. Order of Distribution

There are a number of statements in reported cases, law review articles, and legal texts praising the theme of equality of distribution to creditors in bankruptcy proceedings. Such statements must be using the term "equality" in the *Animal Farm* sense; in bankruptcy, some creditors are clearly "more equal" than others. Some unsecured claims

---

11. To illustrate, assume that on January 11, D repays C the $1,000 he owes her. On February 2, D files a bankruptcy petition. On May 5, D's bankruptcy trustee recovers the $1,000 from C as a section 547 preference. Under section 502(h), C has an allowable claim for $1,000.

must be fully satisfied before any distribution is made to other unsecured claims.

Section 726 establishes the rules for distribution in a Chapter 7 case to the holders of unsecured claims. Basically, the distribution is to be as follows:

(1) priorities under section 507 (section 507 is considered below)

(2) allowed unsecured claims which were either timely filed or tardily filed by a creditor who did not know of the bankruptcy

(3) allowed unsecured claims which were tardily filed by creditors with notice or actual knowledge of the bankruptcy

(4) fines and punitive damages

(5) post-petition interest on pre-petition claims.

Each claim of each of the five classes must be paid in full before any claim in the next class receives any distribution. Each claimant within a particular class shares pro rata if the proceeds from the liquidation of the property of the estate is insufficient to satisfy all claims in that class.

Assume, for example, that there is $20,000 available to pay to holders of unsecured claims and the following unsecured claims:

$11,000—claims entitled to priority under section 507

$4,800—claim by X that was timely filed

$7,200—claim by Y that was timely filed

$3,000—claim by Z that was not timely filed even though Z knew of the bankruptcy proceedings.

The distribution would be:

$11,000 to holders of priority claims

$3,600 to X [12]

$5,400 to Y.

In the very unlikely event that the sale of the "property of the estate" yields enough to satisfy each claim in each of the five "classes" listed above, the surplus is paid to the debtor.

a. Priorities

The task of distributing the proceeds from the sale of the property of the estate is complicated by the fact that claims do not come neatly labelled "claims entitled to priority under section 507." Instead, it is necessary to recognize which claims are entitled to priority under section 507.

In the typical Chapter 7 case, administrative expenses allowed under section 503(b) and fees and charges assessed against an estate under Chapter

---

12. The first $11,000 must be used to pay priority claims. The remaining $9,000 ($20,000–$11,000) must be distributed pro rata to $12,000 ($4,800 + $7,200) of timely filed claims. Accordingly, each timely filed claim will be paid at the rate of 75¢ on the dollar. ($9,000/$12,000). Accordingly, X will receive $3,600 for its $4,800 claim.

123 of Title 28 are accorded first priority,[13] section 507(a)(1). Administrative expenses include the costs of maintaining, repairing, storing, and selling the property of the estate; taxes the trustee incurs in administering property of the estate; the trustee's fee; the debtor's attorney's fees; the trustee's attorney's fee; and limited expenses of certain creditors.

In the typical Chapter 7 case,[14] each section 507(a)(1) administrative expense claimant shares pro rata if the proceeds from the sale of the property of the estate is less than the total amount of all claims entitled to this priority. If the proceeds

13. Section 364(c) empowers the bankruptcy court to authorize a bankruptcy trustee or debtor in possession to obtain credit or incur debt that has a priority over all administrative expenses. Section 364(c) is considered infra at page 325.

Section 507(b) grants a holder of a secured claim whose "adequate protection" proved to be less than adequate a "superiority" over all administrative expenses. "Adequate protection" is considered supra at pages —; section 507(b) is considered supra at pages 169–170.

These provisions apply only if the bankruptcy trustee or a Chapter 11 debtor in possession is authorized to operate the business. In the typical Chapter 7 case, the bankruptcy trustee is *not* authorized to operate the business. Accordingly, in a typical Chapter 7 case, sections 364(c) and 507(b) do not apply. Accordingly, in a typical Chapter 7 case, administrative expenses are accorded a first priority after indefeasible liens.

14. Some Chapter 7 cases start as Chapter 11 or Chapter 13 cases and are converted to Chapter 7, sections 1112, 1307. In such a case, the administrative expenses incurred in the Chapter 7 liquidation are paid in full before any payment is made for the administrative expenses incurred while the case was under Chapter 11 or 13, section 726(b).

from the sale of the property of the estate is more than the total amount of all claims entitled to a first priority, second priority claims are next paid.

In an involuntary case, the second priority is accorded to claims arising in the ordinary course of the debtor's business after the commencement of the case but before the earlier of the appointment of a trustee or the order for relief. For example, the creditors of an all-night Chinese restaurant, Wok Around the Clock, Inc., W, file an involuntary Chapter 7 petition on January 11. On January 12, C makes his usual weekly delivery of vegetables to W. C's claim will be entitled to a second priority under section 507(a)(2).

Section 507(a)(2) only applies in involuntary bankruptcy cases. If the Chapter 7 case was debtor-initiated, or if all second priority claims are satisfied, it is necessary to look to the third priority.

Section 507(a)(3) grants a third priority to wage claims. This third priority includes claims for vacation pay, severance pay, and sick leave pay. It is subject to two limitations:

(1) Time—only compensation earned within 90 days before the bankruptcy petition. (If the debtor's business ceased operations before the bankruptcy petition, the 90 day period is measured from the cessation of business operations.)

(2) Amount—only $2,000 per employee.

Assume, for example, that D files a Chapter 7 petition on December 31. It owes C, $5,000 for November and December salary. $2,000 of C's wage claim would be entitled to a third priority under section 507(a)(3); the remaining $3,000 of his claim would be an unsecured claim.

Claims for contributions to employee benefit plans receive a fourth priority under section 507(a)(4). This priority for fringe benefits is also subject to time and amount limitations:

(1) Time—only for services rendered within 180 days of the bankruptcy petition. (If the debtor's business ceased operations before the bankruptcy petition, the 180 days is measured from the cessation of business operation.)

(2) Amount—[$2,000 × number of employees] − total payment to employees under section 507(a)(3) + total payments to other employee benefit plans.

Note that payments under section 507(a)(4) will be made to the benefit plan, not directly to individual employees. Note also that section 507(a)(4) focuses on the aggregate of other payments to all employees covered by the plan, not the payments to an individual employee.

Section 507(a)(5) grants farmers a fifth priority for claims against grain storage facilities and fishermen a fifth priority against fish processing facilities. This priority is limited to $2,000 per individual claimant.

Section 507(a)(6) grants a sixth priority to consumers who made a money deposit for property or services that were never provided. If, for instance, D pays $2,500 for five years of dance lessons at C Dance Studios, Inc., and C files a Chapter 7 petition before providing dance lessons, $900 of D's claim will be entitled to a sixth priority. The sixth priority is limited in amount to $900 per claimant.

Certain specified tax claims enjoy a seventh priority.[15] Taxes entitled to this seventh priority include:

(1) income taxes for the three tax years immediately preceding the filing of the bankruptcy petition,[16] and

(2) property taxes assessed before the filing of the bankruptcy petition and last payable without a penalty one year before that date, and

(3) if the debtor is an employer, taxes withheld from employees' paychecks.

To review, section 507(a) establishes seven classes of priority claims. Each claim of a class must

---

15. Remember that under section 724(b), a tax claim secured by an indefeasible lien is paid after fifth priority claims but before sixth priority claims. Section 724(b) is considered supra at pages 260–263.

16. The three-year period is measured from the last date including extensions for filing a return to the date of the bankruptcy petition. If, for example, D files a bankruptcy petition on April 15, 1980, claims for taxes for 1979, 1978, and 1977 would be entitled to a priority. If, however, D files a bankruptcy petition on December 7, 1980, only claims for taxes for 1979 and 1978 would be entitled to a priority.

be paid in full before any claim in the next class receives any distribution. After all of the priority claims have been fully satisfied, distributions are made to unsecured claims that are timely filed, section 726(a)(2).

b. Subordination

Section 507, the priority provision, has the effect of moving certain specified claims to the head of the line. Section 510, the subordination provision, has the effect of moving some claims further back in the line.[17]

Section 510 requires subordination in two instances:

(1) when there is a subordination agreement that would be enforceable under non-bankruptcy law, section 510(a)

(2) when a seller or purchaser of equity securities seeks damages or rescission, section 510(b).

Additionally, the court has the discretion after notice and hearing to subordinate any claim to other claim or claims "under principles of equitable subordination," section 510(c). According to legislative history, these equitable principles are defined by case law. A student note summarized the case law on equitable subordination as follows:

"The federal courts have employed equity powers to subordinate claims valid under state law in two

17. Section 726, which governs the order of distribution in a Chapter 7 case, is prefaced "Except as provided in section 510."

broad classes of cases. Where a claimant has engaged in inequitable conduct toward other claimants, the bankruptcy court will often subordinate his claim. * * * Secondly, courts have subordinated valid claims of persons holding positions of control whose actions have caused damage to the estate." Note, Bankruptcy: Power to Subordinate on Equitable Grounds Claims Valid Under State Law, 67 Colum.L.Rev. 583, 586–7 (1967).

CHAPTER XV

LEASES AND EXECUTORY CONTRACTS

The effect of bankruptcy on a debtor's leases and executory contracts is governed primarily by section 365. Under section 365, a bankruptcy trustee can either

    1. reject a lease or executory contract;

    2. assume and retain a lease or executory contract;

    3. assume and assign a lease or executory contract.

In order to understand section 365 and assess these three options, a law student or lawyer must be able to answer the following questions:

A. What is the effect of rejecting a lease or executory contract, of assuming a lease or executory contract?

B. What is the procedure for rejecting or assuming a lease or executory contract?

C. What are the limitations, if any, on rejecting a lease or executory contract?

D. What are the limitations, if any, on assuming or assigning a lease or executory contract?

E. What is an executory contract?

A. EFFECT OF REJECTION, ASSUMPTION, ASSIGNMENT

Floyd Lawson, L, leases a building for his barbershop from Mayberry Realty Corp., M. The lease agreement provides for a ten year term and monthly rentals of $250. L files a bankruptcy petition. What is the effect of the bankruptcy trustee or debtor in possession rejecting the lease? Assuming the lease? Assigning the lease?

If the lease is rejected, L has no further right to use the building for his barbershop. If the lease is rejected, L has no further personal liability on the lease. The rejection of the lease is, of course, a breach of the lease, section 365(g). M will have an allowable unsecured claim against the bankrupt estate for back rent and future rentals, section 502(g), 502(a)(6). The amount that M will receive on this unsecured claim will depend on the property of the estate in a Chapter 7 case and will depend on the provisions of the plan in a Chapter 11 or Chapter 13 case.

If the lease is assumed, the leasehold continues to be an asset of the estate. L can continue to operate his barbershop in the building. Assumption covers the burdens of the lease as well as the benefits. By assuming the lease, the trustee or debtor in possession is obligating the estate to make all payments under the lease.[1] This obligation is a first priority administrative expense.

1. Compare the Bankruptcy Code's treatment of the debtor's landlord with its treatment of the debtor's secured creditor. If

What if the trustee or debtor in possession assumes the barbershop lease and sells the lease to Aunt Bea Taylor who wants to open an adult bookstore in the building? Such an assignment "relieves the trustee and the estate from any liability for any breach of such contract or lease occurring after such assignment," section 365(k). After the assignment, M can look only to Aunt Bea for the payment of the post-assignment obligations under the lease.

B. PROCEDURE FOR REJECTION OR ASSUMPTION

Section 365(a) contemplates court approval of rejection or assumption. Rule 6006 provides that the assumption or rejection is a contested matter governed by Rule 9014. Neither the Code nor the

a Chapter 11 or Chapter 13 debtor wants to retain a building that she is leasing, the debtor must continue to make all payments called for by the lease. Section 365 does not provide for the alteration or modification of leases; under section 365, the lease is either rejected or assumed, as is.

In contrast, if a Chapter 11 or Chapter 13 debtor wants to keep a building that is subject to a mortgage, the debtor can "impair" or "modify" the rights of the mortgagee in her plan, sections 1123(b)(1); 1322(b)(2).

To illustrate, D Corp. files a Chapter 11 petition. D is using two buildings. It is leasing one of the buildings from X at a rental of $2,000 a month. Y is financing D's purchase of the other building. The D–Y loan agreements grant Y a mortgage on the building and call for monthly payments of $3,000. D can keep the leased building only if it continues to pay X $2,000. D has greater flexibility with respect to retention of the building subject to Y's mortgage.

Rules indicate what standard the court should apply in determining whether to grant or withhold its approval. Most, but not all, cases seem to apply a business judgment test.

1. Chapter 7 Cases

There is a 60 day rule in Chapter 7 cases. Leases and executory contracts that are not assumed within 60 days after the order for relief are deemed rejected, section 365(d)(1).

2. Chapters 11 and 13

Section 365(d)(4) provides the same 60 day time limit in Chapter 11 and Chapter 13 cases for leases of non-residential real property. There is no time limit in Chapter 11 and Chapter 13 cases for the assumption or rejection of residential leases, personal property leases, or other executory contracts. Such leases and contracts can be assumed or rejected in the Chapter 11 or Chapter 13 plan or can be assumed or rejected prior to the formulation of the plan, sections 365(d)(2), 1123(b)(2), 1322(b)(7).

C. LIMITATIONS ON THE REJECTION OF A LEASE OR EXECUTORY CONTRACT

There are four situations in which the power of a trustee or debtor in possession to reject a lease or executory contract is limited:

1. Section 365(h) limits the effect of rejection of a lease of real property when the debtor is the

landlord. A trustee for a debtor who owns rental real property may not use section 365 to evict tenants. Even if the trustee decides to reject the debtor/lessor's leases, the tenant has a right to remain in possession. Assume, for example, that Hulk Hogan invests some of his earnings in an office building; your law firm rents an office in the building. If the Hulkster later files for bankruptcy and rejects the lease, your firm can still remain in possession of the leasehold.

The trustee for the debtor/lessor may, however, use rejection to terminate some of the services required by the lease such as maintenance. The lessee may then offset any damages caused by such termination against its rent obligation.

2. Sections 365(h) and (i) provide similar limitations on a debtor/seller's rejection of a timeshare contract.

3. Section 365(i) provides similar limitations on the debtor/seller's rejection of an installment land sales contract.

4. Section 1113 limits the rejection of collective bargaining contracts in Chapter 11 cases. Paragraph (f) of section 1113 prohibits a debtor/employer from unilaterally changing a pre-bankruptcy collective bargaining agreement. Paragraph (e) provides for court approval of interim changes pending court action on a request to reject a collective bargaining agreement. Paragraph (b) requires post-petition negotiations with and disclosures to the union as a condition precedent to rejection of

the collective bargaining agreement. And, paragraph (c) sets out the standard the court is to apply in ruling on a motion to reject a collective bargaining agreement.

D. LIMITATIONS ON ASSUMPTION AND ASSIGNMENT

1. Leases and Executory Contracts That Cannot Be Assumed or Assumed and Assigned

There are some leases and executory contracts that cannot be assumed and assigned.

A lease or contract that has terminated before bankruptcy cannot be assumed.[2] D leases Blackacre from L. D defaults. L takes the steps required by state law to evict D and terminate the lease. D later files for bankruptcy. D cannot assume the lease. Regardless of religious views, there is no such thing as a born-again lease.

A loan commitment or other financing arrangement cannot be assumed, section 363(c)(2). C agrees to provide D with a $250,000 line of credit. D files a bankruptcy petition before drawing on this line of credit. D cannot assume this executory contract and compel C to loan the $250,000.

---

2. The 1984 amendments added section 365(c)(3) that prohibits the assumption of a lease of non-residential real property that has terminated prior to the order for relief. It can be questioned whether this was a necessary addition. There are numerous pre-1984 cases holding that terminated leases cannot be assumed.

Contracts that are not assignable under state law are not assignable in bankruptcy, section 365(c)(1). Batman contracts to patrol the streets of Gotham City. Batman later files a bankruptcy petition. Batman cannot assign this contract to Madonna.

Contract clauses that prohibit or limit the assumption and assignment of leases and executory contracts in bankruptcy will not be effective. The trustee or debtor in possession can assume a lease even though the lease agreement provides in the lease for automatic termination or a right of termination because of bankruptcy or insolvency, section 365(e).

2. Requirements for Assumption and Assignment

Paragraph (b) of section 365 sets out the requirements for assumption of a lease or executory contract. Note that paragraph (b) only applies if there has been a default other than breach of a provision relating to bankruptcy filing or insolvency. Assume, for example, that Kinky Friedman's Kosher Fried Chicken, Inc., K, rents a building from Colony Square Mall, Inc., C. K files a bankruptcy petition. At the time of the bankruptcy petition, K is current on all of its obligations under the lease. If K decides to assume the lease, section 365(b) does not apply.

The principal requirement of section 365(b) is "adequate assurance." [3] Section 365(b) requires

---

3. This standard sounds similar to but is apparently different from the standard applied in stay litigation. Section 362(d)

"adequate assurance" of future performance and a cure of all defaults or "adequate assurance" that all defaults will be promptly cured. The term "adequate assurance" is not statutorily defined. Section 365(b)(3) indicates what constitutes "adequate assurance" if the lease covers real property that is a part of a "shopping center." [4]

"Adequate assurance" is also a condition precedent to assignment of a lease or executory contract. Remember that after assignment, the other party to the lease or executory contract can look only to the assignee for the performance of the debtor's post-assignment obligations under the lease or contract. To protect the non-bankrupt party, section 365(f)(2) requires that the assignee provide "adequate assurance" of future performance as a condition to any assignment.

E. DEFINITION OF EXECUTORY CONTRACT

Section 365 applies to leases and executory contracts. The Bankruptcy Code does not define the term "lease." There is probably no need for a definition. When there is a problem as to whether a "lease" of personal property is a disguised credit

protects the holder of secured claims by requiring "adequate protection" of the creditor's interest in the collateral. Section 365(b) protects the lessor of property by requiring "adequate assurance" of the lease obligations.

4. The term "shopping center" is not statutorily defined. Because of section 365(b)(3), a lessor of a shopping center enjoys greater protection than a lessor of other real property.

sale, bankruptcy courts look to the definition of "security interest" in UCC section 1–201(37).

Similarly, the Bankruptcy Code does not define the phrase "executory contract." The most frequently cited and most thorough discussion of executory contracts in bankruptcy is a two-part, 142 page article written prior to the enactment of the Bankruptcy Code by Professor Vern Countryman. Professor Countryman concludes that an executory contract for purposes of bankruptcy is one that is so far unperformed on both sides that the failure of either party to complete her performance would be a material breach excusing further performance from the other party. See Countryman, Executory Contracts In Bankruptcy, 57 Minn.L.Rev. 439 (1973); 58 Minn.L.Rev. 479 (1974). Most of the reported cases under the Bankruptcy Act of 1898 and the Bankruptcy Code seem to follow the Countryman definition. There are, however, cases that use a different definition of "executory contract."

CHAPTER XVI

DISCHARGE

Most individuals who file voluntary bankruptcy petitions expect that the bankruptcy case will wipe out all of their debts. These expectations are not always realized. Bankruptcy "discharges" *certain* debtors from *certain* debts.

As the last sentence suggests, there are three major discharge issues:

1. Which debtors receive a discharge § 727(a)
2. Which debts are discharged §
3. What is the effect of a discharge.

A. WHICH DEBTORS RECEIVE A DISCHARGE

1. Chapter 7

In counseling a beleaguered debtor about Chapter 7, it is very important to ascertain her eligibility for discharge—to determine whether any of the grounds for withholding discharge can be established by the bankruptcy trustee or a creditor. If the debtor is denied a discharge, she loses two ways. The debtor will leave the bankruptcy proceeding without her section 541 property yet owing the same debts that she owed at the time of the filing of the bankruptcy case less any distribution that creditors received from the trustee.

The grounds for withholding a discharge, i.e., objections to discharge, are set out in section 727(a). These ten grounds are exclusive. Unless the bankruptcy trustee or a creditor is able to establish one of these ten objections, the debtor in a Chapter 7 case will receive a bankruptcy discharge.

Section 727(a)(1) denies a discharge to corporations and partnerships.[1] Only an individual is eligible to receive a discharge in a case under Chapter 7 of the Bankruptcy Code.[2]

The next six grounds for withholding discharge have as their foundation some form of dishonesty or lack of cooperation by the individual debtor.

A fraudulent conveyance may be the basis for an objection to discharge. Section 727(a)(2) denies a discharge to a debtor who transfers property "with an intent to hinder, delay or defraud" within the twelve months immediately preceding the filing of the bankruptcy petition or after the filing of the bankruptcy petition.

---

1. Section 727(a)(1) is intended to prevent "trafficking in corporate shells and partnerships." Generally, the owners of a bankrupt corporation do not need a bankruptcy discharge. Since the corporation is a separate legal entity, they are protected from personal liability for the corporation's debts.

2. A corporation may receive a discharge under Chapter 11, section 1141(d), considered infra at pages 341–343.

An objection to discharge may be based on the unjustified failure to keep or preserve financial records, section 727(a)(3). A section 727(a)(3) objection raises the following issues of fact: (1) Has the debtor failed to keep financial records? (2) Is such failure "justified under all of the circumstances of the case"? and (3) Is it still possible to ascertain the debtor's financial condition and business transactions? The standards applied in resolving these fact questions will reflect the nature of the debtor's business and his assets and liabilities.

Section 727(a)(4) lists four acts which tend to deprive the bankruptcy trustee of property of the estate or of information necessary to discover or collect property of the estate:

    1. making a false oath or account in connection with the bankruptcy case;

    2. presenting or using a false claim against the estate;

    3. receiving or giving consideration for action or inaction in the bankruptcy proceeding; or

    4. withholding books and records from the bankruptcy trustee.

Proof that the debtor "knowingly and fraudulently" committed one of these acts will bar discharge.[3]

---

3. Proof that the debtor "knowingly and fraudulently" committed one of these acts will also subject the debtor to criminal sanctions: a fine of not more than $5,000 and/or imprisonment for not more than five years, 18 U.S.C.A. section 152. The standard of proof under 18 U.S.C.A. is beyond a reasonable doubt; section 727(a)(4) merely requires a preponderance of the

The fifth ground for denial of discharge is the failure to explain "satisfactorily" any loss or deficiency of assets, section 727(a)(5). Section 727(a)(5) focuses on the truth of the debtor's explanation, not on the wisdom of his or her expenditures.

Under section 727(a)(6), a debtor may be denied discharge if he refuses to testify after having been granted immunity or after improperly invoking the constitutional privilege against self-incrimination.

The seventh ground for withholding discharge is the debtor's commission of any act specified in section 727(a)(2)–(6) no more than a year before the filing of the bankruptcy petition in connection with another bankruptcy case concerning an "insider," section 727(a)(7). The term "insider" is defined in section 101(28). An individual's relatives, partners, partnership and corporation all come within the definition.

Section 727(a)(8) and section 727(a)(9) limit the frequency of discharge relief. If a debtor has received a discharge in a Chapter 7 or Chapter 11 (or XI) case in the past six years, she will be denied discharge, section 727(a)(8). If a debtor has received a discharge in a Chapter 13 (or XIII) case within the past six years she will be denied a discharge unless (a) payments under the plan totalled at least 100% of the allowed unsecured claims, *or* (b) payments under the plan totalled at least 70% of the allowed unsecured claims *and* the

evidence. Accordingly, section 727(a)(4) focuses on commission of the act, not conviction for the crime.

plan was proposed in good faith *and* was the debtor's "best effort," section 727(a)(9).

The six years are measured from filing date to filing date. So, if X obtains a bankruptcy discharge on April 5, 1986, in a bankruptcy proceeding filed on December 7, 1985, section 727(a)(9) would not bar X's bankruptcy discharge in a Chapter 7 case filed on December 8, 1991.

Section 727(a)(8) and section 727(a)(9) only limit the availability of a discharge in a Chapter 7 case. They do not affect the debtor's right to file a voluntary petition or creditors' right to file involuntary petitions.

Section 727(a)(10) recognizes certain waivers of discharge. A debtor's waiver will bar discharge only if it is:

(1) in writing, and

(2) executed after the filing of the bankruptcy petition, after the order for relief, and

(3) approved by the court.

Remember that section 727(a) is not self-executing. The bankruptcy trustee or a creditor must object to discharge, section 727(c)(1). The time for and form of objection are governed by Rules 4004 and 7001.

Rule 4004 sets the time for filing complaints objecting to discharge. Any such complaint must be filed within 60 days of the first date set for the meeting of creditors. The court may "for cause" extend the time for filing a complaint objecting to discharge on motion of a party in interest. Such a motion, however, must be filed within the 60 day period.

If any creditor files an objection to discharge, the bankruptcy court tries the issue of the debtor's right to a discharge. Such a trial is an "adversary proceeding" governed by Part VII of the Bankruptcy Rules, Rule 4004(d). If no objection to discharge is filed, and the debtor has not waived his right to a discharge, has not failed to attend the meeting of creditors, and has paid the filing fees, the court shall grant the discharge, section 727(a), Rule 4004(c).

After the court has determined whether to grant a discharge, the court must hold a hearing and the debtor must appear in person, section 524(d). The hearing must be held within 30 days of the order granting or denying a discharge. Rule 4008. At the hearing, the court informs the debtor that a discharge has been granted, or why a discharge has not been granted.

2. Chapter 11

In Chapter 11, the confirmation of the plan operates as a discharge, section 1141(d). The following hypothetical points out the practical significance of this rule: D Corp. owes X $100,000. D Corp.'s Chapter 11 plan proposes to pay X $70,000 over three years. On confirmation, D's only obligation to X is to pay it $70,000 over three years as provided in the plan. The remainder of the debt has been discharged.

The grounds for denying a discharge in a Chapter 11 case are different from the grounds for denying a discharge in a Chapter 7 case. A Chapter 11 debtor will be denied a discharge only if *all* of the following requirements are satisfied:

1. the plan provides for liquidation of all or substantially all of the property of the estate; AND

2. the debtor does not engage in business after consummation of the plan; AND

3. the debtor would be denied a discharge if the case were in Chapter 7, section 1141(d)(3).

The following hypotheticals illustrate the application of section 1141(d)(3).

(1) D Corp. files a Chapter 11 petition. Its Chapter 11 plan provides for the sale of all of its assets, distribution of the proceeds from the sale to creditors, and termination of business operations. D Corp. would not receive a discharge.

(2) D Inc.'s Chapter 11 plan provides for the sale of six stores and continued operations of five stores. If its plan is confirmed, D Inc. will receive a discharge.

(3) D, an individual who owns and operates several small businesses as sole proprietorships, files a Chapter 11 petition. D's Chapter 11 plan provides for the continued operation of these businesses. Because of her "bankruptcy history," D would be

denied a Chapter 7 discharge under section 727(a) (9). If her Chapter 11 plan is confirmed, D will receive a discharge.

3. Chapter 13

In Chapter 13 cases, unlike Chapter 11 cases, the confirmation of the plan does not effect a discharge. In Chapter 13, the question of whether a debtor will receive a discharge cannot be resolved until the debtor either completes her payments under the plan or completes her efforts to make payments under the plan, section 1328.

Section 1328(a) makes mandatory the discharge of a debtor who has completed all of the payments required by his Chapter 13 plan. Section 1328(b) gives the court discretion to grant a "hardship" discharge to a debtor who has failed to make all of the payments required by his Chapter 13 plan. Section 1328(b) lists three factors that the court should consider in exercising this discretion. Section 727 is not included in the list; section 727 is not applicable in Chapter 13 cases.

A discharge under section 1328(b) is not as comprehensive as a discharge under section 1328(a). As indicated on pages 354, 55 infra, more debts are excepted from a section 1328(b) discharge.

B. WHICH OBLIGATIONS ARE AFFECTED BY A BANKRUPTCY DISCHARGE

Even when the debtor receives a discharge, she is not necessarily freed from all of her obligations.

[*300*]

Certain obligations are not affected by a discharge. In determining whether a discharge affects an obligation, it is necessary to consider the following three questions.

1. Is the obligation a "debt" as that term is defined in section 101?

Sections 727(b), 1141(d), and 1328 discharge the debtor from "debts." [4]

2. If so, when did the obligation become a debt?

Subject to limited exceptions, a Chapter 7 discharge reaches only "debts that arose before the date of the order for relief," section 727(b). A Chapter 11 discharge covers debts that "arose before the date of such confirmation," section 1141(d)(1)(A). A Chapter 13 discharge reaches debts "provided for by the plan," section 1328(a), (c). This includes pre-petition debts and post-petition debts that come under section 1305.

3. Is section 523 applicable?

Section 523 excepts certain debts from the operation of a discharge. Section 523 applies in all

---

4. Remember that section 101 defines "debt" in terms of a "claim" and that section 101's definition of "claim" is very broad. Virtually all of a debtor's obligations will come within the term "debt." Current cases are raising a couple of issues in this regard. In the Manville cases, the courts are wrestling with the question of whether people who are developing asbestosis because of exposure to Manville products but are not yet aware of the disease have "claims." In *Kovacs* and other environmental cases, the courts are considering whether clean-up obligations give rise to "debts." The latter question is considered infra at pages 317–318.

Chapter 7 cases, in Chapter 11 cases involving individual debtors, and in Chapter 13 cases in which the debtor receives a section 1328(b) "hardship discharge," sections 727(b), 1141(d)(2), and 1328(c).

The next eight pages cover section 523 and point up the extent to which Chapters 7, 11, and 13 differ with respect to debts affected by a discharge.

1. Chapter 7

In a Chapter 7 case, a discharge relieves a debtor from personal liability for debts that are both

1. incurred prior to the time of the order for relief and

2. not within one of the exceptions to discharge set out in section 523.

It is very important to understand the difference between section 727(a) objections to discharge and section 523(a) exceptions to discharge. If an objection to discharge has been established, all creditors may attempt to collect the unpaid balance of their claims from the debtor. If a creditor establishes an exception to discharge, only that creditor may attempt to collect the unpaid portion of its claim from the debtor; all other pre-petition claims remain discharged. Proof of an objection to discharge benefits all creditors; proof of an exception to discharge benefits only the creditor that establishes the exception.

Section 523(a) sets out ten exceptions to discharge.

Bankruptcy affords very little relief to the delinquent taxpayer. Most taxes are not discharged in bankruptcy. Section 523(a)(1) excepts from the bankruptcy discharge all income and excise taxes for the three tax years immediately preceding bankruptcy.[5] And, taxes more than three years old are non-dischargeable if (a) a return was not filed, or (b) a return was filed within two years of the filing of the bankruptcy petition, or (c) a "fraudulent return" was filed.

Section 523(a)(2) excepts from discharge debts for money, property, or services obtained through fraud, false pretenses, or false representations. Section 523(a)(2) replaces section 17(a)(2) of the Bankruptcy Act of 1898. Section 17(a)(2) was the most frequently invoked exception to discharge, usually by lending institutions, finance companies, credit unions, or credit sellers contending that the debtor obtained money or goods through fraud in that she failed to disclose *all* existing debts in the financial data form she submitted when she applied for credit.

Section 523(a)(2)(B) deals specifically with false financial statements. A creditor seeking an excep-

5. Taxes that are entitled to a priority are excepted from discharge, section 523(a)(1)(A). Section 507(a) provides a priority for taxes for "a taxable year ending on or before the date of the filing of the petition for which a return, if required, is last due, including extensions, after three years before the date of the filing of the petition."

tion to discharge based on the debtor's providing false or incomplete financial information must establish:

(1) materially false written statement respecting the financial condition of the debtor or an "insider";

(2) its *reasonable* reliance on the statement; [6]

(3) the debtor's intent to deceive.

Section 523(a)(2)(B) presents hard problems of proof for a creditor. Merely establishing the falsity of the debtor's financial data will not be sufficient. The creditor will also have to establish its reliance, the reasonableness of such reliance, and, most difficult of all, the debtor's intent to deceive.

6. In consumer loan refinancings, a creditor may have relied on the false financial data only with respect to part of the debt. For example, D owes Friendly Finance $1,200. D wants to borrow an additional $300. To induce, Friendly Finance to lend $300 more, D submits a false financial statement. Friendly Finance combines the $300 of fresh cash with a renewal of the $1,200 of existing debt into a single new note with consolidated payments. If D files a bankruptcy petition, how much of Friendly Finance's $1,500 claim will be excepted from discharge under section 523(a)(2)?

In re Danns, 558 F.2d 114 (2d Cir.1977) excepted only the claim for the new credit saying that there was no evidence that the original loan was renewed in reliance on the false representation. *Danns* does not establish the rule that only the "fresh cash" claim is excepted for discharge. If the creditor is able to establish that it relied on the false financial data in refinancing the original loan, the entire claim will be excepted from discharge.

According to Senator DeConcini, section 523(a)(2)(B) "codifies the reasoning expressed by the Second Circuit in *In re Danns*." Congressional Record, October 6, 1978, S. 17412.

The 1984 amendment to section 523(a)(2) *seems* to add exceptions from discharge for certain obligations for luxury goods and services and for certain cash advances. Note, however, that new section 523(a)(2)(C) provides that such debts are "presumed to be non-dischargeable." How can this presumption be rebutted? Section 523(a)(2)(C) begins with the phrase "for purposes of subparagraph (A) of this subsection." Section 523(a)(2)(A) deals with false representations. When a person buys something on credit, he impliedly represents (1) an ability to pay and (2) an intent to repay. Section 523(a)(2)(C) seems to presume that with respect to the described luxury purchases and cash advances the debtor lacks that ability and/or intent. Accordingly, it would seem that the debtor can avoid section 523(a)(2)(C)'s exception from discharge by showing that he had both the ability and the intent to repay at the time of the transaction.

It is necessary to read section 523(d) together with section 523(a)(2). A creditor who unsuccessfully asserts a section 523(a)(2) exception to the discharge of a consumer debt may be required to pay the debtor's costs including an attorney's fee. Section 523(d)'s test is whether the creditor was "not substantially justified." Even if the position of the creditor was "not substantially justified," it can avoid section 523(d) liability if "special circumstances would make the award unjust."

Unscheduled debts are excepted from discharge by section 523(a)(3). A creditor needs to know that its debtor is involved in a bankruptcy case. Only a creditor that timely files a proof of claim shares in the distribution of the "property of the estate." How does a creditor learn that its debtor is in bankruptcy? Section 521 requires the debtor to file a schedule of liabilities, and the bankruptcy court sends a notice to each creditor on the list. A creditor whose debt was not scheduled will not receive any notice; a creditor that does not receive the notice will not file a proof of claim unless it knows of the bankruptcy case; a creditor that does not file a proof of claim will not be paid from the property of the estate. Accordingly, section 523(a) (3) excepts from discharge a debt not timely scheduled unless the creditor had notice or actual knowledge of the bankruptcy case.

Section 523(a)(4) excepts from bankruptcy discharge liabilities from "fraud or defalcation while acting in a fiduciary capacity." It also makes nondischargeable all embezzlement and larceny liabilities, whether the debtor is a fiduciary or not.

Section 523(a)(5) makes certain domestic obligations nondischargeable: child support and alimony for the maintenance or support of a spouse. The debt may have been incurred in connection with a property settlement so long as it is actually in the nature of alimony, maintenance, or child support. Liabilities which are a part of a property settlement which are not in the nature of alimony, maintenance or child support are dischargeable.

Section 523(a)(6) excepts from the operation of the bankruptcy discharge any debt arising from the debtor's "willful and malicious" injury of person or property. There is considerable confusion as to the meaning of the limiting phrase "willful and malicious." The exact same phrase was used in the exception to discharge provisions in the Bankruptcy Act of 1898. The Supreme Court in Tinker v. Colwell, 193 U.S. 473 (1904), held that those provisions excepted a criminal conversation judgment stating that "a *willful disregard* of what one knows to be his duty, * * * which necessarily causes injury and is done intentionally may be said to be done willfully and maliciously."

Since section 523(a)(6) uses the same language as the Bankruptcy Act of 1898, it would seem that *Tinker v. Colwell* would be authority for the meaning of "willful and malicious" in section 523(a)(6). However, the Committee reports that accompanied a late draft of the Bankruptcy Code expressly reject *Tinker v. Colwell.*

Most of the litigation under section 523(a)(6) involves an unauthorized sale of encumbered property by the debtor. For example, S has a security interest in D's tractor. The security agreement provides that D shall not sell the tractor without prior written authorization from S. D makes an unauthorized sale of the tractor, spends the proceeds, and files for bankruptcy. While this sale is an injury to property for purposes of section 523(a)(6), is it "willful and malicious"?

[*307*]

There is a line of cases that read section 523(a)(6) as requiring a conscious intent to harm the creditor; these cases hold that an unauthorized sale of encumbered property is not "willful and malicious." Other cases interpret section 523(a)(6) as merely requiring that the debtor know that his action will harm the creditor; these cases hold that an unauthorized sale of encumbered property is "willful and malicious."

Fines, penalties, or forfeitures that the debtor owes to a governmental entity are nondischargeable unless the debt is compensation for an actual pecuniary loss or a tax penalty on a dischargeable tax,[7] section 523(a)(7). Section 523(a)(8) contains an exception to discharge for certain educational debts: the debtor's obligations on a student loan made or guaranteed by a governmental unit or a nonprofit institution may be discharged in bankruptcy only if the bankruptcy petition was filed more than five years after the commencement of the repayment period unless the court finds that repayment of the loan will "impose undue hardship on the debtor and the debtor's dependents." Section 523(a)(9) excepts from discharge debts that were or could have been listed in a prior case in which the debtor did not receive a discharge.[8]

---

7. Claims for fines, penalties, and forfeitures have a very low priority in bankruptcy, section 726(a)(4).

8. Compare section 523(a)(9) with section 523(b). Section 523(a)(9) denies dischargeability; section 523(b) provides for dischargeability. Section 523(a)(9) looks to debts from a prior bankruptcy case in which a discharge was withheld (i.e., objec-

Section 523(a)(9) [9], added in 1984, excepts from discharge obligations incurred as a result of the debtor's driving while intoxicated. Note, however, the exact statutory language. It can at least be argued that if D files for bankruptcy before a judgment is entered against her assessing liability for damages caused as a result of her driving while intoxicated, section 523(a)(9) does not apply.

Exceptions to discharge based on section 523(a) (2), (4), or (6) must be asserted in bankruptcy

tion to discharge under section 727) for reasons other than the six-year bar. Section 523(b) applies when there was a prior bankruptcy case in which a discharge was granted but certain debts were excepted from the discharge because of a "time problem" such as the three year tax period or the five year educational loan period. If there is no longer a time period problem, then the debts that were nondischargeable in the earlier case are now dischargeable. Consider the following illustrations:

(1) 8/85, D files a bankruptcy petition.

D denied a discharge because of falsification of records, section 727(a)(3):

Four years later, D again files a bankruptcy petition; Any of the pre-1985 debts still unpaid are excepted from discharge by section 523(a)(9).

(2) 9/85, X files a bankruptcy petition.

X receives a discharge;

X's debt to Y is not discharged because it was not timely scheduled;

9/87, X again files a bankruptcy petition;

If X's debt to Y is still unpaid and is not timely scheduled, the debt can be discharged, section 523(b).

9. That's right, two different provisions with the same subparagraph number.

court.[10] Unless the creditor's motion is timely made, the debt is discharged. When a creditor is relying on section 523(a)(1), (3), (5), (7), (8), or (9), there is no requirement that the matter be heard in bankruptcy court. If no request is filed with the bankruptcy court, the dischargeability issue may arise in connection with the creditor's collection efforts in a non-bankruptcy forum. For example, D owes C $1,000. D files a bankruptcy petition. D fails to list her debt to C on her schedule of liabilities. D receives a bankruptcy discharge. Six months later, C sues D in state court for the $1,000. If D asserts her bankruptcy discharge as a defense, C can counter by asserting a section 523(a)(3) exception to discharge.

10. Rule 4007(c) sets a deadline for filing complaints contending that a particular debt is excepted from discharge by section 523(a)(2), (4), or (6). It is similar to the rule for filing complaints objecting to discharge, i.e., it sets a deadline of 60 days following the first date set for the meeting of creditors. This 60-day time period can be extended if a motion is filed before the expiration of the 60-day period. See Rules 4007(c) and 9006(b)(1). A motion filed after the expiration of the 60-day period will not be successful. The bankruptcy court does *not* have the discretion to extend the time to file a section 523(c) complaint after the expiration of the 60 days. See Rule 9006(b) (3). A creditor or the debtor may at "any time" file a complaint with the bankruptcy court to determine whether a particular debt is excepted from discharge by section 523(a)(1), (3), (5), (7), (8), or (9), Rule 4007(b). If no such complaint is filed with the bankruptcy court, the dischargeability issue may arise in connection with the creditor's collection efforts in a non-bankruptcy forum.

2. Chapter 11

The answer to the question which debts are affected by a discharge is different in Chapter 11 than in Chapter 7 in two significant respects.

First, recall that generally a Chapter 7 discharge is limited to debts that arose before the date of the order for relief, section 727(b). A Chapter 11 discharge reaches debts that arose before the date of confirmation of the plan.

Second, every Chapter 7 discharge is subject to the exceptions to discharge of section 523. In Chapter 11, section 523 only applies if the debtor is an individual, section 1141(d)(2). Section 523 does not apply if the Chapter 11 debtor is a corporation or a partnership.

3. Chapter 13

In Chapter 13 cases, the answer to the question which debts are covered by the discharge depends on the nature of the Chapter 13 discharge. If the debtor has made all of the payments required by the plan and received a discharge under section 1328(a), the discharge affects all debts provided for by the plan except

1. claims for alimony and child support and

[*311*]

2. certain long term obligations such as a house mortgage on which the payments extend beyond the term of the plan, section 1328(a). [11]

As noted earlier, the "hardship" discharge under section 1328(b) is not as comprehensive as the section 1328(a) discharge. If the debtor receives a discharge under section 1328(b), all of the exceptions to discharge in section 523 apply, section 1328(c).

C. EFFECT OF A DISCHARGE

1. What a Discharge Does

a. *Protection from Personal Liability*

A discharge protects the debtor from any further personal liability on discharged debts. Section 524(a) provides that a discharge voids a judgment on discharged debts and enjoins any legal "action" to collect such a debt from the debtor or property of the debtor. A discharge also bars extrajudicial collection "acts" such as dunning letters or telephone calls to collect discharged debts.

11. Note that section 1328(a), unlike section 523(a)(1), does not except unpaid taxes from the operation of a discharge. Section 1328(a) should be read together with section 1322(a)(2) which in essence requires that all Chapter 13 plans provide for full payment of the taxes covered by section 523(a)(1).

b. Protection from Reaffirmation Agreements

A reaffirmation agreement is an agreement to pay a debt dischargeable in bankruptcy. Under contract law principles, an express promise to pay a debt that has been discharged in bankruptcy is enforceable even though there is no consideration or detrimental reliance to support the promise. Section 524(c) and (d) limit the enforceability of reaffirmation agreements by

1. requiring that the agreement be executed before the discharge is granted, section 524(c)(1);

2. giving the debtor a right to rescind, section 524(c)(4);

3. requiring that the agreement include a clear and conspicuous statement of the right to rescind, section 524(c)(2);

4. requiring the agreement be filed with the court, section 524(c)(3);

5. requiring a hearing if the debtor is an individual, section 524(d).

If the debtor was represented by an attorney in negotiating the reaffirmation agreement, section 524(c)(3) also requires an affidavit from the attorney. The affidavit must state that (1) the debtor was "fully informed," (2) the agreement was "voluntary," and (3) the agreement does not impose an "undue hardship." If the debtor was represented by an attorney in negotiating the reaffirmation agreement, the judge does not scrutinize the sub-

[*313*]

stance of the agreement. If an individual debtor was not represented by an attorney in negotiating the reaffirmation agreement, the judge must test the reaffirmation agreement by the standards set out in section 524(a)(6) unless the debt was fully secured by real property.

To review,

1. sections 524(c)(1), (2), (3), and (4) apply to all reaffirmation agreements.

2. section 524(d)'s hearing requirement applies only if the debtor is an individual.

3. section 524(c)(3)'s affidavit requirement applies only if debtors are represented by attorneys in reaffirmation negotiations;

4. section 524(d)'s hearing requirement applies only to individual debtors;

5. section 524(c)(6) applies only to individual debtors not represented by attorneys in negotiating the reaffirmation agreements.

c. *Protection from Discrimination by a Governmental Unit or an Employer*

Subject to very limited exceptions, a governmental unit may not deny a debtor a license or a franchise or otherwise discriminate against a debtor *"solely because"* the debtor (i) filed for bankruptcy, (ii) was insolvent prior to and/or during bankruptcy, or (iii) refuses to pay debts *discharged* by his, her or its bankruptcy, section 525(a). The 1984 amendments added similar protection from discrimination by employers. A private employer cannot fire an employee or "discriminate with respect to employment" *"solely because"* (i) the employee filed for bankruptcy, (ii) was insolvent prior to or during the bankruptcy, or (iii) refuses to pay debts *discharged* by his or her bankruptcy, section 525(b).

The italicized language in the preceding paragraph emphasizes the limitations on the protection from discrimination provided by section 525. If an employer dismisses an employee because of lack of financial ability and responsibility, can it consider the employee's bankruptcy along with other information? If a debtor's educational loans are excepted from discharge, can a state college withhold her transcript until the educational loans are paid?

2. What a Discharge Does *Not* Do

A discharge does not cancel or extinguish debts. It only protects the debtors from further personal liability on the debt.

a. *No Protection of Co-debtors*

Section 524(e) limits the protection of the discharge to the debtor. A bankruptcy discharge does not automatically affect the liability of other parties such as co-debtors or guarantors. For example, the discharge of an insured tortfeasor does not affect the liability of the insurance company.

b. No Effect on Liens

A bankruptcy discharge has no effect on a lien. See, e.g., Long v. Bullard, 117 U.S. 617 (1886); United Presidential Life Ins. Co. v. Barker, 31 B.R. 145 (N.D.Tex.1983). This rule is important with respect to abandoned or exempt property. To illustrate, D owes C $10,000. The debt is secured in part by D's car which is worth $6,000. D files for relief under Chapter 7. The trustee abandons the car to the debtor under section 554. D receives a discharge. The discharge does not extinguish C's security interest. If D is in default, C can repossess the car under section 9–503. The discharge does, however, wipe out C's rights against D personally. If C repossesses and resells the car, C can not obtain a deficiency judgment against D.

3. Discharge and a Debtor's Obligations Under State Law

What is the effect of a bankruptcy discharge on a debtor's obligations under state laws such as environmental laws, consumer protection statutes, and criminal codes? A discharge affects "debts", sections 727(b), 1141(d), 1328. Debt is defined in section 101 as "liability on a claim," and "claim" is defined in section 101 as "right to payment" or "right to equitable remedy for breach."

Numerous reported bankruptcy court decisions have considered the question of whether a restitution obligation imposed as a part of a criminal sentence is a "claim" affected by a bankruptcy discharge. The bankruptcy courts are divided on this question. Compare In re Brown, 39 B.R. 820, 11 B.C.D. 1048 (Bkrtcy.M.D.Tenn.1984), with In re Mead, 41 B.R. 838 (Bkrtcy.Conn.1984).

Recently, the Supreme Court dealt with the effect of a bankruptcy discharge on obligations under state environmental laws. In Ohio v. Kovacs, 105 S.Ct. 705 (1985), the Supreme Court held that the Chapter 7 debtor's obligation to clean-up toxic wastes gave rise to a "claim" within the meaning of the Bankruptcy Code and could be discharged. Kovacs had been the chief executive officer of a corporation that operated a waste disposal site in Ohio. Ohio sued the corporation and Kovacs, alleging violation of the environmental laws. Kovacs later signed a consent judgment, requiring him to remove all industrial wastes from the site within twelve months. Because of Kovacs' noncompliance with the order, the state court appointed a receiver who was directed to take control of all of Kovacs' assets and clean up the site. Kovacs then filed for bankruptcy.

In holding that a bankruptcy discharge relieved Kovacs of his duty to clean up toxic wastes, the Supreme Court emphasized Kovacs' lack of control over the site because of the appointment of a receiver. "What the receiver wanted from Kovacs after bankruptcy was money to defray cleanup costs." 105 S.Ct. at 710. "On the facts before it, and with the receiver in control of the site, we

[*317*]

cannot fault the Court of Appeals for concluding that the cleanup order had been converted into an obligation to pay money, an obligation that was dischargeable in bankruptcy." 105 S.Ct. at 711. "[W]e do not address what the legal consequences would have been had Kovacs been taken into bankruptcy before a receiver was appointed." Id.

CHAPTER XVII

CHAPTER 11

The Bankruptcy Act of 1898 contains four separate chapters for the reorganization of businesses: Chapter VIII which deals with railroad reorganizations; Chapter IX which covers corporate reorganizations; Chapter XI for the arrangement of unsecured debts by corporations, partnerships and individuals; and Chapter XII which is available to non-corporate debtors who own encumbered real estate. Chapter 11 of the Bankruptcy Code replaces these four chapters. [1] It contains some principles from each of the above chapters and some new concepts.

A. COMMENCEMENT OF THE CASE

1. Filing the Petition

A case under Chapter 11 is commenced by the filing of a petition. The petition may be filed by either the debtor or creditors.

Insolvency in not a condition precedent to a voluntary Chapter 11 petition. With two exceptions, any "person" that is eligible to file a voluntary bankruptcy petition under Chapter 7 is also

---

1. Chapter 13 is also available to certain business debtors, i.e., "individuals with a regular income" and less than $100,000 of unsecured debts and $350,000 of secured debts. Chapter 13 is considered infra at pages 344–362.

eligible to file a petition under Chapter 11. The first exception is stockbrokers and commodity brokers: they are eligible for Chapter 7, but not Chapter 11. The second exception is railroads: railroads are eligible for Chapter 11, but not Chapter 7.

If the Chapter 11 petition has been filed by an eligible debtor, no formal adjudication is necessary. The filing of the petition operates as an "order for relief," section 301.

The requirements for a creditor-initiated Chapter 11 case are the same as the requirements for an involuntary Chapter 7 case, section 303. These requirements are discussed supra at pages 153–156.

2. Notifying and Organizing the Creditors

How will creditors learn of a Chapter 11 filing? Sections 521 and 342 provide a partial answer.

Section 521 obligates the debtor to file a list of creditors. Section 342 requires appropriate notice of the order for relief. Rule 2002 governs the content of and time for the notice.

Generally, a creditor whose claim is included on a Chapter 11 debtor's list of creditors will not have to file a proof of claim. Unless the claim is scheduled as disputed, contingent, or unliquidated, a proof of claim is "deemed" filed by section 1111(a). Rules 3001 and 3003 govern the filing of a proof of claim in a Chapter 11 case.

The Bankruptcy Code requires a meeting of creditors, section 341. Section 343 indicates that the debtor is to be examined under oath at the meeting. Section 341(c) prohibits the bankruptcy judge from presiding at or attending the meeting. [2]

In most Chapter 11 cases, the debtor has hundreds if not thousands of creditors. It would not be practical for the Chapter 11 debtor to attempt to negotiate with each creditor individually. Accordingly, section 1102 directs the bankruptcy court to appoint a committee of unsecured creditors as soon as practicable after the order for relief. [3] A pre-petition creditors' committee will be continued if it was "fairly chosen and is representative of the different kinds of claims to be represented," section 1102(b)(1). In the absence of any such pre-petition

---

2. This prohibition is consistent with the Bankruptcy Code's goal of limiting the judge to adjudicatory functions. At a creditors' meeting, the judge might obtain a great deal of extraneous information without the constraints of adversarial trial procedure.

3. Under Chapter XI of the Bankruptcy Act of 1898, creditors' committees were elected, not appointed. Professor King suggests the following explanation and criticism of the change: "Too often in the past, attorneys sought creditor clients to obtain control of the election and to have themselves retained by the committee. Since election frequently served only the purposes of the attorneys, rather than the democratic process, changing to an appointment system was thought to be more appropriate. Unfortunately, section 1102(b)(1) leaves the door open to questionable practices by permitting the continuance of a pre-petition committee if it was fairly chosen and is 'representative of the different kinds of claims to be represented.'" King, *Chapter 11 of the 1978 Bankruptcy Code,* 53 Am.Bankr. L.J. 107, 112 (1979).

committee, the court is instructed to appoint the seven largest unsecured creditors willing to serve, section 1102(b). On request of a party in interest and after notice and hearing, the court may change the membership or size of a committee if it is not sufficiently representative, section 1102(c).

A creditors' committee performs a number of functions. It may:

(1) consult with the trustee or debtor in possession concerning the administration of the case [4]

(2) investigate the debtor's acts and financial condition

(3) participate in the formulation of the plan

(4) request the appointment of a trustee [5]

(5) "perform such other services as are in the interest of those represented," section 1103(c). The creditors' committee may also appear at various hearings as a party in interest, section 1109(b). And, the committee may file a plan in those situations where the debtor ceases to have the exclusive right to do so, section 1121. [6]

B. OPERATION OF THE BUSINESS

Successful rehabilitation of a business under Chapter 11 generally requires the continued opera-

4. Debtor in possession is considered infra at page 323.

5. The appointment of a trustee in a Chapter 11 case is considered infra at pages 323, 324.

6. The question of who may file a Chapter 11 plan is considered supra at pages 319, 320.

tion of the business. No court order is necessary in order to operate the debtor's business after the filing of a Chapter 11 petition. Section 1108 provides: "Unless the court . . . orders otherwise, the trustee may operate the debtor's business."

1. Who Operates the Business

Notwithstanding section 1108's use of the word "trustee," the debtor will remain in control of the business in most Chapter 11 cases. Pre-bankruptcy management will continue to operate the business as a "debtor in possession" unless a request is made for the appointment of a trustee and the court, after notice and a hearing, grants the request.

Section 1104 sets out the grounds for the appointment of a trustee. A trustee is to be appointed if there is cause (fraud, dishonesty, mismanagement, or incompetence) or if the appointment of a trustee is "in the interest of creditors, any equity security holders, and other interests of the estate." Section 1104 specifically instructs the court to disregard the number of shareholders or the amount of assets and liabilities of the debtor in deciding whether to appoint a trustee.

If a trustee is appointed, she must be "disinterested," as defined in section 101(13). The duties of a trustee are enumerated in section 1106. Essentially, the trustee has responsibility for the operation of the business and formulation of the Chapter 11 plan.

If a trustee is not appointed, the court may appoint an "examiner." Section 1104(b) sets out the requirements for the appointment of an examiner:

(1) a trustee was not appointed, *and*

(2) appointment of an examiner was requested by a party in interest, *and*

(3) the debtor's nontrade, nontax, unsecured debts exceed $5,000,000, *or* "such appointment is in the interests of creditors, any equity security holders, and other interests of the estate."

An "examiner" does not operate the business. Rather he investigates the competence and honesty of the debtor and files a report of the investigation, sections 1104(b), 1106(b).

2. Obtaining Credit

One of the first problems confronting a debtor in possession or a Chapter 11 trustee is financing the operation of the business pending the formulation and approval of a plan of rehabilitation. Obtaining credit is essential to almost every Chapter 11 case. Section 364 deals with obtaining credit. It provides a number of inducements to third parties to extend credit to a debtor that has filed a Chapter 11 petition.

A post-petition unsecured credit transaction in the Chapter 11 debtor's "ordinary course of business" automatically has administrative expense priority [7] over pre-petition creditors, section 364(a). The court may, after notice and hearing, provide administrative expense priority for credit transactions that are not in the ordinary course of business, section 364(b).

[Note the two differences between paragraphs (a) and (b) of section 364. First, paragraph (a) applies to ordinary course of business credit transactions; paragraph (b) applies if the credit transaction is not in the ordinary course of the debtor's business. Second, paragraph (b) requires "notice and hearing"; there is no notice and hearing requirement in paragraph (a).]

If priority over pre-petition unsecured creditors is not a sufficient inducement, the bankruptcy court may, after notice and hearing, authorize obtaining credit with:

(1) priority over other administrative expenses, *or*

(2) a lien on the debtor's unencumbered property, *or*

(3) a lien on the debtor's encumbered property, section 364(c).

Section 364(d) is the "last resort" provision. If the debtor is unable to otherwise obtain credit, the court may authorize the debtor to grant its post-petition creditors a "superpriority," i.e., a lien on

7. The priority afforded administrative expenses is considered supra at pages 277–279.

encumbered property that is equal or senior to existing liens. The court may authorize such a "superpriority" only if there is "adequate protection" of the pre-petition secured creditor's interest.

3. Use of Encumbered Property

In the typical Chapter 11 case, most of the personal and real property that the debtor owns at the time of the filing of the Chapter 11 petition is encumbered by liens.

The personal and real property that the debtor acquires after the filing of the Chapter 11 petition is generally protected from pre-petition liens. Property acquired by the debtor after it files a Chapter 11 petition will not be "subject to any lien resulting from any security agreement entered into by the debtor before the commencement of the case," section 552(a). After-acquired property clauses are not recognized in cases under the Bankruptcy Code.

Assume, for example, that Reems Organ Co. files a Chapter 11 petition. If First Bank has contracted for a security interest in "all of Reems' inventory, now owned or hereafter acquired," section 552(a) will limit First's lien to organs manufactured by Reems before the Chapter 11 petition was filed.

First Bank's lien will probably also reach the proceeds from the sale of such pre-petition organs. The Bankruptcy Code does recognize a right to "proceeds, product, offspring, rents, or profits," section 552(b). Under section 552(b), a pre-petition security interest continues to reach proceeds acquired after the bankruptcy petition was filed "except to any extent that the court, after notice and a hearing and based on the equities of the case, orders otherwise." [8]

Section 362(a), considered supra at pages 167, 168 stays a creditor with a lien on the property of a Chapter 11 debtor from repossessing the encumbered property. Section 362(d), considered supra at pages 164–172, provides for relief from the stay in limited situations.

Section 363 empowers the debtor in possession or trustee to continue using, selling, and leasing encumbered property. The interest of the lien creditor is safeguarded by section 363's requirement of "adequate protection," section 363(e). (The concept of "adequate protection" is dealt with by section 361. Section 361 is dealt with on pages 165–172).

Encumbered property that is not "cash collateral" as defined in section 363(a) may be used, sold, or leased in the ordinary course of business without a prior judicial determination of "adequate protection," section 363(c)(1). [9] On "request" of the

8. The "equities of the case" exception covers situations where property of the estate is used in converting the collateral into proceeds. If, for example, Reems incurs costs of $1,000 in selling organs for $7,000, the court may limit First Bank's lien on the proceeds to $6,000.

9. Section 363(c)(1) is applicable only if "the business of the debtor is authorized to be operated." In a Chapter 11 case, the

lien creditor, the court shall condition the use, sale, or lease of encumbered property so as to provide "adequate protection," section 363(e). In other words, if D Department Stores, Inc., D files a Chapter 11 petition and C Bank, C, has a perfected security interest in D's inventory, D may continue to sell inventory in the ordinary course of business. D will not have to obtain court permission in order to make such sales; rather, C will have the burden of requesting the court to prohibit or condition such sales so as to provide "adequate protection" of C's security interest.

Notice and a hearing [10] on the issue of "adequate protection" is required before a Chapter 11 debtor uses, sells, or leases encumbered property in a manner that is *not* in the ordinary course of business, section 363(b). If for example, D, after filing its Chapter 11 petition, decides to discontinue its furniture department and wants to make a bulk sale of its furniture inventory, C must be first given notice and the opportunity for a hearing on the issue of "adequate protection."

Encumbered "cash collateral" may only be used if the court after notice and hearing on adequate protection authorizes such use, section 363(c)(2). "Cash collateral" is defined in section 363(a):

trustee or debtor in possession is authorized to operate the business "unless the court orders otherwise," section 1108.

10. Remember that "notice and hearing" means "such notice as is appropriate in the particular circumstances, and such *opportunity* for a hearing as is appropriate in the particular circumstances," section 102(1)(A).

"cash, negotiable instruments, documents of title, securities, deposit accounts, or other cash equivalents." A bank account is "cash collateral"; accounts receivable are not. Accordingly, D may not withdraw funds from its bank account to pay employees or the utilities without bankruptcy court authorization. And, D may not spend the cash it receives from post-petition sales of inventory without such authorization. Unless the debtor in possession or trustee is authorized to use cash collateral, all such cash collateral coming into the debtor in possession or trustee's possession must be segregated and accounted for, section 363(c)(4).

C. PREPARATION OF THE PLAN OF REHABILITATION

1. Who Prepares the Plan

A Chapter 11 plan may be filed at the same time as the petition or any time thereafter. Unless a trustee has been appointed, the debtor has the exclusive right to file a Chapter 11 plan. "Only the debtor may file a plan until after 120 days after the date of the order for relief under this chapter," section 1121(b). If the debtor does file a plan within this 120 day period, no other plan may be filed during the first 180 days of the case, section 1121(c)(3). [11] Section 1121(d) empowers the

11. Note that the time is to be measured from the date of the order of relief, not the date that the Chapter 11 plan was filed. Assume, for example, that D files a Chapter 11 petition on January 12, and files its Chapter 11 plan on February 22.

bankruptcy court to extend or reduce the 120 day and 180 day periods.

If a trustee is appointed, the trustee, the debtor, a creditor, the creditors' committee, and any other party in interest may file a plan, section 1121(c). More than one plan may be filed. Similarly, if the debtor fails to file a plan and obtain creditor acceptances [12] within the specified time periods, any party in interest may file a plan and more than one plan may be filed.

Regardless of who files the plan, the creditors' committee will probably play a major role in formulating the plan, cf. section 1103(c)(3).

2. Terms of the Plan

Section 1123 governs the provisions of a Chapter 11 plan. Subparagraph (a) sets out the mandatory provisions of a Chapter 11 plan ("shall"); subparagraph (b) of section 1123 indicates the permissive provisions of a Chapter 11 plan ("may").

A Chapter 11 plan may alter the rights of unsecured creditors, secured creditors, and/or shareholders. Section 1123 contemplates that the plan will divide creditors' claims into classes and treat each claim in a particular class the same.

No other plan may be filed until after July 11 (180 days from January 12).

12. Acceptance of a Chapter 11 plan by creditors is considered infra at pages 333–337.

Section 1122 governs classification of claims in Chapter 11 plans. Section 1122(b) authorizes the segregation of all small claims into a single class if "reasonable and necessary for administrative convenience." [13] Section 1122(a) provides the general test for "inclusion"—for determining whether a claim *can* be included in the same class. All claims within a class must be "substantially similar." Section 1122(a) does not provide any test for "exclusion"—for determining whether a claim *must* be included in the same class. No language in section 1122 expressly limits the discretion of the drafter of the plan in placing "substantially similar" claims in different classes. To illustrate, assume that X, Y, and Z are creditors of Chapter 11 debtor, D. If D's plan places all three creditors' claims in the same class, section 1122(a) controls. It is clear from section 1122(a) that D cannot place the claims of X, Y, and Z in a single class unless all three claims are "substantially similar." If, however, D's Chapter 11 plan places each creditor's claim in a separate class, section 1122(a) does not control. What limits D's discretion in placing claims in a separate class is not clear from the Bankruptcy Code.

13. A Chapter 11 debtor will often find it advantageous to pay small claims in full. A class of claims that receives full cash payment on the effective date of the plan is not "impaired," section 1124(3)(A). A class that is not impaired under a plan is deemed to have accepted the plan, and solicitation of acceptances with respect to such class is not required, section 1126(f).

3. Funding for the Plan

Compliance with the requirements of section 1123 is not the difficult part of preparing a plan for the rehabilitation of a business under Chapter 11. Rather, the hard questions are how much will creditors be offered by the plan and how will the plan be effectuated.

Chapter 11 debtors often use money borrowed from third parties to make distributions to creditors under Chapter 11 plans. Sale of assets is another major source for Chapter 11 payments.

A Chapter 11 plan may provide for the sale of all or substantially all of the debtor's assets, section 1123(b)(4). Often, a Chapter 11 plan offers creditors the debtor's debt or equity securities, rather than cash. Generally, the issuance of a security requires expensive and time-consuming federal and state registration. Section 1145(a)(1) exempts the issuance of the debtor's securities under a Chapter 11 plan from federal and state registration requirements. A creditor's resale of a security received under a Chapter 11 is also exempted from federal and state registration requirements, section 1145(b). [14]

14. Section 4(1) of the Securities Act of 1933 states in essence that transactions by any person who is not an "issuer, underwriter, or dealer" need not be registered. Section 1145(b)(2) provides an exemption to creditors who resell securities obtained under a Chapter 11 plan by indicating that such creditors are not "underwriters."

D. ACCEPTANCE

1. Disclosure

"The premise underlying * * * Chapter 11 * * * is the same as the premise of the securities law. If adequate disclosure is provided to all creditors and stockholders whose rights are to be affected, then they should be able to make an informed judgment of their own, rather than having the court or the Securities and Exchange Commission inform them in advance whether the proposed plan is a good plan," H.R. 95–595, p. 226. Accordingly, the bankruptcy court does not review a Chapter 11 plan before it is submitted to creditors and shareholders for vote. Instead, the bankruptcy court reviews the information provided to creditors and shareholders to insure that their judgment is an "informed judgment."

Section 1125 requires full disclosure before postpetition solicitation of acceptances of a Chapter 11 plan. Creditors and shareholders must be provided:

(1) a copy of the plan or a summary of the plan, and

(2) "a written disclosure statement approved, after notice and a hearing, by the court as containing adequate information."

Section 1125(b).

[*333*]

"Adequate information" is defined in section 1125(a) as information which it is "reasonably practicable" for this debtor to provide to enable a "hypothetical reasonable investor" who is typical of the holders of the claims or interests to make an informed judgment on the plan. What constitutes "adequate information" thus depends on the circumstances of each case—on factors such as (1) the condition of the debtor's books or records, (2) the sophistication of the creditors and stockholders, and (3) the nature of the plan.

2. Who Votes

Both creditors and shareholders vote on Chapter 11 plans. According to section 1126(a), creditors with claims "allowed under section 502" and shareholders with interests "allowed under section 502" vote on Chapter 11 plans. The statutory requirement of "allowed under section 502" is generally satisfied by the Bankruptcy Code's "double-deeming." In a Chapter 11 case, section 1111 deems filed a claim or interest that is scheduled and is not shown as disputed, contingent, or unliquidated. And, section 502 deems allowed any claim or interest that is filed and not objected to by a party in interest.

Statutory "deeming" also eliminates voting by two classes of claims or interests. First, if a class is to receive nothing under the plan, it is deemed to have rejected the plan, and its vote need not be solicited, section 1126(g). Second, if a class is not "impaired" under the plan, the class is deemed to have accepted the plan and again its vote need not be solicited, section 1126(f).

a. Impairment of Claims

The concept of "impairment" is unique to Chapter 11. Section 1124 is entitled "Impairment of Claims or Interests." Under section 1124, a class of claims or interests is impaired unless

(1) the legal, equitable, and contractual rights of the holder are left "unaltered;"

[If the plan in any way changes the rights of the holder, it alters and thus impairs the holder. It is not necessary to determine whether the change adversely affects the holder.] *or*

(2) the only alteration of legal, equitable, or contractual rights is reversal of an acceleration on default by curing the default and reinstating the debt; *or*

(3) cash payment to (A) a creditor on the effective date of the plan is equal to the allowed amount of the claim; *or* (B) cash payment to a shareholder on the effective date of the plan is equal to the greater of the share's redemption price and its liquidation preference.

b. 1111(b) Elections

Section 1111(b), like section 1124, deals with a concept that is unique to Chapter 11. Generally, a creditor whose debt is only partially secured has two claims—a secured claim measured by the value of its collateral and an unsecured claim for the remainder, section 506(a). Assume, for example, that C's $100,000 claim against D is secured by real property owned by D that is valued at $70,000. Under section 506(a), C has a $70,000 secured claim and a $30,000 unsecured claim. Under section 1111(b), C can elect to have a $100,000 secured claim and no unsecured claim.[15]

Let's use the hypothetical in the previous paragraph to consider the advantages and the disadvantages of a section 1111(b) election:

Advantages of section 1111(b) election:

(1) If C makes the section 1111(b) election, its secured claim will be impaired under section 1124(3), considered above, unless the Chapter 11 plan provides for a cash payment of $100,000.

(2) If C makes the section 1111(b) election, section 1129(b), considered infra at pages 340, 341, requires that C be paid at least $100,000 under the plan.

Disadvantages of section 1111(b) election:

(1) If C makes the section 1111(b) election, it will not be able to vote its $30,000 unsecured claim.

---

15. Note that section 1111(b) provides for election by classes of secured claims, not by individual holders of secured claims. Generally, each holder of a secured claim will be in a separate class. Note also that some classes of secured claims are not eligible to make a section 1111(b) election.

(2) If C makes the section 1111(b) election, it will not participate in the distribution to holders of unsecured claims.

3. Needed Majorities

A class of claims has accepted a plan when more than one half in number and at least two thirds in amount of the allowed claims actually voting on the plan approve the plan, section 1126(c). The following hypothetical illustrates the application of section 1126(c):

D files a Chapter 11 petition. D's schedule of creditors shows 222 different creditors and $1,000,000 of debt. D's Chapter 11 plan divides creditors into four classes. Class 3 consists of 55 creditors, with claims totalling $650,000. Only 39 of the creditors in Class 3 vote on the plan. Their claims total $450,000. If at least 20 Class 3 creditors (more than ½ of 39) with claims totalling at least $300,000 (²/₃ of 450,000) vote for D's plan, the plan has been accepted by Class 3.

A class of interests has accepted a plan when at least two thirds in amount of the allowed interests actually voting on the plan approve the plan, section 1126(d).

E. CONFIRMATION

Section 1128 requires that the bankruptcy court hold a hearing on confirmation and give parties in interest notice of the hearing so that they might raise objections to confirmation.

While it is possible for more than one plan to be filed and accepted, only one plan may be confirmed. If more than one plan meets the confirmation standards of section 1129, the court "shall consider the preferences of creditors and equity security holders in determining which plan to confirm," section 1129(c).

Subparagraphs (a), (b), and (d) of section 1129 contain the confirmation standards. Section 1129(d) prohibits confirmation of a plan whose "principal purpose" is the avoidance of taxes or the avoidance of registration of securities. Subparagraph (a) and (b) are discussed below.

1. Standards for Confirmation

a. Plans Accepted by Every Class

Subject to the limited exception of section 1129(c) and 1129(d), a plan that has been accepted by every class of claims and every class of interests must be confirmed by the bankruptcy court if the 11 enumerated requirements of section 1129(a) are satisfied. Section 1129(b) does not apply to plans that have been accepted by every class of claims and every class of interests.

Most of the requirements of section 1129(a) are easy to understand, easy to apply. Two of the requirements are somewhat complex. Section 1129(a)(7) creates a "best interests of creditors" test. It requires that each dissenting member of a class—even dissenting members of classes that approve the plan—receive at least as much under the plan as it would have received in a Chapter 7 liquidation.[16]

Section 1129(a)(9) provides special treatment for priority claims. A holder of an administrative expense claim or a claim for certain postpetition expenses in an involuntary case must be paid in cash on the effective date of the plan unless the *claim holder* otherwise agrees, section 1129(a)(9) (A). Wage claims, claims for fringe benefits, and certain claims of consumer creditors must be paid in cash on the effective date of the plan unless the *class* agrees to accept deferred cash payments that have a present value equal to the amount of the claims, section 1129(a)(9)(B). Each priority tax claim must receive deferred cash payments that have a present value equal to the amount of the claim, section 1129(a)(9)(C).[17]

b. *Plans Accepted by Less Than Every Class*

Plans accepted by less than every class can be confirmed only if the additional requirements of

16. Section 1129(a)(7) looks to the value of the distribution under the plan as of the effective date of the plan. If for example the plan calls for payment to Creditor X of $100 a month for 20 months, the value of the payment to X "as of the effective date of the plan" is clearly less than $2,000.

17. Section 1129(a)(9)(C) fails to reflect the change in numbering in section 507. It refers to 507(a)(6); it should refer to section 507(a)(7).

section 1129(b) are satisfied. Section 1129(b) requires that

    1. at least one impaired class of claims has accepted the plan;

    2. the plan does not discriminate unfairly;

    3. the plan is fair and equitable.

Section 1129(b)(2) sets out three different tests for determining whether a plan is "fair and equitable" depending on whether the dissenting class is a secured claim, unsecured claim, or ownership interest.

The section 1111(b) election, considered supra at page 335, affects whether a Chapter 11 plan is fair and equitable to a holder of a secured claim. Section 1129(b)(2)(A)(i) requires that (1) the holder of the secured claim retain its lien, (2) the payments at least equal the amount of the allowed secured claim, and (3) the payments have a present value equal to the value of the collateral. The following hypothetical points out the relationship between these three requirements and section 1111(b).

Assume that D owes C $100,000. C has a lien on D's equipment that has a value of $85,000. D files for Chapter 11 relief. C makes a section 1111(b) election. C does not accept the plan. The plan will be fair and equitable with respect to C if (1) it provides that the security interest will remain on D's equipment to secure the entire $100,000 debt, (2) C is paid at least $100,000 over the life of the plan, and (3) the deferred payments to be made to

C under the plan have a present value of at least $85,000.

The "fair and equitable" standard is satisfied with respect to a dissenting class of unsecured claims if junior claims and interests neither receive nor retain anything, section 1129(b)(2)(B)(ii). To illustrate, D Corp. files for Chapter 11 relief. Its Chapter 11 plan provides for payment of 70 cents on the dollar to a class of holders of unsecured claims and for its stockholders to retain their D Corp. stock. This plan is not "fair and equitable" under section 1129(b)(2)(B)(ii). Stockholders are junior to the dissenting class and stockholders are retaining property under the plan.

A comprehensive consideration of the other "fair and equitable" provisions in section 1129(b) is beyond the scope of this basic student text.

2. Effect of Confirmation

After confirmation of a Chapter 11 plan, the debtor's performance obligations are governed by the terms of the plan. The provisions of a confirmed Chapter 11 plan bind not only the debtor but also the debtor's creditors and shareholders "whether or not such creditor, equity security holder, or general partner has accepted the plan," section 1141(a). Subject to limitations noted below, confirmation of a Chapter 11 plan operates as a discharge, section 1141(d). The following hypothetical illustrates the possible application of section 1141(a) and section 1141(d).

D's confirmed Chapter 11 plan provides for monthly payments to creditors. Each creditor in Class 2 is to receive 5% of its claim each month for 15 months. After making two payments under the plan, D defaults. At the time of the filing of the petition D owed C $10,000. C has received $1,000 under the plan. C's claim against D is now limited to $6,500. (75% × $10,000 – 1,000).

Chapter 11 withholds discharge from some debtors and some debts. The plan may limit discharge, section 1141(d)(1). The order of confirmation may limit discharge, section 1141(d)(1). The exceptions to discharge in section 523 are applicable to individual debtors, section 1141(d)(2). The objections to discharge in section 727 are applicable only if (1) the plan provides for the sale of all or substantially all of the debtor's property, *and* (2) the debtor does not engage in business after the consummation of the plan, section 1141(d)(3).

The following chart compares Chapter 11 discharge rules with those of Chapter 7, considered supra at pages 293–318.

	Chapter 7	Chapter 11
Corporations, Partnerships	Not eligible for discharge	Eligible for discharge unless plan is a liquidating plan and the debtor terminates business
Section 523	Applicable to individuals	Applicable to individuals

CONFIRMATION

	Chapter 7	Chapter 11

Grounds for withholding discharge	Section 727	1. provision in plan,
		2. provision in confirmation order,
		3. Section 727 *if*
		  a. liquidating plan, and
		  b. termination of business operations

CHAPTER XVIII
CHAPTER 13

A. COMMENCEMENT OF THE CASE

Chapter 13 of the Bankruptcy Code replaces Chapter XIII of the Bankruptcy Act of 1898. Chapter XIII was limited to a "wage earner," i.e., "an individual whose principal income is derived from wages, salary, or commissions."

Chapter 13 is open to more debtors. Subject to limited exceptions,[1] the source of income is not an eligibility test. A debtor may file for Chapter 13 relief if she:

(1) *is an individual, and*

[Chapter 13 is not available to corporations or partnerships.]

(2) *has a "regular income," and*

[The phrase "individual with a regular income" is statutorily defined in section 101(27) as "an individual whose income is sufficiently stable and regular to enable such individual to make payments under a plan under Chapter 13 of this title."]

---

1. Neither a stockbroker nor a commodity broker may file a petition under Chapter 13, section 109(e).

(3) *has fixed unsecured debts of less than $100,000 and fixed secured debts of less than $350,000,* section 109(e).

[Note that the debt limitation does not include contingent, unliquidated claims. For example, Dr. Frank Burns is sued for $400,000 for malpractice on April 4. He could still file a Chapter 13 petition on April 5.]

Chapter 13 is similar to Chapter 7 and Chapter 11 in that the case begins with the filing of a bankruptcy petition, section 301. Chapter 13 is different from Chapter 7 and Chapter 11 in that only the debtor may file a Chapter 13 petition. There are no involuntary, i.e., creditor-initiated, Chapter 13 cases.

The filing of a Chapter 13 petition triggers the automatic stay of section 362. Section 362 is discussed supra at pages 159–172. A Chapter 13 petition also stays civil collection activities directed against codebtors of the individual who filed the petition, section 1301.

B. CODEBTOR STAY

Section 1301 restrains a creditor from attempting to collect a debt from the codebtor of a Chapter 13 debtor.

The following hypothetical illustrates the application of section 1301's codebtor stay: D borrows money from C to buy a pair of contact lenses. Her mother, M signs the note as a comaker. D later incurs financial problems and files a Chapter 13 petition. Section 362 stays C from attempting to collect from D; section 1301 stays C from attempting to collect from M.

Section 1301's stay of collection activities directed at codebtors is applicable only if:

(1) the debt is a consumer debt, and

(2) the codebtor is not in the credit business.

This codebtor stay automatically terminates when the case is closed, dismissed, or converted to Chapter 7 or 11.

Section 1301(c) sets out three grounds for relief from the codebtor stay. Section 1301(c) requires notice and hearing and requires the court to grant relief if any of the three grounds are established.

First, the stay on collection from the codebtor will be lifted if the codebtor, not the Chapter 13 debtor, received the consideration for the claim, section 1301(c)(1). For example, if in the above hypothetical, M, not D, filed for Chapter 13 relief, C could petition for relief under section 1301(c)(1) so that it could attempt to collect from D. Section 1301(c)(1) also covers the situation in which the Chapter 13 debtor is merely an accommodation endorser.

Second, when the Chapter 13 plan has been filed, a creditor may obtain relief from the codebtor stay to the extent that "the plan filed by the debtor proposes not to pay such claim," section 1301(c)(2). Assume, for example, that D still owes C $200. D's

Chapter 13 plan proposes to pay each holder of an unsecured claim 70 cents on the dollar. As soon as the plan is filed, D can obtain relief from the stay so that it can obtain $60 from M. A motion to lift the stay under section 1301(c)(2) is deemed granted unless the debtor or co-debtor files a written objection within 20 days, section 1301(d).

Third, section 1301(c)(3) requires the court to grant relief from the codebtor stay to the extent that "such creditor's interest would be irreparably harmed by continuation of such stay." The running of a state statute of limitations is not a basis for relief under section 1301(c)(3). Section 108(c) guarantees the creditor at least 30 days after the termination of the stay to file a state collection action against the codebtor.

C. TRUSTEES

There will be a trustee appointed in every Chapter 13 case, section 1302(a). In many districts, the bankruptcy judge appoints a standing trustee who serves as trustee in every Chapter 13 case, section 1302(d).

Remember that in a number of pilot districts, trustees are appointed by United States trustees, section 1501.[2] In such a district, the United States trustee appoints the standing trustee, section 151302. In such a district, the United States trus-

2. The United States trustee is considered at page 148 supra.

CHAPTER 13

tee serves as trustee in Chapter 13 cases if there is
no standing trustee.

The trustee in a Chapter 13 case is an active
trustee. She has all of the avoidance powers discussed supra in Chapter XI.[3] Section 1302 imposes
a number of duties on a trustee in a Chapter 13
case. Operation of the debtor's business is *not* one
of the duties there enumerated. If a debtor engaged in business files a Chapter 13 petition, section 1304(b) contemplates that the business will be
operated by the debtor, not by the trustee, "unless
the court orders otherwise."

3. The Bankruptcy Code does not clearly indicate whether a
Chapter 13 trustee can assert the avoidance provisions. The
statutory arguments for a Chapter 13 trustee being able to
avoid preferences and other pre-bankruptcy transfers are

1. section 103 which indicates that provisions in chapter 5
such as section 547 are applicable in Chapters 7, 11, and 13;

2. use of the word "trustee" in section 547 and the other
avoidance provisions.

The statutory argument for a Chapter 13 trustee *not* being
able to avoid preferences and other pre-bankruptcy transfers
focuses on section 1302(b)'s exclusion of section 704(1). If a
Chapter 13 trustee is not empowered to "collect the property of
the estate," is she able to avoid pre-bankruptcy transfers?

An excellent law review article by Professor Ralph Peeples
considers this question and properly concludes that a Chapter
13 trustee should be able to assert the avoidance provisions.
Peeples, *Five Into Thirteen: Lien Avoidance in Chapter 13*, 61
N.C.L.Rev. 849 (1983).

D. PREPARATION OF THE CHAPTER 13 PLAN

Only a debtor may file a Chapter 13 plan, section 1321. The court may dismiss a Chapter 13 case or convert it to Chapter 7 for "failure to file a plan *timely* under section 1321 of this title," section 1307(c)(3). The Code leaves the question of the meaning of "timely"—of how many days the debtor has to file such a plan—to the rules.

Section 1322 governs the contents of a Chapter 13 plan. Subsection (a) of section 1322 specifies what the plan must provide; subsection (b) specifies what the plan may provide. A Chapter 13 plan must provide for full payment in cash of all claims entitled to priority under section 507 [4] unless the holder of the claim otherwise agrees, section 1322(a)(2). A Chapter 13 plan may provide for less than full payment to other unsecured claims. It may not, however, arbitrarily pay some holders of unsecured claims less than others. Rather, the plan must either treat all unsecured claims the same or classify claims and provide for the same treatment of each unsecured claim within a particular class, sections 1322(a)(3), 1322(b)(4).

A Chapter 13 plan may also modify the rights of most holders of secured claims. It may modify the rights of creditor *A* who has a security interest on the Chapter 13 debtor's car. It may modify the

---

4. The priority rules of section 507 are considered supra at pages 278–284.

rights of Creditor *B* who has a mortgage on the Chapter 13 debtor's store. It may not, however, modify the rights of Creditor *C* who has mortgage *only* [5] on the Chapter 13 debtor's principal residence, section 1322(b)(2).

In the typical Chapter 13 case, the source of the payments proposed by the plan will be the debtor's wages. This is not, however, a statutory requirement. Section 1322(a)(1) only requires that the plan provide for submission of "such portion of future earnings * * * of the debtor to the supervision and control of the trustee as is necessary for the execution of the plan." Payments under the plan may also be funded by sale of property of the estate, section 1322(b)(8).

Section 1322(c) limits the payment period under a Chapter 13 plan to three years except that the court may approve a payment period of as long as five years.

E. CONFIRMATION OF THE CHAPTER 13 PLAN

In Chapter 13, creditors do not vote on the plan. Chapter 13 requires only court approval. The standards for judicial confirmation of a Chapter 13 plan are set out in section 1325.

Section 1325(a)(1) requires that the plan satisfy the provisions of Chapter 13 and other applicable

---

5. Note the word "only" in section 1322(b)(2). If C loaned D $100,000 and obtained a mortgage on both D's residence and D's store, it would seem that the plan could modify D's rights.

bankruptcy law requirements. Section 1325(a)(2) conditions confirmation on payment of the $60 filing fee. Section 1325(a)(3) sets out a "good faith" standard.

Section 1325(a)(4) protects the holders of unsecured claims by imposing a "best interests of creditors" test: the present value of the proposed payments to a holder of an unsecured claim must be at least equal to the amount that the creditor would have received in a Chapter 7 liquidation.[6]

Section 1325(a)(4) now needs to be read together with section 1325(b) which was added in 1984. New section 1325(b) requires that a Chapter 13 plan either provide for payment in full of all claims or commit all of the debtor's "disposable

---

6. The following hypothetical illustrates the practical significance of the "present value" language in section 1325(a)(4). Assume these facts:

D owes C $1,000;

D files a Chapter 13 petition;

If D had filed a Chapter 7 petition, the sale of the property of the estate would have yielded a sufficient sum to pay all priority creditors in full and pay unsecured creditors like C 36¢ on the dollar;

D's Chapter 13 petition proposes to pay C $10 a month for 36 months.

This plan does not satisfy the requirement of section 1325(a)(4). Payment of $360 over a thirty-six month period does not have a "present value" of $360.

This hypothetical is probably somewhat unrealistic. In the typical Chapter 7 case, an unsecured creditor would receive little if anything. Accordingly, in the typical Chapter 13 case, section 1325(a)(4) will be easily satisfied.

income" for three years to payments under the plan. The phrase "disposable income" is defined in section 1325(b)(2). The following hypothetical illustrates the application of section 1325(b). D files a Chapter 13 petition. She earns $1,200 a month. $900 of the $1,200 is "reasonably necessary" to support and maintain D and her dependents. D's Chapter 13 plan must commit $300 a month for 36 months.[7]

Section 1325(a)(5), considered supra at pages 259–260, protects the holders of secured claims "provided for by the plan" by requiring one of the following:

(A) acceptance of the plan by such a creditor; *or*

(B) continuation of the lien and proposed payments to such a creditor of a present value that at least equals the value of the collateral; *or*

(C) surrender of the collateral to the creditor.

Section 1325(a)(6) requires a determination of ability to perform; it requires that the debtor "will be able to make all payments under the plan and to comply with the plan."

A confirmed Chapter 13 plan is binding on the debtor and all of his creditors, section 1327(a).

---

7. What if D's income or living expenses change so that her "disposable income" changes? Section 1325(b) seems to require the court to determine what D's disposable income will be over the next three years. If there is an unanticipated change, then the debtor or a creditor can request a modification of the plan under section 1329; section 1329 is considered infra at page 353.

Unless the plan or the order confirming the plan otherwise provides, confirmation of a plan vests all of the "property of the estate" in the debtor free and clear of "any claim or interest of any creditor provided for by the plan," section 1327(c).

After confirmation, the plan is put into effect with the debtor generally making the payments provided in the plan to a Chapter 13 trustee who acts as a disbursing agent.

A Chapter 13 plan can be modified after confirmation. Section 1329 expressly provides for post-confirmation modification on request of the debtor, the trustee, or the holder of an unsecured claim. The 1984 amendments added the language that expressly empowers an unsecured creditor to request modification of a Chapter 13 plan. This suggests that if the income of a Chapter 13 debtor increases after she has obtained confirmation of her plan but before she completes the payments under the plan, a creditor can request that payments under the plan be increased.

F. DISCHARGE

After completion of the payments provided for in the Chapter 13 plan, the debtor receives a discharge, section 1328(a). A section 1328(a) discharge is *not* subject to all of the exceptions from discharge set out in section 523. The only debts excepted from a section 1328(a) discharge are:

(1) allowed claims not provided for by the plan,

(2) certain long-term obligations specifically provided for by the plan,[8] and

(3) claims for alimony and child support.

The bankruptcy court may grant a discharge in a Chapter 13 case even though the debtor has not completed payments called for by the plan. Section 1328(b) empowers the bankruptcy court to grant a "hardship" discharge if:

(1) the debtor's failure to complete the plan was due to circumstances for which she "should not justly be held accountable;" *and*

(2) the value of the payments made under the plan to each creditor at least equals what that creditor would have received under Chapter 7; *and*

(3) modification of the plan is not "practicable."

A section 1328(b) "hardship" discharge is not as comprehensive as a section 1328(a) discharge. A "hardship" discharge is limited by all of the section 523(a) exceptions to discharge, section 1328(c).

---

8. A Chapter 13 plan may not provide for a payment period of more than five years, section 1322(c). Some of the debtor's debts may have a longer payment period. Assume, for example, that D buys a new mobile home on January 10, 1985. She obtains financing from B Bank; the note provides for payments of $300 a month for 120 months. On March 30, 1986, D files a Chapter 13 petition. Her Chapter 13 plan provides for payments of $300 a month to B Bank for the 36 months of the plan, cf. section 1322(b)(5). On completion of the plan, D's obligation to B Bank for the remaining payments is excepted from discharge by section 1328(a)(1).

If a debtor receives a discharge under either section 1328(a) or section 1328(b), he may not receive a discharge in a Chapter 7 case filed within six years of the date that the Chapter 13 case was filed unless payments under the plan totalled at least 70% of the allowed unsecured claims, and the plan was the "debtor's best effort," section 727(a) (9). A discharge under section 1328(a) or section 1328(b) does not affect the debtor's right to future Chapter 13 relief.

G. DISMISSAL AND CONVERSION

A debtor who files a Chapter 13 petition may change his mind. He may at any time request the bankruptcy court to dismiss the case or convert it to a case under Chapter 7, section 1307(a), (b).

The bankruptcy court may also dismiss a Chapter 13 case or convert it to a case under Chapter 7 on request of a creditor. The statutory standard for such creditor-requested conversion or dismissal is "for cause." Section 1307(c) sets out eight examples of "cause."

Section 1307(d) gives a bankruptcy court the power to convert from Chapter 13 to Chapter 11 before confirmation of the plan on request of a party in interest and after notice and hearing. Section 1307(e) protects farmers from creditor-requested conversions from Chapter 13 to Chapter 7 or Chapter 11.

Converting a case from Chapter 13 to Chapter 7 raises questions about the treatment of post-petition claims and post-petition property. For example, assume that D files a Chapter 13 petition on January 15 and converts to Chapter 7 on April 5. What about the claims against D that arise from January 15th to April 5th? According to sections 1305 and 348(d), claims arising in the period between filing of the Chapter 13 petition and conversion to Chapter 7 are allowable claims and cases have consistently so held.

The treatment of property acquired between January 15th and April 5th is less clear. Is it property of the estate? If D had filed a Chapter 7 petition, the property that D acquired after January 15th would not be property of the estate, section 541. However, property acquired after the filing of a Chapter 13 case is property of the estate under section 1306. Under section 348, the conversion from 13 to 7 does not "effect a change in the date of the filing of the petition." It is not clear, however, whether section 348 means that D should be regarded as having filed a Chapter 13 case on January 15th or a Chapter 7 case on that date. Cases are divided as to whether property acquired in the gap between filing for Chapter 13 relief and conversion to Chapter 7 is property of the estate.

H. COMPARISON OF CHAPTERS 7 AND 13

Only a debtor may file a Chapter 13 petition. Each debtor who files a Chapter 13 petition could instead have filed a Chapter 7 petition. Before

COMPARISON OF CHAPTERS 7 AND 13

filing, the debtor's attorney should carefully compare Chapters 7 and 13. The following chart provides such a comparison:

	Chapter 7	Chapter 13
1. Automatic Stay	Automatic stay of section 362 protects the debtor from creditors' collection efforts	Automatic stay of section 362 protects the debtor from creditor's collection efforts. Automatic stay of section 1301 protects co-debtors
2. Loss of Property	"Property of the estate" as described in section 541 is distributed to creditors	Except as provided in the plan or in the order of confirmation, debtor keeps "property of the estate"
3. Availability of Discharge	Section 727(a) lists ten grounds for objection to discharge	Section 727 is inapplicable. Discharge depends on completion of payments required by the plan, section 1328(a). Section 1328(b) provides for a "hardship" discharge to a debtor who makes some but not all payments required by the plan

	Chapter 7	Chapter 13
4. Debts Excepted From Discharge	Section 523(a) excepts nine classes of claims from the operation of a discharge	A section 1328(a) discharge is only subject to the exception for alimony and child support. A section 1328(b) discharge is subject to all of section 523(a)'s exceptions to discharge
5. Effect on Future Chapter 7 Relief	A debtor who receives a discharge in a Chapter 7 case may not obtain a discharge in another Chapter 7 case for six years	A Chapter 13 discharge does not affect the availability of discharge in a future Chapter 7 case if the Chapter 13 plan was the debtor's "best effort" and paid 70% of all general claims
6. Whether debtor's post-petition earnings are property of the estate	No, section 541(a)(6)	Yes, section 1306
7. Debtor's ability to terminate the case	"Only for cause", section 707	"On request of the debtor at any time," section 1307(b)

	Chapter 7	Chapter 13
8. Relief from taxes	Ability to satisfy taxes not a condition to discharge; most taxes unaffected by discharge	Subject to limited exceptions, plan must provide for full payment of all taxes, section 1322(a)(2); payment of taxes may be deferred over five year life of plan; no exception from discharge
9. Amount required to be distributed to holders of claims	Property of the estate, section 541	Plan controls; confirmation requires that holders of claims receive at least as much as they would in 7 and that plan commits all disposable income, sections 1325(a)(4); 1325 (b).

I. COMPARISON OF CHAPTERS 11 AND 13

Any debtor who files a Chapter 13 petition could instead have filed a Chapter 11 petition. Accordingly, before filing, the debtor's attorney should carefully compare Chapters 11 and 13. Chapter 13 would seem to offer an eligible debtor [9] the following advantages:

9. Remember that Chapter 13 is not available to all debtors. Corporations and partnerships are not eligible for Chapter 13,

1.   Codebtors are protected by the automatic stay, section 1301.

2.   A business debtor desiring to continue operating his or her business is probably less likely to be replaced by a trustee in Chapter 13 than in Chapter 11.[10]

3.   Only the debtor may file a plan in Chapter 13.

4.   Chapter 13 makes no provision for creditors' committees.

5.   Chapter 13 does not require creditor acceptance of a plan of rehabilitation.

6.   The objections to discharge set out in section 727 do not apply in Chapter 13; these objections do apply in Chapter 11 liquidation cases, section 1141(d)(3).

7.   A Chapter 13 discharge can be more comprehensive than a Chapter 11 discharge.   If a debtor completes her payments under the Chapter 13 plan and receives a discharge under section 1328(a), she will not be affected by the exceptions to discharge in section 523.   If an individual debtor receives a Chapter 11 dis-

and individuals have to meet the $100,000/$350,000 debt limits of section 109(e).

10.   Section 1303 sets out the duties of a Chapter 13 trustee. It does not mention operating the business.   The phrase "Unless the court orders otherwise" in section 1304(b) is, however, statutory authority for the court turning over the operation of the debtor's business to the Chapter 13 trustee.

charge, she will be affected by the exceptions to discharge in section 523, section 1141(d)(2).

There are, however, also reasons for an individual debtor to use Chapter 11 rather than Chapter 13:

1. In Chapter 11, the plan can modify the payment obligations on the debtor's home mortgage, section 1123(b)(1). A Chapter 13 plan cannot modify the payment obligations on the debtor's home mortgage, section 1322(b)(2).

2. Classification of claims in a Chapter 13 plan cannot "discriminate unfairly," section 1322(b)(1). Classification of claims in a Chapter 11 plan is subject to a "discriminate unfairly" test only if the requisite majority of that class fails to accept the plan, sections 1122, 1129(b)(1).

3. A Chapter 13 plan must either pay all claims in full or commit all of the debtor's "disposable income" for the next three years to the plan, section 1325(b). There is no comparable requirement in Chapter 11.

4. A debtor receives a discharge "earlier" in Chapter 11 than in Chapter 13. A debtor receives a Chapter 11 discharge when her plan is confirmed, section 1141(d). In Chapter 13, confirmation does not effect a discharge. A Chapter 13 debtor does not receive a discharge until she has completed payments under the plan or has been excused from making payments because of hardship, section 1328.

CHAPTER XIX

ALLOCATION OF JUDICIAL POWER OVER BANKRUPTCY MATTERS

The question of which court has the power to adjudicate the litigation that arises in bankruptcy can be an important one. Many attorneys that represent parties with claims against the bankrupt or parties against whom the bankrupt has claims prefer to litigate in some forum other than the bankruptcy. Some believe that the bankruptcy judge has a pro-debtor bias; others are simply more comfortable or more familiar with state court procedures.

In considering the question of which court has the power to adjudicate the litigation that arises in bankruptcy, it is helpful to consider the kinds of matters that can arise in bankruptcy.

Some will involve only bankruptcy law. For example, D files a Chapter 13 petition. C, a creditor of D, files a motion to dismiss alleging that D does not meet the eligibility standards of section 109(e) in that D owes more than $350,000 of unsecured debt. D's answer raises the question of whether section 109(e) includes disputed debts.

Other matters will involve both bankruptcy law and non-bankruptcy law. For example, D files a Chapter 7 petition. C files a secured claim that describes its Article 9 security interest. The bankruptcy trustee takes the position that C's security interest is invalid. If this is litigated, it will probably involve both the Bankruptcy Code's invalidation provisions and the Uniform Commercial Code's perfection provisions.

And, still other matters will not involve substantive bankruptcy law. For example, D. Inc., a Chapter 11 debtor, files a breach of contract claim against X.

A. HISTORY

The allocation of judicial power over bankruptcy matters has been and still is one of the most controversial bankruptcy issues. A general familiarity with prior statutory schemes and prior controversies is helpful to understanding the present situation.

1. 1898 Act

Under the Bankruptcy Act of 1898, bankruptcy courts had limited jurisdiction. This jurisdiction was commonly referred to as "summary jurisdiction." (The phrase "summary jurisdiction" is somewhat misleading. First, it incorrectly implies that under the Bankruptcy Act of 1898, bankruptcy courts had a second, non-summary form of jurisdiction. Summary jurisdiction is the only form of jurisdiction that a bankruptcy judge possessed under the Bankruptcy Act of 1898. Bankruptcy courts had only summary jurisdiction; other courts had plenary jurisdiction. Second, it incorrectly implies that in resolving controversies the bankruptcy judge always conducted summary proceedings.)

Summary jurisdiction extended to (1) *all* matters concerned with the administration of the bankruptcy estate and (2) *some* disputes between the bankruptcy trustee and third parties involving rights to money and other property in which the bankrupt estate claimed an interest. The tests for which disputes with third parties were within the bankruptcy judge's summary jurisdiction turned on issues such as whether (1) the property in question was in the actual possession of the bankrupt at the time of the commencement of the case, (2) the property in question was in the constructive possession of the bankrupt at the time of the commencement of the case, and (3) the third party actually or impliedly consented to bankruptcy court jurisdiction.

There was considerable uncertainty over which disputes were within the summary jurisdiction of the bankruptcy court. This uncertainty gave rise to considerable litigation.

2. 1978 Code

Apparently for the above reasons, Congress in 1978 decided to create a bankruptcy court with pervasive jurisdiction. Apparently for political reasons, Congress also decided that this bankruptcy court should *not* be an Article III court.

As you recall from your Constitutional Law course in law school or civics in high school, Article III of the Constitution vests the judicial power of the United States in the United States Supreme Court and such inferior tribunals as Congress might create. To insure the independence of the judges appointed under Article III (the so-called constitutional courts), Article III provides them with certain protections. These include tenure for life, removal from office only by congressional impeachment, and assurance that their compensation will not be diminished. The constitutional courts created under Article III include the United States Supreme Court, the United States Courts of Appeal, and the United States District Courts. The United States Customs Court (now the Court of International Trade) is an Article III court; its judges may be, and often are, assigned to hear cases in the district courts and the courts of appeals.

Congress, in the exercise of its legislative powers enumerated in Article I of the Constitution, may create other inferior federal tribunals—the so-called legislative courts. Judges of these legislative courts need not be granted tenure for life. In addition, they can be removed by mechanisms other than congressional impeachment, and their salaries are subject to congressional reduction. Historically, these Article I legislative courts and their judges have been granted jurisdiction over limited and narrowly defined subject matters, like the Tax

[*365*]

Court. In other instances, jurisdiction has been limited to narrowly defined geographical territories, such as the territorial courts, the District of Columbia courts, etc.

In enacting the 1978 Code, Congress gave bankruptcy judges none of the protections found in Article III of the Constitution. Nevertheless, in enacting the 1978 Code, Congress gave bankruptcy judges much of the power and responsibilities of an Article III judge. Since bankruptcy debtors can be just about any kind of individual or business entity, this meant that litigation in the bankruptcy courts could deal with almost every facet of business and personal activity.

3. Marathon Pipeline Decision

The 1978 grant of pervasive jurisdiction to a non-Article III bankruptcy court was successfully challenged in the *Marathon* case.

Northern Pipeline, a Chapter 11 debtor, filed a breach of contract lawsuit against Marathon Pipeline in bankruptcy court. There was no question as to whether the bankruptcy court had jurisdiction over this lawsuit under 28 USC section 1471(c). Marathon Pipeline did, however, question whether section 1471(c) conferred Article III judicial power on non-Article III courts in violation of the separation of powers doctrine and filed a motion to dismiss. The bankruptcy judge refused to dismiss; he was reversed by the district judge. On direct appeal, a divided Supreme Court sustained

Marathon's challenge in Northern Pipeline Constr. Co. v. Marathon Pipeline Co., 102 S.Ct. 2858 (1982).

The Court in *Marathon* was so divided that there was no majority opinion. Justice Brennan's opinion was joined by three other justices. Additionally, two justices concurred in the result. The holding of these six is perhaps best summarized in footnote 40 of Justice Brennan's plurality opinion which indicates that (1) the 1978 legislation does grant the bankruptcy court the power to hear Northern Pipeline's breach of contract claim, (2) the bankruptcy court, a non-Article III court, cannot constitutionally be vested with jurisdiction to decide such state law claims, and (3) this grant of authority to the bankruptcy court is not severable from the remaining grant of authority to the bankruptcy court.

The Supreme Court in *Marathon* stayed the entry of any judgment until October 4, 1982, to allow Congress time to enact new legislation allocating judicial power over bankruptcy matters. When Congress failed to act, the stay was extended to December 24, 1982. Again, Congress failed to act.

4. Emergency Rule

In December of 1982, all of the district courts adopted an Emergency Rule on allocation of judicial power over bankruptcy matters. The Rule was proposed by the Director of the Administrative Office of the United States Courts at the instruction of the Judicial Conference. The Emergency

Rule was based on questionable assumptions such as the assumption that the district courts still had bankruptcy jurisdiction after *Marathon.* Nevertheless, all of the courts of appeal that considered constitutional challenges to the Rule upheld its validity.

The Emergency Rule provided for a general reference from the district court to the bankruptcy court of all bankruptcy litigation covered by section 28 USC 1471. Paragraph (d)(3) of the Rule created a special category of proceedings, "civil proceedings that, in the absence of a petition in bankruptcy, could have been brought in a district court or a state court"; in such "related proceedings," the bankruptcy court could not enter a judgment unless the parties consented, but, like a special master, was to submit findings and a proposed judgment to be reviewed by the district court.

5. 1984 Amendments

After *Marathon,* Congress was urged to solve the constitutional dilemma by establishing bankruptcy courts as Article III courts. Congress rejected this solution. Instead, the 1984 amendments make the bankruptcy court a part of the federal district court, confer jurisdiction in bankruptcy on the district court, and allocate judicial power in bankruptcy matters between the federal district judge and the bankruptcy judge. It is easy for any lawyer or law student to criticize the provisions allocating judicial power over bankruptcy matters.

It is more difficult (but probably more important) for a lawyer or law student to understand how these provisions operate.

B. OPERATION OF 1984 AMENDMENTS

In understanding the 1984 amendments allocating judicial powers over bankruptcy matters, it is necessary to understand three separate, new sections to title 28: (1) 151, (2) 1334, and (3) 157.

1. Bankruptcy Court as Part of the District Court, Section 151

Section 151 refers to a bankruptcy judge and a bankruptcy court as a "unit" of the district court. It is important to keep this reference in mind when reading other sections in Title 28 dealing with the allocation of judicial power in bankruptcy matters. When the term "district court" appears in section 1334 or section 157, it could be referring to the United States district judge and/or the bankruptcy judge. After all, the bankruptcy judge is a part of the district court—a "unit" of the district court.

2. Grants of Jurisdiction to the District Court, Section 1334(a) and (b) [1]

Section 1334(a) vests original and exclusive jurisdiction in the district court over all *cases* arising under the Bankruptcy Code. "Case" is a term of art used in both the Bankruptcy Code and the

---

1. Section 1334(c) which deals with abstention will be separately considered later in this chapter.

Bankruptcy Rules. "Case" refers to the entire Chapter 7, 9, 11, or 13—not just some controversy that arises in connection with it.

The term "case" is to be distinguished from the term "proceeding." A specific dispute that arises during the pendency of a case is referred to as a "proceeding." Section 1334(b) provides that the district courts have original but not exclusive jurisdiction over all civil proceedings, "arising under title 11, or arising in or related to cases under title 11."

To review, if the Sunshine Cab Co. files a Chapter 11 petition, section 1334(a) gives the district court jurisdiction over Sunshine's Chapter 11 case itself. And, section 1334(b) gives the district court jurisdiction over a complaint filed by Sunshine's trustee alleging that payments to Louie De Palma were preferential or a complaint filed against Sunshine by Elaine Nardo alleging sex discrimination.

3. Role of the Bankruptcy Court, Section 157

Clearly, section 1334 confers jurisdiction over bankruptcy matters to the district court. It is equally clear that most federal district judges have neither the time nor the inclination to exercise this jurisdiction. Accordingly, section 157 empowers the district judge to refer bankruptcy matters to the bankruptcy judge.

Note the title of section 157, "Procedures." As this title suggests, section 157 is not a jurisdictional provision. It does not confer jurisdiction on the bankruptcy judge. Rather, it deals with procedure—the role that the bankruptcy judge, a unit of the district court under section 151, is to play in exercising the jurisdiction conferred by section 1334 on the district court.

Section 157 differentiates between "core" and "non-core" proceedings. A non-exclusive list of core proceedings is set out in section 157(b)(2). [Sunshine Cab's section 547 action against Louie is an easy example of a core proceeding.] Generally, in core proceedings, the bankruptcy judge conducts the trial or hearing and enters a final judgment.

Obviously, if a matter is not a core proceeding, it is a "non-core proceeding." "Non-core proceeding" is neither defined nor illustrated in the statute. [Elaine's sex discrimination action against the Sunshine Cab Co. is an obvious example of a non-core proceeding.] In non-core proceedings, the bankruptcy judge still can hold the trial or hearing, but generally cannot issue a final judgment. She instead submits proposed findings of fact and law to the district court for review, section 157(c)(1).

The bankruptcy judge is empowered to determine whether a matter is a core proceeding or a non-core proceeding, section 157(b)(3). Note that a determination that a proceeding is *non*-core does not mean that the matter is withdrawn from the bankruptcy judge. Remember that a bankruptcy judge can hear non-core proceedings and prepare findings of facts and law.

Section 157(d) authorizes the district judge [2] to withdraw a case or proceeding from a bankruptcy judge. The first sentence of section 157(d) provides for permissive withdrawal "for cause shown." The second sentence of section 157(d) requires withdrawal of a proceeding on timely motion of a party if both the Bankruptcy Code and another federal law must be considered.[3]

4. Abstention Under Section 1334(c)

Withdrawal under section 157(d) moves a matter from the bankruptcy judge to the federal district judge. Abstention under section 1334 moves the litigation from the federal courts to a state court.

Section 1334(c)(1) provides for permissive abstention. If the district court believes that abstention would be "in the interest of justice" or "in the interest of comity with State courts or respect for State law," it has the option of abstaining. Section 1334(c)(2) provides for mandatory abstention; if the

2. Section 157(d) uses the phrase "district court." In this context, however, it would seem that "district court" should be limited to the district judge. How can a bankruptcy judge decide that she should withdraw a reference to herself?

3. Note the statutory phrase "requires consideration of both." What does this mean? In re White Motors Corp., 42 B.R. 693, 12 B.C.D. 235 (N.D.Ohio 1984), the federal district court concluded that section 157(d) mandates withdrawal only if the resolution of the dispute requires a "substantial and material" consideration of non-bankruptcy law. The obvious questions the *White Motors* decision raise are (1) what is the statutory basis for a "substantial and material" test?, and (2) what is "substantial and material?"

following requirements of section 1334(c)(2) are satisfied, the district court must abstain:

1. A party to the proceeding must timely file a motion to abstain.

Section 1334(c)(2), unlike section 157(d), makes no provision for the court to act on its own motion. Nor does section 1334(c)(2) indicate what "timely" means.

2. The proceeding is based on a State law claim or cause of action.

3. The matter is a "related to" proceeding, as contrasted with an "arising under" or "arising in" proceeding.

Section 1334(b) uses all three of these phrases. Section 1334(c)(2) limits mandatory abstention to its certain "related to" proceedings. There is no statutory definition of "arising under," "arising in," or "related to." Obviously, Sunshine Cab's preference action against Louie is an example of "arising under"—it is a cause of action created by the Bankruptcy Code. Obviously, Elaine's sex-discrimination action against Sunshine Cab is either "arising in" or "related to." It is not obvious from existing case law whether Elaine's action is "arising in" or "related to."

4. The action could not have been commenced in federal court in the absence of the jurisdiction conferred by section 1334. If there is any other basis for federal court jurisdiction, mandatory abstention is not available. This requirement means

that mandatory abstention would not be available in the *Northern Pipeline* case because of the diversity of citizenship between the parties.

5. An action is commenced in state court. There is a question as to whether this means that the state court action must be pending at the time of the bankruptcy filing.

6. The state court action can be timely adjudicated.

C. QUESTIONS ABOUT ALLOCATION OF JUDICIAL POWER UNDER THE 1984 AMENDMENTS

As is obvious from the above discussion of the operation of the 1984 amendments, there are a number of still unanswered questions about the allocation of judicial power over bankruptcy matters. In addition to the questions raised above, consider

1. What constitutes "consent" for purposes of section 157(c)(2)?

2. Can the bankruptcy judge's "core"/"non-core" determination under section 157(b)(3) be appealed?

3. Can the district court act sua sponte under the second sentence of section 157(d)? [Note the first sentence of section 157(d) expressly mentions "on its own motion."]

4. When does "district court" include the bankruptcy judge? In section 1334(c)—can a bankrupt-

cy judge decide a mandatory abstention motion? In section 157(b)(5)—can the bankruptcy judge try a personal injury claim and submit proposed findings of fact and conclusions of law? In section 157(d)—can the bankruptcy judge play any role in withdrawal motions?

5.   Do the references to "personal injury tort" in sections 157(b)(2)(B) and 157(b)(5) and 1411 include products claims that are based on a breach of UCC warranty theory?

6.   Are the 1984 provisions on allocation of judicial power in bankruptcy constitutional?   Are the *Northern Pipeline* tests—whatever they are—satisfied?

*

INDEX

References are to Pages

[*377*]

INDEX
References are to Pages

[*378*]

INDEX
References are to Pages

[*381*]

INDEX
References are to Pages